NELSON'S WAY

D0238599

SJ – to my friends in Dubai – SD, DL, AS, JF, LV, MB, MC – with thanks for being such great mates!

JG – to my colleagues at the Centre for Leadership Studies – TD, ED, DL, NO, RB, AM, PC, SM, JB, KG, AC, VR – you are great to work with!

NELSON'S WAY

Leadership Lessons
from the Great Commander

Stephanie Jones & Jonathan Gosling

NICHOLAS BREALEY
PUBLISHING

BOSTON • LONDON

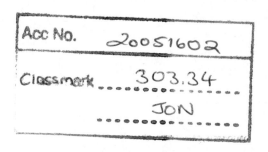
First published by
Nicholas Brealey Publishing in 2005

3–5 Spafield Street
Clerkenwell, London
EC1R 4QB, UK
Tel: +44 (0)20 7239 0360
Fax: +44 (0)20 7239 0370

100 City Hall Plaza, Suite 501
Boston
MA 02108, USA
Tel: (888) BREALEY
Fax: (617) 523 3708

http://www.nbrealey-books.com

ISBN 1-85788-371-3

British Library Cataloguing in Publication Data
A catalogue record for this book is available from the
British Library.

Printed in Finland by WS Bookwell.

CONTENTS

FOREWORD

by N.A.M. Rodger

IT IS NOTEWORTHY, AND RATHER SURPRISING, THAT NELSON has never before been presented as a model for modern managers, though other historical heroes have been fashionable subjects for some time. Perhaps writers have been put off by a legend still rather obviously encrusted with fictions. Perhaps they have been deterred by the complexities of the naval world in which Nelson achieved greatness, the difficulty of mastering a lost technology that very few modern writers or readers have encountered. Either way, this is a good time to take courage, for recent historians have done a lot to dispel the Nelson myths and reveal the realities of his remarkable career.

It is worth distinguishing three aspects of Nelson's life: the heroic, the embarrassing and the mundane. The heroism has always received most attention and many popular biographies of the past looked no further. Unfortunately, much of the heroic legend was indeed legendary, and there is still much work to be done to understand Nelson as a real hero with real achievements that seemed to his contemporaries to be almost incredible, but that were rooted in the practical circumstances of his age and his career. We need to know more about Nelson as a leader, of both officers and men. In particular, we know much too little of the ways in which the great mutinies of 1797 disturbed the discipline of the navy; it is already clear that Nelson's instinctive sympathy with the common man was a huge professional asset in the post-1797 navy, where every thinking officer could see that discipline had to be rebuilt on a new footing, but few admirals had any idea how to go about it.

The embarrassing aspects of Nelson's career were more or less ignored by the first generation of biographers, but in more recent times the balance has tipped the other way as he has fallen into the hands of writers interested only in his private life. His professional achievements took place in a remote and difficult world with which these authors do not wish to trouble their readers, or themselves. The result is a genre of trivia that has more to do with certain modern magazines and television programmes than with the realities of Nelson's life. What we need, and seldom get, are biographers who are able to confront and understand the episodes (not all of them connected with Emma Hamilton) that cast doubt on Nelson's judgement and even sense of duty. We need an integrated portrait of Nelson the man and the officer that makes sense both of his heroism and of his weakness.

Finally, we must consider the mundane aspects of Nelson's greatness that have hardly ever been noticed. Admirals have to be managers as well as leaders. A squadron of warships, especially one operating in hostile waters far from support, is a complex organisation and a major management challenge. Military operations present further management difficulties – and an eighteenth-century admiral had very few staff to help him. Nelson was equally outstanding as a manager and as a leader, which was an unusual combination among British admirals of the day. His contemporaries included officers like Lord Keith, who made a successful career as a capable manager of large-scale operations without ever demonstrating any flair as a leader or tactician. Nelson was as good a manager as Keith – but he was a great deal more besides.

Nelson had another quality that was distinctive, though not unique; he went on getting better and better. It is a commonplace of any large organisation that many people rise because they were very good when they started in junior positions. This is how people are identified as potential leaders, because they are very good at their jobs. The problem is that those who make good lieutenants do not necessarily make good captains or admirals. People are promoted beyond their abilities. Those who possess in abundance the qualities necessary for success in junior positions fail to learn or develop the different qualities needed for high command. This has been a frequent phenomenon in the Royal Navy, which has always been better at training junior officers than forming them for high command.

Nelson exemplifies the reverse trend. Stripped of the heroic legend, his early career shows a surprisingly high level of mistakes, some of them serious. His self-confidence matured more quickly than his judgement. As he grew older and more senior, he learnt continually and matured the qualities that he needed for high command. He was a better captain than he had been a lieutenant, and went on to be a better admiral still. In this too he is an unusual and educative model for managers and leaders today.

For all these reasons *Nelson's Way* arrives at the right time and on the right lines. It addresses the realities of Nelson's career, asking pragmatic questions in search of practical answers that can be applied to real careers today. It shows us how much Nelson still has to teach us, and how much we still have to learn from him as well as about him.

N.A.M. Rodger
London and Exeter
June 2005

INTRODUCTION

Why Nelson?

'It was felt in England as something more than a public
calamity. Men started at the intelligence and turned pale,
as if they had heard of the loss of a dear friend. An object
of our admiration and affection, of our pride and of our
hopes, was suddenly taken from us, and it seemed as if we
had never, till then, known how deeply we loved and
reverenced him.'
Robert Southey, Life of Nelson, *1813*

THERE IS NO DOUBT THAT NELSON IS ADMIRED. IN JUNE
2005, 167 ships from 57 nations, and 300,000 people, gathered
in Portsmouth to watch a re-enactment of the Battle of
Trafalgar. In 2002, in the BBCtv series *Great Britons* in which viewers
voted for their favourites, Nelson was in the top ten. He came second
behind Cromwell in having the most portraits hanging in the National
Portrait Gallery, and second behind Newton in having the most streets
named after him in Britain. There are streets, villages, towns and cities
named after Nelson all over the world. Over 1,000 books and over 20
films and documentaries have told his story. Of historical characters and

military and naval heroes, only his old enemy Napoleon outsells Nelson in books and popular merchandise. Dozens of statues have been erected in his memory, with his own square in London. Hundreds of public houses up and down the land are adorned with his name and picture, some simply called 'The Hero'. Every year on 21 October toasts are drunk to 'The Immortal Memory' at naval bases all over the world, even by Americans, who numbered among his enemies. The Nelson Society, founded in 1981, and the 1805 Club, founded in 1990, have a large and growing following.

Nelson was certainly a leader. From his early teens he was commanding boats and cutters with up to 20 oarsmen, and from the age of 18 he was in charge of a watch and took command of ships taken as prizes. By 21 he was a captain, responsible for hundreds of men. By his last campaign, he was ordering the destiny of 40 ships and tens of thousands of men. Through his close network of captains, his 'band of brothers', he was responsible for the men in battle, but that was only a small part of the story. He was also responsible for feeding them, keeping up their morale, and maintaining their ships in fighting trim, for years at a time.

Why is he still admired as a leader 200 years later? He was widely seen as Britain's first national hero, great in his own lifetime and jettisoned to stardom by his death at the moment of victory. The outpouring of popular grief at his death was, like that surrounding John F. Kennedy and Princess Diana, something nobody could forget. His series of sea battles ensured Britain's supremacy of the oceans for 100 years. His approach to naval tactics was not new, but its execution was devastating, and in his battles the enemy was annihilated, not just defeated. In this respect he revolutionised war at sea. With history and biography outselling nearly every other category in bookshops, Nelson's memory lives on.

Nelson's story makes a rattling good yarn, with spectacular characters and fast-paced action, over the top in places and larger than life. It comes over as a good story because he wrote it in his letters as he lived it, and the legends are interwoven with the facts because many of them were created in his lifetime. His writing style is vivid and colourful, racy and breathless, peppered with quotations from Shakespeare and the Bible. He gave interviews to the press and leaked his own accounts of battles, competing with his superiors. He was ahead of his time in his media-savvy approach to public relations. He spoke, wrote and even made signals in soundbites, such as the famous 'England expects that every man will do his duty'. This was not just for his men; it was a message for posterity.

Nelson won the hearts of ordinary people, on land and at sea. He went on tour in England and worked the crowds. He cared about individuals; he remembered the names, faces and characteristics of hundreds of sailors. He visited sailors in hospital. He wrote to their mothers. His death plunged his officers and men, and the nation, into mourning for a classless everyman's hero who was no patrician, no aristocrat.

Nelson was also a man of the moment. His personal ambition was exactly aligned with the needs of the country. Britain was on the edge after many long years of war and only 22 miles from the enemy. The British people were terrified by the prospect of invasion, especially on the south coast. Naughty children were told that 'Boney will get you' and local militia were being raised in every village, reaching a crisis in the summer of 1805. The country needed a hero to unite it against Napoleon. He was at the right place at the right time.

Nelson was clearly courageous. He fought from the front and took part in over 100 battles, skirmishes and assaults on forts and towns, attacking other ships at sea and in port. He was wounded several times in action, undergoing the amputation of his arm (smashed by a musket ball) without anaesthetic and suffering a long and painful recovery. Then he immediately volunteered for active service again. As a commander he had the courage of his convictions throughout his campaigns, and as a manager he had the moral courage to run the fleet as he saw fit. He made the ultimate sacrifice (this was certainly how it was seen at the time) by laying down his life for his country.

Nelson was famous. He was instantly recognisable, with his star-spangled uniform, empty sleeve and bejeweled cocked hat. He was mobbed in London, in Portsmouth, everywhere he went. Thousands of cheap souvenirs emblazoned with his image filled the shops after his death. Nearly everyone had their Nelson mug, milk jug or reproduction medal, just as people today collect Manchester United football shirts or team posters.

Nelson's life and achievements were controversial. He was generous but ruthless, fair but prejudiced, professional but impulsive, revolutionary but conservative, intensely loyal but guilty of seducing (or being seduced by) his friend's wife. He looks different in all his portraits, and interpretations of his contribution vary in every book written about him. Complex and full of contradictions, no one will ever say the last word.

We are both new-generation Nelson fans. As young teenagers we nailed our colours to Nelson's mast, fascinated by his inspirational story, his heroic exploits and his immortality, fuelled by his dramatic death at the hour of victory.

Having both pursued careers in teaching and consulting in leadership and management, and having worked together for years without realising our mutual interest in Nelson, we have often reflected on Nelson's way of leadership. We have both trained and consulted to business executives who face the same questions as Nelson, helping them to come up with their own answers.

Nelson's Way differs from other Nelson books because our focus is on the challenges facing today's leaders. Leadership lessons and their applications are therefore the key theme of the book. We also show how the echo of Nelson's leadership still reverberates on the themes confronted by contemporary leaders. There is no substitute for a well-proven example, and there is still so much we can learn from Nelson.

Nelson was much more than an exemplary naval commander. Although in singular circumstances, he speaks to us of universal ideals and common challenges. Each chapter in *Nelson's Way* deals with a phase in his life, delineated by major events. In telling the story of his life, we articulate the virtues that he practised and the ideals he held before him. These are universally recognised and, we believe, help explain Nelson's lasting appeal, as values to which we can all aspire.

But ideals alone do not explain either his genius or his popularity. He faced practical challenges common to all who take up leadership roles. His responses to these challenges were his own, and may not be appropriate for everyone. But these challenges must be answered by every leader, consciously or not.

In *Nelson's Way* we ask these key questions of every reader who is, or who aspires to be, a leader. Nelson's answers, as he practised them, constitute Nelson's Way, but any leader has to answer these for him- or herself:

- ⚓ Why be a leader? What motivates you to take this challenge? Nelson wanted heroism, fame and glory: what are you looking for?
- ⚓ Do you have to be an expert to be a leader in your field? Do you need a vocation? All naval officers had to climb through the ranks and Nelson had to know his business inside out. But do you? And is it the most necessary feature of leadership in your context?
- ⚓ Do you want to lead from the front and be always visible and courageous? Nelson did, inspiring his officers and men by taking the flak. But there is much to be said for quiet leadership, behind the scenes. Which is your approach?
- ⚓ How do you handle your public and private life, balancing love and duty? Nelson wore his heart on his sleeve with his great passions for both his romantic interest and his career. How do you achieve your work/life balance?
- ⚓ Why be a team player? Is it necessary and more effective to share leadership? Nelson thought so, in terms of the trust he invested in his 'band of brothers' and the loyalty he inspired. To what extent are you prepared to share ideas and plans, and devolve authority and initiative to your team?
- ⚓ Can leaders be managers too? Is it important to be a good, diligent administrator and resource manager as well as a visionary leader? Nelson was; it was essential for winning battles. Can you be both, in the context in which you work? Do you think it's necessary?
- ⚓ Why should others follow you? Nelson's officers and men were inspired by him and were convinced he would lead them to victory and to glory. Are your team members following you because they have to or because you are inspirational? Are you consciously helping them achieve their potential?
- ⚓ What will be your legacy? For Nelson it was naval supremacy for over 100 years and a tradition of professionalism, heroism, teamwork,

inspiration and glory. What will you leave behind as the mark of your leadership?

We hope that the story of Nelson is able to prompt you to answer these questions for yourself and that it will provide leadership lessons for you. And you may choose not to lay down your life in the attempt!

1

HEROISM

The making of a legend, 1758–1770s

'Difficulties and dangers do but increase my desire of
attempting them... this presaged my character.'
Nelson

The most famous naval signal ever transmitted, as much for posterity as for the encouragement of the sailors on 21 October 1805 – a famous Nelson soundbite. *'Nelson's Signal' by Thomas Davidson, undated.*

IT WAS SIX IN THE MORNING OF 20 NOVEMBER 1777 WHEN THE frigate *Lowestoffe*, commanded by Captain William Locker, was patrolling the American coast and sighted two sails to northward. The frigate gave chase, and after four hours fired a cannon and ten double-shotted swivel guns at one, the *Resolution* brig, an American privateer on its way to North Carolina. Outgunned, it offered little resistance and its consort, a schooner carrying gunpowder for the American colonies, escaped. In the afternoon, as the brig was brought close by, a fierce storm blew up, threatening to engulf both the *Lowestoffe* and its prize.

Driving rain, gales and heavy seas smashed into both vessels, and Captain Locker called on the First Lieutenant, Charles Sandys, to board and secure the prize. Sandys, a commissioned officer of four years' standing, had already shown himself to be an incompetent officer, described as 'vulgar' and a 'dolt' and 'bringing discredit on the naval service'. He was also a drunkard, liking 'a cup of grog as well as ever'.

Accounts of what happened next vary. One report said that Sandys tried to reach the prize but was driven back by the furious waves, and another version maintained that he never left the frigate, rummaging around below decks for his sword. But whatever the case, Sandys flunked the job and Locker stormed around the deck in consternation, shouting above the din of the waves: 'Have I no officer in the ship who can board the prize?'

The ship's boat had already been launched and was pitching and tossing in the waves as the storm worsened. The ship's master stepped forward to the job, but young Second Lieutenant Horatio Nelson, newly promoted and just 19 years old – but looking about 16 – stopped him. 'It is my turn now,' he recorded in his memoirs, 'and if I come back it is yours.'

Meanwhile the brig was shipping a great deal of water, and other observers described how Nelson's small boat ploughed through mountainous waves, one of which took him right over the deck of the prize and across the other side, 'out again with the scud'. But Nelson finally made it, clambered on board and hoisted the navy's colours. The weather continued so foul that the prize separated, despite Nelson's attempts to follow Locker's orders by keeping it under the frigate's stern. The captain feared that the prize – and Nelson – were lost, but four days later both the frigate and the brig made it back to Port Royal, Jamaica.

The prize was worth good money to be taken into the service, but there was much more value in its capture than mere cash. Locker and Nelson learned from the Americans that the French at St Nicholas Mole (from where the brig had embarked) would soon enter the war in aid of the rebellious colony and against Britain. A fleet carrying thousands of soldiers was about to arrive on the north coast of Haiti.

Looking back, Nelson was to reflect that the incident 'presaged my character' by demonstrating 'that difficulties and dangers do but increase my desire of attempting them'. The story – one of many – became another of Nelson's canonical feats of heroism and courage, inspiring one of the stirring paintings that were engraved, published and sold in vast numbers after his death. Junior officers corroborated the event, though it was barely mentioned in the ship's log, but Nelson made it into an epic tale, part of the legend.

This and other possibly apocryphal stories were 'manufactured' for the creation of the persona. They increased in the telling by shipmates, relatives and friends, who dined out on the stories. Mythology has been described as the continual bane of the Nelson student, difficult to expunge because so much of it was created by contemporaries to whom we might otherwise look for authoritative accounts of events. Over 200 years later we are still doing it – a picture of the heroic feat described above illustrates our cover.

Nelson may have wanted to be a hero from the beginning, but he had a tough start. Joining his uncle's ship as a homesick 12-year-old on a cold March day in 1771 in metropolitan Chatham in Kent, the weakly provincial boy searched for a friendly face. There were none, and Uncle Maurice was nowhere to be found. Miserably pacing the deck of this strange, smelly, heaving wooden world, he must have asked himself if he had made the right choice.

Horatio Nelson was born at Burnham Thorpe in the county of Norfolk on 29 September 1758. His was a middle-class clergyman's family and he was the sixth of eleven children, living in a quiet, coastal setting. The only possible indicator of the potential for later fame and fortune came with the family's connections to the powerful Walpoles. Nelson's mother was the grand-niece of Sir Robert Walpole, the first British Prime Minister. Nelson knew death from a young age, with a number of siblings dying in childhood or as young adults, and his mother died when he was only nine. It was a difficult childhood, with a strict, disciplinarian father, freezing cold winters, a succession of inhospitable boarding schools and few home comforts for a fairly poor family with many mouths to feed.

It was against this background that Nelson jumped at the idea of going to sea, with his late mother's brother, Captain Maurice Suckling. Once Nelson had persuaded his father to write, Suckling responded with a robust acknowledgement of the cheapness of life and the ever-presence of death in the mid-eighteenth century:

> *what has poor Horatio done, who is so weak, that he, above all the rest, should be sent to rough it out at sea? But let him come, and the first time we go into action, a cannon ball may knock off his head and provide for him at once.*

Nelson, though still a young boy, wanted to take part in the wars that had been a constant backdrop to his childhood. He wanted to follow in the footsteps of brave Uncle Maurice, who told stirring stories of high adventure in the Seven Years War in the magical West Indies. He would not see his home again for ten years.

Perhaps being alone in the world from an early age accounts for his later obsession with duty and single-minded attention to his goals. He never forgot these initial days on his first ship, when no one was expecting him and everyone ignored him. He was still a small boy, missing his mother, and was to feel his loss for the rest of his life. Even past 40, he wrote, 'the thought of former days brings all my mother to my heart, which shows itself in my eyes'. Unused to women and without female company for many years, Nelson was vulnerable to the charms of a succession of women, some highly respectable, many dubious. Lonely and isolated, his levels of ambition reached unreasonable proportions, perhaps as a substitute for love and domesticity. He was not a settled nor a satisfied man. Happiness was always brief and interrupted.

Early tales of heroism

The second half of the eighteenth century was an age of exploration. On a voyage to the Arctic, legend describes how the young Nelson, aged 14, ran off over the ice and tried to attack a polar bear. As was to become usual with him, he went too far. The musket misfired and the bear, around seven feet tall, turned to attack him. Why did he do this, his concerned but annoyed captain asked. 'Sir, I wished to kill the bear that I might carry the skin to my father.'

This story was possibly invented or at least exaggerated, as only one in ten logs and diaries of the expedition mentions it at all, but it has a long vintage in Nelson lore. Nelson did not refer to it in his own account of his exploits, and the story was told some years after the event by one of the captains:

> As a proof of that cool intrepidity which our young mariner possessed... notwithstanding the extreme bitterness of the cold... young Nelson was discerned at a considerable distance on the ice, armed with a single musket, in anxious pursuit of an immense bear.

But it does give us a clue to the early motivations of the heroic impulse. He wanted to please his remaining parent, he wanted others to be proud of him, and he wanted to collect trophies to attest to his heroism for all to see. These motivations remained with him throughout his life. Doing things that no one else would dare became his trade mark.

This kind of story captured the imagination of a less cynical age, at a time when bravery and physical courage were almost a daily requirement. We should not forget that Britain had been at war for much of the century, and fortunes and reputations were made through war, exploration, discovery and outright piracy. These stories were told by people anxious to be associated with Nelson. They hoped to profit by connection to the man, but they were also reassured and enthused by the idea of heroism, which fitted the spirit of the age so well. All naval and military personnel were subject to this expectation, but Nelson was to take it to heart more than others. Heroic deeds might lead to fame and fortune; but for Nelson, being a hero was most important. The fame came with the heroism though the fortune was elusive, materialising only after his death.

Many commentators date Nelson's specific and identifiable 'discovery' of heroism to a form of epiphany experienced during a long and feverish illness on a voyage in the tropical East Indies. His moods could always be volatile. In a black depression, hovering between illness and recovery, even life and death, Nelson's mind wandered. Concerned that he did not have enough patronage to succeed (although he had benefited considerably from Uncle Maurice's influence), and frustrated with his poor health, he described a dramatic change of heart.

> *After a long and gloomy reverie, in which I almost wished myself overboard, a sudden glow of patriotism was kindled within me, and presented my king and country as my patron; my mind exulted in the idea. 'Well then', I exclaimed, 'I will be a hero, and confiding in providence, I will brave every danger.'*

However doubtful this story, fever-induced visions resulting in life-changing experiences are not unknown. But few of the worldwide pantheon of heroes before or since can pinpoint so exactly the moment of their decision to be a hero, if this is indeed what was happening here. Perhaps Nelson exaggerated the story, or it was embellished with the advantage of hindsight. Nonetheless, a country at war – as Britain was for most of Nelson's life – calls for an emotional response and commitment beyond personal careers. A transcendent sense of purpose, expressed as patriotic service, is essential for any warrior setting out for glory into the uncertainties of war.

How did Nelson consciously develop himself into a hero? It was through his commitment to the cause, his impressive and well-communicated achievements, his long-term and well-maintained relationships with key superiors, peers and anyone who would help spread the message. Even his disasters helped in the hero-creation process, turning the loss of the sight of his eye and his right arm to his advantage, as part of the heroic branding. When his ship was challenged in the Baltic for identification he pointed to his missing arm: 'I am Lord Nelson. See, here's my fin!' He wrote thousands of letters (including hundreds designed as 'press releases'), had his portrait painted and was sculpted an estimated 40 times, with all his medals and decorations – which he enjoyed showing off – so that even those who had never seen him knew what he looked like.

Nelson's rise to fame as a 'pop hero' also coincided with the emergence of a mass media and mass production of souvenirs or 'merchandise'. Combined with his carefully engineered press coverage was his presence at ceremonies and civic receptions around Britain, and public gestures giving away swords and medals and a summary of his heroic deeds to date, all well reported in the press. He gave interviews to journalists even on his short final leave in England before Trafalgar. Even Napoleon had a bust of Nelson in his dressing room at the Tuileries, and was to copy and adapt Nelson's famous Trafalgar signal. Imitation is the sincerest form of flattery.

Nelson's heroism was also closely geared to the needs of the navy and the objectives of national defence in wartime; as Joseph Conrad wrote, Nelson 'brought heroism into the line of duty'. He was not a rebel without a cause nor a hero of romantic fiction but a hero doing a much-needed job, playing a leading role in defending the country against Napoleon. In a defensive rather than aggressive role, Nelson can be seen as a different kind of hero from the seadogs of the Elizabethan era, such as Drake, Raleigh and Grenville, who were more in buccaneering and privateering mode. Nelson, as an 'official hero' – at least by the time of his death – inspired generations of future leaders, creating committed followers to polish the image. Dying in action, a sacrifice in the hour of victory, secured him at the apogee of heroism. Surviving two centuries, his is still a contemporary image, providing leadership lessons transcending time, place and context.

Nelson's heroism was a sign but not the measure of his greatness. There was much more than this: his dedication, his ability to inspire, to manage, to win loyalty. However, the conscious manufacturing and manipulation of the image, the communication of the heroic message, the showmanship, the public relations in an early form, the spin that he successfully employed to build the living legend, the narcissism – these were also part of the story. The successful creation of a persona is not just about being a hero, but making sure that everyone knows.

This included publicising his own version of events, as at the Battle of Cape St Vincent. Despite playing a prominent part in the battle, his name was omitted by his admiral from the official dispatches. Arguably, the popular mythology of that battle today is more Nelson's side of the story than the official version, especially as most accounts are to be found in Nelson biographies. Would that have been the case if Nelson had not written such eloquent and effective reports? Or would his role in the battle have received so much attention if he had not broadcast it so effectively? Surely not. He instinctively appreciated the importance in leadership of symbolic gestures and stories. If his superiors failed to appreciate them, Nelson certainly did not.

How Nelson remained focused on his ambition to be a hero and rise to the top of his profession, through unemployment, illnesses, wounds and defeats, is all part of the story. Obsessive, slightly crazy, restless for glory, he jumped at every opportunity to carry out some new aspect of his perceived duty. He was, of course, egged on by the public, who desperately needed a heroic figure to set against the enormous presence of Napoleon. Nelson and Napoleon – who could ask for more larger-than-life hero and villain characters?

One reason for Nelson's willingness to plunge himself into danger was the role of religion and spirituality in his life. His father, a country vicar, brought him up to believe that it was the poor parson's family who enjoyed privileged communion with God, not the wealthy landowners who held temporal, but not spiritual, power. Nelson's belief that God was on his side, and would help him overcome any hardships, came to play a major part in his leading-from-the-front mentality.

His commitment to the heroic image meant that dying a martyr's death at the moment of victory was an outcome to be envied, not avoided. In the meantime, God was somehow protecting him, leading him to his destined sacrifice. The echoes of Christian archetypes are hard to avoid.

Nelson described his protection by the Almighty when writing in his journal, and there is no reason to doubt its authenticity and sincerity:

> *When I lay me down to sleep, I recommend myself to the Care of Almighty God. When I awake I give myself up to His direction, amidst all the evils that threaten me, I will look up to Him for help, and question not but that He will either avert them or turn them to my advantage. Though I know neither the time nor the manner of my death, I am not at all solicitous about it because I am sure that He knows them both, and that He will not fail to support and comfort me.*

As we shall describe throughout this book, Nelson built on a series of heroic exploits to win the hearts of his men, his officers and the people of Britain at a time of great fear and threat of invasion. With only the strength and reputation of the navy as protection, Britain fought against most of Europe, with Napoleon at the height of his powers. The British needed to focus on a hero to rally their spirits and morale. There were other gallant officers at sea and others who had won major fleet actions – but none had Nelson's personality, his commitment, visibility, courage and ability to inspire.

Nelson's Way
Heroism

The approach to leadership exemplified by Nelson involves a transcendent sense of purpose and a level of ambition that can only be described as obsessive. Behind the romantic image of the hero and the elegant and persuasive prose, Nelson took determination and persistence to almost ruthless extremes, overcoming political obstacles, personal hardships, tactical errors and mortal dangers.

This leadership style is not for the faint-hearted. It means a 24/7 focus, to be pursued at all costs, to the point of being seen as unconventional, hyperactive and unable to relax until the objective has been achieved. In Nelson's case, there was no other way.

Heroes are legendary figures, endowed with great strength or ability, and admired for noble achievements and qualities such as courage and bravery. They are grand, noble, potent, impressive, epic, victorious and celebrated. They need to be role models, an ideal type in their chosen field. Their job is to lead others, being both courageous and magnanimous. They come to the fore when they are needed, especially in a crisis.

To be a hero as a leader you need to be talked about for specific achievements and qualities. You need to be outstanding in your chosen area – be it ideas, execution, relationships or any other way of making progress – and to be known for this. As in heroic verse and in the way of heroes of ancient times, you need to be dramatic, colourful and famous.

No organisation can cope with too many heroes in this full-blooded sense, with their tendency to be egotistical and larger than life; nor is everyone cut out for heroism. But most companies could do with more leaders who are inspirational, exciting and vibrant. Heroic qualities can be identified in existing and potential staff, through looking for determination, energy, outstanding achievements both at and outside work, courageous tendencies from a young age, being looked up to by others, and being fond of self-publicity.

Do candidates for jobs in your organisation bring articles about themselves to show you? Are they outstanding in their field? Do they support particular causes? Most importantly, will other people see in them the qualities they most admire in themselves? They could be heroes!

Leadership comments
John Adair

Nelson has always been a great hero of leadership writer John Adair and features prominently in his book *Great Leaders*. 'Nelson is as close as we've had to someone with a touch of genius for leadership,' he maintains. 'As with anything else, it is by studying those with genius that we progress our knowledge of leadership.' As he goes on to explain, 'We should, by using modern understanding, be able to identify universal principles of leadership exemplified in Nelson's career.'

And this is what he has done. Adair has used Nelson's leadership lessons extensively in the hundreds of leadership programmes he has delivered across the world and in many industry sectors, in the military and in civilian life, emphasising Nelson's heroism, his achievements and qualities, his iconic status as a role model, his emergence at a time of need, his commitment to his chosen cause.

Adair sees a fundamental of heroism as the need to have great ability, and thus he talks of Nelson's 'authority of knowledge – he had strong mastery of his trade'. Courage had to be there too, but physical courage was almost taken for granted: 'Nelson got used to battle from a very early age. Professional soldiers get used to it, and carry on as normal. Conditions that we would find extraordinary – cannon balls and splinters flying about – were something he was quite used to.'

In identifying and training leaders, Adair emphasises the existence of courageous tendencies from a young age, and evidence of volunteering for independent action at time of need, as a vital part of heroism. 'The primal act of leadership is leading from the front in action,' he comments. 'Nelson advertised himself – he enjoyed a touch of the heroics.'

As Adair explains, for you to be a hero, people have to tell stories about you. You have to be at least a bit of a celebrity. Thus, officers and sailors told stories about Nelson, such as 'even at Merton – his home – he would come down to breakfast in full uniform. There is a pleasing touch of vanity about him – it makes him human.' They told stories about his 'patent bridge for boarding first rates', his courage during the amputation of his arm, the way he turned a blind eye at Copenhagen. Nelson represented their own values in these colourful episodes. 'What stories do people tell about you?' Adair asks those in his leadership classes. 'Nelson virtually invented personal PR,' he maintains.

Another vital aspect of heroism that Adair learned from Nelson was 'that he was an extraordinarily good manager – he found the energy and commitment to do all the paperwork early in the day so he could devote the rest of the day to leading', to acts of heroism that were real and genuine. As Adair reminds us, 'The navy was the biggest organisation in Europe – it took a lot of work to run it!' In teaching leadership, Adair emphasises both heroic and apparently non-heroic aspects.

Nelson's respect for his officers and men, his understanding of their values and ability to build their trust, meant he had to be in touch with them. For this he used the mechanism practised in the navy that 'any sailor could present a petition to the Admiral at any time – he didn't have to go through a bureaucratic rigmarole'. Adair talks of this technique being used by Peter Davies when he took over as CEO of Sainsbury's: 'He invited anyone in the company to email him directly.' The thousands of letters that Nelson received and answered show his amazing ability as a communicator.

Being a role model was key to Nelson's ability to inspire, another fundamental of being a hero. 'All these men pent up on ship built up huge corporate emotion – he was a lightning rod to redirect this energy.'

The model of leadership presented by Adair takes a holistic view. 'If we were to compare Nelson with other heroes such as Montgomery, in the three roles of leader, colleague and subordinate, he would score high on all three.'

'He was extraordinary in that he could win eminence and glory without arousing the envy of his colleagues and seniors,' Adair adds. 'Like Haydn and Mozart – Haydn recognised that Mozart, the younger man, had the edge on him, had a special kind of genius.'

There are also words of warning for modern-day followers of Nelson, according to Adair. 'Unless you are of Nelsonian stature, the focus on personal glory would be a mistake,' he advises. There is much to be said for quiet heroism, for promoting team spirit, for being genuinely respected by a small circle. Especially because, unlike in the Nelsonic context, it is challenging to keep exceeding previous acts of glory, sustaining it right to the end. Perhaps this is the greatest challenge of being a hero – being consistent, keeping up the legend, which can be so easily lost. Many leaders have subsequently lost the plot – and lost respect.

Leadership lessons
Heroism

⚓ Why do you want to be a leader? There are many good reasons for taking on this role, and heroism may have little to do with it. But even on a small scale, to be admired and respected is important for most leaders.

⚓ Decide if you want to be a hero as a leader and be honest with yourself – have you got the energy and commitment for it?

⚓ Then volunteer for tough but high-profile assignments, which give you opportunities for independent action.

⚓ Be an excellent communicator – you can't be any kind of leader without it, and certainly not a heroic one. Get a good PR person onto it if you can't do it yourself.

⚓ Spread the word about your achievements with stories that will be repeated, to inspire others and remind them of the values they most admire. It is not enough simply to sing your own praises.

⚓ If you want to be a hero, be a real one, showing genuine and robust heroic qualities – courage, passion, loyalty – not just the spin.

⚓ Choose a profession or organisation where you can rise to the top with prestige and honour, and which is congruent with your own values. Start by being a hero to your peers.

⚓ Identify and represent important values that can earn trust and respect – and fame.

⚓ You can't be the heroic leader all the time, so you have to be good at what you do and be a good manager as well.

⚓ Have deep and unshakeable faith in what you do and feel good about it.

⚓ Keep it up right to the end!

2

VOCATION

Learning the ropes, 1771–1793

'I returned a practical seaman... with a saying common
with the seamen, "Aft the most honour, forward the
better man."'
Nelson

A painting started when Nelson successfully passed his lieutenant's examination and completed when he was promoted to captain. The fort of San Juan in Nicaragua, one of his first engagements, was added in to the background.
'Captain Horatio Nelson' by John Francis Rigaud, 1781.

ON 9 APRIL 1777, A NERVOUS YOUNG NELSON APPEARED AT the Navy Office in London wearing his best uniform to sit for his examination for lieutenant. Clutching the journals of his voyages and certificates of service from his different captains, Nelson headed for Seething Lane and Crutched Friars. A lieutenant's commission – which hopefully would soon follow if he passed the examination – would be issued at the Admiralty, but the job of examining candidates was delegated to the Navy Board, partly because the ships' books used to corroborate claims of service were stored there.

The examiners would be looking for evidence of Nelson's ability to handle a ship and his eligibility for a lieutenant's commission. They were unlikely to ask him about naval warfare, strategy, tactics, combat training or how promising he might be as a leader. If the examiners had connections with the candidate, there may be just a few simple questions. It was unlikely to be a walkover, however. There were many middle-aged midshipmen who had repeatedly failed their examinations.

So Nelson had swotted up on his knowledge of seamanship and navigation, but he was more worried about the fact that he was only 18 while a commissioned officer was supposed to be at least 20. He looked even younger, too – what if one of the examiners made a point of enquiring about his age? And what about the six years of sea service he needed, when one of these had been with a merchant ship?

His nervousness must have been allayed, nevertheless, by discovering that next to the two strangers in the examination room, Captains John Campbell and Abraham North, resplendent in full-dress uniforms and sat behind a large table, sat none other than the Comptroller of the Navy Board himself, Captain Maurice Suckling – Nelson's uncle.

Nelson's brother William later denied that patronage had played a role, suggesting that Uncle Maurice did not reveal his relationship with the candidate until after Nelson had successfully passed the examination. According to William, Suckling said, 'I did not wish the younker to be favoured. I felt convinced that he would pass a good examination, and you see, gentlemen, that I have not been disappointed.' It is now thought that the connection between Nelson and his uncle would have been obvious from Nelson's documents. The other examiners would have seen that Nelson's first ship was Suckling's *Raisonable* and drawn their own conclusion – this is how most aspiring young officers gained their entry point into the service.

Nelson was very lucky and must have been relieved to see his uncle, especially because Suckling not only confirmed that the young Nelson could 'splice, knot, reef a sail, &c. and is qualified to do the duty of an able seaman and midshipman', but he also initialled Nelson's passing certificate attesting that the candidate 'appears to be more than twenty years of age'. Nelson was even luckier when, the following day, he was appointed lieutenant of the *Lowestoffe*, a frigate fitting out at Sheerness for the Jamaica station. He was to serve under an officer who came to replace Suckling as patron and mentor, Captain William Locker. Against the backdrop of the American Wars of Independence, there was a real chance of action and prize money.

Writing to brother William, studying at Christ's College, Cambridge, Nelson joked:

> *I passed my degree as Master of Arts on the 9th instant [that is, passed the Lieutenant's examination] and received my commission on the following day for a fine frigate of 32 guns. So I am now left in the world to shift for myself, which I hope I shall do, so as to bring credit to myself and friends.*

Thrilled to be officially launched on his career at last, Nelson sat for his first portrait. The Rigaud painting was finished in 1781 when Nelson was a slim and confident 22 year old. A recent X-ray of this work shows the original sketch begun before what was to be a momentous trip to the West Indies: a boyish, chubby-faced 18 year old, a hat under his arm, proudly setting forth on his career. Nelson's technical knowledge, his patronage and his ambition had already set him on a path to adventure.

In this early phase of Nelson's career, he clearly appreciated that 'learning the ropes' was vital to progress. First of all, to cross the hurdle of the lieutenant's examination. Secondly, to help him in tactical decision making in the future. Thirdly, to prove his commitment to the navy – this was his vocation. Just doing the job was not enough.

So Nelson needed to be a practical seaman to rise to the top of his profession. He had to learn navigation, seamanship, the handling of all vessels from a ship's tender to a ship of the line, and all aspects of what it took to be an able seaman, midshipman and ultimately a captain. The basis for respect as a captain, and as a leader of any rank in the Navy, was and still is all-round competence in charge of a ship in all weathers. The way to learn was through undertaking voyages, but there were few available in peacetime. He needed war to make it happen. During the peace of 1788 to 1793 he spent five years of unemployment waiting for command of a ship. There was nothing else he wanted to do; none of the possibilities of the day – business, the merchant navy, farming – held any attractions for him.

Technical knowledge was expected of a junior naval officer of the day; in this the navy differed from the army, in which commissions could be purchased. This meritocracy opened the service to middle-class families and gave it the status of a profession, defined largely by very clear areas of competence. However, developing a career in the navy called for more than technical skill. As we shall see in later chapters, captains had to be able to command large groups of men, to administer supplies of various kinds, and to be a trustworthy political and diplomatic representative. But to get into a position to learn these capabilities, aspiring officers first needed to understand and work within the process of patronage, finding prominent supporters to promote their careers and provide the much-needed openings.

Nelson made the most of every opportunity to learn from skilled mentors and sought experiences that would both be demanding and get him noticed. He was given command of ships' boats and cutters as a young teenager, taking soundings, delivering messages and ferrying officers – and commanding the boat's crew of up to 15 men. This was the first step in a career that stretched ahead through command of a ship, then a squadron, and then taking charge of an expedition or task-force, then a whole fleet.

At each stage, thorough practice was the only way to gain a real appreciation of the problems involved. Nelson took many risks in his approach to war and navigation, and was by no means always right in his judgement. But he could almost always claim that he had himself done whatever he asked others to do.

Promotion in the navy also demanded the resilience to survive malnutrition, disease and constant exposure to damp and discomfort, as well as the good fortune to avoid shipboard accidents and random cannon balls that came with every skirmish. It was important to be a survivor, and yet still to be prepared to take risks and make sacrifices – or to seek a more comfortable and less dangerous vocation.

Nelson's first ship was Suckling's *Raisonable*, where he gained an understanding of the way of life on board ship, its structure and ordered routine, its hierarchy and its people. Everyone knew their place, laid down by the rigid Articles of War, yet each ship was in many ways a world unto itself. It could be a success or a failure, happy or miserable, efficient or chaotic, depending on the personality and ability of the captain and senior officers. In his first two decades at sea, Nelson was to experience at first hand the effects of good and bad leadership, and to learn by observation, practice and his ability to form lasting relationships with people of all classes and ranks.

Uncle Maurice introduced the young Nelson to these powerful formative influences. Life in the midshipmen's berth and the job of being a captain's servant included the hardship, discomfort and danger of working the ship; the rudiments of seamanship, navigation and the operation of the guns; and the handling of the ship's boats. As a 'young gentleman of the quarterdeck' Nelson had to sleep in a hammock, keep himself in a presentable condition as an officer, and jump at orders. It was a tough life, but a prestigious, adventurous and popular profession, and naval officers walked ashore with pride. The navy was the foundation of security, independence and prosperity for Britain in the eighteenth century, and was to remain so for generations.

Nelson attended lessons in seamanship and navigation from the ship's sailing master and kept logs of his daily observations of wind and position (which he carried on doing all his life). He was taught signalling and supervising watches, but it was the boat work that he especially enjoyed.

However, when peace came the *Raisonable* was paid off, and Nelson knew he would need to remain active to keep learning. He had six years' service to get under his belt before he could apply for his lieutenant's examination, and even with Uncle Maurice adding on a few months here and there and backdating the log entries, he was not going to make the progress he needed in peacetime.

Soon afterwards Suckling was given command of the *Triumph*, a Thames guardship, but this was still not especially active. Fortunately and again drawing on his 'interest', Nelson was offered the opportunity to join a merchant ship. This was the only time in his career that he left the navy for another service, and he came away with a more positive impression of the merchant marine than he expected.

The merchant navy offered more money, less danger, more predictable voyages and more comfort (or at least, less discomfort) than the fighting force. But there was no honour or glory, no heroism, no legends to be made. The merchant service was not organised into a structured unit. Many ships were owned individually or by several investors who required captains to share the financial risks. Thus promotion was limited to those with the capital to buy a share of the vessel and its cargoes. This fragmented group of vessels plying their trade across the world could not offer Nelson the career track he craved. A clear hierarchy offering advancement in status was much more attractive.

The long merchant voyage of more than a year did, however, give the young Nelson the chance to explore the romantic and exciting West Indies and to learn the serious art of seamanship. He survived the dangers of the fever-ridden tropical climate, coming to respect and understand the practical seamen with whom he worked. They might not have thought much of him in his midshipman's uniform from the dreaded navy, well known for pressing experienced and capable merchantmen into the king's service. But he was keen and hard-working, and grateful for the help they gave him. He bought into the seamen's dictum of 'aft the more honour, forward the better man', although this in no way diminished his desire for honour.

Returning to the *Triumph* – and careful to count his time with the merchant service as naval experience – Nelson commanded the ship's tender, for the first time instructing grown men in their duties in rowing and navigating. He was still only 14, but he was learning skills that were to pay dividends in later life: gaining the trust of his men and understanding the complexities of inshore and coastal navigation.

The waters around the Pool of London and the Nore became very familiar to him. As he was to reflect, this experience made him 'confident of myself amongst rocks and sands, which has many times since been of great comfort to me'. Commanding a small vessel – even just a tender – was held out as a reward for his continuing efforts.

To the Arctic

This was the age of exploration, and when Nelson heard about two ships fitting out for the Arctic – the *Racehorse* and the *Carcass* – he wanted to be there. 'We're not taking boys,' he was told, but he and his obliging uncle lied about his age and, as Nelson claimed 'I fancied I was to fill a man's place, I begged I be his coxswain which, finding my ardent desire for going with him', the captain agreed.

The ships were bomb vessels, with powerful hulls built to withstand the recoil of heavy mortars. They were small enough to handle the restricted spaces of the ice channels and strong enough to break through the ice. It was an exciting voyage of exploration, with innovative food on board, such as cakes of soup containing meat boiled with oatmeal and vegetables. Ice saws were loaded, together with special apparatus for distilling salt from seawater. Two whalemen had been hired as pilots and there were two Harrison chronometers on board. There was a new device for calculating the speed of a ship and the distance it had travelled. Nelson was issued with six 'fearnought' jackets, two milled caps, two pairs of 'dreadnought' trousers, four pairs of milled stockings, a strong pair of boots, a dozen pairs of milled mittens, two cotton shirts and handkerchiefs. He was still a small 14 year old.

The ships ground and cracked through the ice, but there was no passage to be found. The captains explored islands and much wildlife was killed and eaten. There was a real risk of being trapped in the ice, and at one point the ships had to be hauled, but fortunately the ice broke up. Appalling storms dogged the homeward voyage. The expedition was a failure – they never came close to reaching the Pole – but Nelson notched up another exciting experience in an altogether different environment. He learned more seamanship, resourcefulness and resolution, and had grown in confidence, ability and enthusiasm for new challenges. His wages for a six-month voyage were just over £8.

The East Indies

So far, Nelson had been under the kindly protection of his uncle and other moderate officers, but with his next voyage that changed dramatically. On board the *Seahorse*, bound for the East Indies, he witnessed punishment by flogging nearly 100 times in just over two years.

Captain George Farmer of the *Seahorse* was another of Suckling's friends. Nelson learned a great deal on this voyage from Thomas Surridge, the sailing master, who fashioned him into a practical seaman. He took lunar observations against a fixed star, using a quadrant or sextant, and turned them into Greenwich Mean Time through a process of spherical trigonometry. A comparison with local time, ascertained from routine observations, gave an estimate of the ship's longitude.

But Nelson learned more than navigation on this voyage. A total of 130 men and boys were crowded into the *Seahorse*, an old ship of 112 foot (30 metres) length and 32 foot (9 metres) beam. While all the crew members were required to work as a team and observe loyalty to the captain, it was not a happy ship. There was bullying, drunkenness and insubordination. The first lieutenant, named Drummond, would turn up on deck to take the watch in a state of inebriation. He would call his servant to fetch more drink during the watch, and would constantly beat seamen with a rope's end. He openly defied the captain's authority, and was finally court-martialled and dismissed. But Captain Farmer, overly reliant on brutal punishment, had allowed Drummond to get away with too much for too long.

Nevertheless, during these years Nelson enjoyed the company of another young midshipman, Thomas Troubridge, who became a long-term friend and colleague.

In one of the first engagements of Nelson's career, the *Seahorse* attacked a larger Indian warship. Captain Farmer's log records details of the skirmish:

> *at 7 saw two sail standing towards us, which we imagined to be Bombay [East India Company] cruisers... they hauled their wind to the southward... and hoisted Hadir Aly's colours. We immediately tacked, and stood after them. At 8 fired several shot to bring one of them to... one of the [enemy] ketches sent her boat on board us and told us they belonged to Hadir Aly, but as the other ketch did not bring to, or shorten sail, and several other vessels were heaving in sight, which we imagined to be enemy consorts, we kept firing round and grape shot at her until noon... at half past noon the ketch brought to, and struck her colours... we found that we had fired at the above vessel fifty-seven round shot, nine pounders; fifteen grape shot, nine pounders; two double-headed hammer shot, nine pounders; twenty-five round shot, three pounders; and two grape shot, three pounders.*

The *Seahorse* was able to fire its broadsides in rapid succession and the Indiaman struck its colours. The ability of a British naval ship to fire more speedily and accurately than others was a massive advantage. It could attack and beat a larger enemy ship, especially if it could get in very close. Before he was out of his teens, Nelson began to acknowledge the power of the service he had joined, for all its faults. His first four years in the navy had been packed with activity and had given him a wide range of experiences, in different ships and locations. Other officers could have been in the service for 20 years and not experienced so much. It all encouraged his independence, energy and ambition.

For most of 1774 Nelson had to experience the prolonged frustrations of an unpopular but common duty for a naval officer, convoy work. This was inevitably tedious, waiting for merchantmen to gather, shepherding them around and trying to keep them together, and sailing behind or in front of the fleet to intercept enemies. It was all part of learning the ropes, and there was much to see, across the Arabian Sea to Muscat, and then through the straits of Hormuz to Bushire and Bussorah, in modern-day Iran and Iraq.

There were more disciplinary problems on board, again the result of weak leadership, but Nelson kept out of trouble and focused on learning how to tack the ship, a particularly tricky method of changing direction by turning the bow through the wind. Surridge watched with satisfaction as Nelson completed the task with efficiency and authority.

Atlantic convoys

On returning to Britain from the East Indies, Nelson discovered that Suckling, whom he had not seen for a couple of years, was now Comptroller of the Navy and vastly influential. It was at this point that Nelson successfully passed his examination as lieutenant. Not only did Uncle Maurice help him here, he could be relied on to provide even more opportunities, especially through the commission to the *Lowestoffe*. Another reason for celebration – at least for war-hungry Nelson – was the revolt in the American colonies.

If Maurice Sucklng had launched Nelson on his journey to heroism, his captain on the *Lowestoffe* was to set the course and be possibly a greater influence. This was Captain William Locker, who became a life-long friend and mentor. A former protégé of the great mid-eighteenth-century admiral Sir Edward Hawke, Locker introduced Nelson to war at sea. Bearing injuries from hand-to-hand fighting and constantly limping due to a bad splinter wound, Locker taught the young man about fighting and set new benchmarks for his personal courage. It was Locker who coined the phrase 'lay a Frenchman close and you will beat her', emphasising the advantages of superior gunnery enjoyed by the British navy.

A priority now was for Atlantic convoys to be guarded and escorted in the pursuit of their trade, and Nelson and his frigate were sent to

Jamaica for this purpose. This war – a disaster for England – was to give Nelson a range of new experiences, including command, land-based actions, more exposure to disease, politics, romance and marriage. Even when the war was over, Nelson grasped the opportunity to take part in post-war mopping-up operations.

An early letter to Suckling, written on 19 April 1778, clearly shows Nelson's excitement and energy and points to how much he was learning and doing:

> *We haul from the Wharff in two days & then I hope I shall give a good Account of some of the Yankeys... the tender to the* Bristol *[to which he moved after the* Lowestoffe*] was taken by the* Rattlesnake *a ship of 20 guns who have done a great deal of Mischief round the island [Jamaica] as have the* Thunderbolt *a ship of 20 nine pounders... The Rebels have come down the Misisippi plundered our Plantations & carry'd off the Negroes and sold them at New Orleans the* Sylph *&* Hound *are gone to demand them and the* Active *is going down. The* Winchelsea *and* Porpoise *goes with the Convoy on the 25th inst. Providence was taken about six weeks ago by a rebel Privateer assisted by the rebels who live there and all the English vessels burnt or taken, it was retaken by a Kingston privateer who flogg'd the whole Counsel and their Speaker for giving up without firing a Shot.*

Appointment as officer... and command

By the end of 1778, Nelson had heard the sad news that Suckling had died. However, he had already created much of the 'interest' needed to replace his uncle's help. As Nelson wrote to his father on 24 October 1778:

> *I am so very uneasy as you may suppose having just receiv'd the Account of the death of dear good Uncle whose loss falls very heavy on me. His Friendship I am sure I shall always retain a most grateful Sense off. Even in his Illness he did not forget me but recommend'd me in the Strongest manner to Sir Peter Parker who has promis'd me he will make me First Captain. I hope to God your health is recover'd and that you will see your*

Children Flourish in the World. We have just arriv'd from a Pretty Successful Cruize against the French & and I believe I shall share about 400 pounds [prize money]. I hope all my dear Brothers and Sisters are well and all my friends in Norfolk. The Fleet sails to Morrow for England I shall write again by the Pacquet for my Mind is so uneasy at present that I cannot write. Pray write to me. May health Peace & happiness attend you is the Sincere Prayer of Your Ever Dutiful Son, Horatio Nelson.

As it turned out, he had few reasons to be uneasy. Back in the West Indies Nelson, chafing with being only second lieutenant, was again allowed to command the ship's tender, and then was 'made post' in July 1779 and given command of the *Hinchinbrooke*. It was only a frigate, but it was the first rung on the ladder. Promotion now was on the basis of seniority, although distinguished service in action was also a great advantage, and staying alive a necessary requisite.

Admiral Sir Peter Parker made the appointment and became one of the most important influences in Nelson's early life. Margaret, Lady Parker, regarded Nelson as a son, and he wrote to them in 1804 that 'never whilst I breathe shall I forget your kindness for Me, to which I owe all my present honours. May God Bless You My Dear friend and keep you in health many years.' In fact Parker was to be chief mourner at Nelson's state funeral in January 1806.

Another close friend was William Cornwallis, whom Nelson met in the West Indies in 1778. Fourteen years older, Cornwallis was already a war veteran, having served during the Seven Years War, including action with Hawke at Quiberon Bay in 1759. Although their paths were not officially to cross again till Trafalgar, recent evidence suggests that they kept in touch over a quarter century.

Nelson was hungry for command, writing to Sir Peter Parker in January 1780 that his ship was ready for sea as soon as the troops had embarked, and

I beg you will give me leave to represent to you, that in my opinion it will be much for the Good of the Service, that all the Seamen in the Transport Service be left entirely to my direction, and that orders be given to the Commanding Officer of the Land Forces for all Applications

*for Seamen be made to Me, as I shall then be Enabl'd to Send Good Men
and Officers instead of their taking Raw Undisciplin'd Men, and also
that the masters of Transports be Order'd to follow only my directions.*

Although only 22, his confidence in his own ability – and belief in the
navy compared with the efforts of soldiers – is already clearly apparent.
And this expedition was one of the first of his exploits to be mentioned
in the autobiographical *Sketch of My Life*, which he published in 1799.
As he wrote,

*I quitted my ship, carried troops a hundred miles up a river, which none
but Spaniards since the time of the buccaneers had ascended... I
boarded, if I may be allowed the expression, an out-post of the Enemy,
situated upon an island in the river... I made batteries and afterwards
fought them, and was a principal cause of our success.*

This otherwise disastrous expedition would probably have received very
little coverage except for Nelson's role and graphic accounts. The losses
from 'yellow jack' (yellow fever) greatly exceeded losses from combat,
and Nelson himself was invalided home with dysentery, looked after by
his friend Cornwallis. Of the *Hinchinbrooke*'s 200 officers and men, only
10 survived. The episode's place in history was ensured forever when
Nelson asked that it be added to the first portrait ever painted of him,
which he had commissioned and first sat for after passing his lieutenant's examination. Reproduced at the beginning of this chapter, it
shows a confident young man, still looking younger than his years and
so far unmarked by the wounds of battle, with the Nicaraguan fort of
San Juan clearly identifiable in the background.

Nelson was thrilled at the end of May 1780 to be given command of
the brand-new 44-gun frigate the *Janus*, but was too ill to take up the
post.

His next ship was the frigate *Albemarle*, an unhandy and troublesome
former French prize, and it took all of his ability to captain it. Although
he wrote to family and friends that 'I have an exceeding good Ship's
company. Not a Man or Officer I would wish to change. She appears also
to sail very well', he was just being upbeat and optimistic. In reality the

ship was 'so exceedingly crank' that its masts were out of proportion to its beam and length. Nelson used his technical knowledge to deal with the problem, explaining to his commander-in-chief:

> *notwithstanding the 15 tons of Iron Ballast I received here and which have been laid on her Keilson... in a Squall of Wind which lasted about an hour, and was upon the Beam, she stayed so much down on her Broadside that there was much fear she would oversett... I leave to your judgement whether her lower Masts ought to be shortened or whether she should have more than a Twentyfour gunships masts and yards [it was a 28-gun frigate] with her present masts it is very dangerous to go to Sea in her... as we are so much shallower in the Hold and between decks.*

Nelson also faced severe manning problems, having to recruit retired seamen from Greenwich Hospital to fit out the *Albemarle* for sea. He already knew managing a convoy was a difficult job, especially in this case as 'very few of the Ships paid the least Regard to any Signals that were made for the better conducting them safe home'.

Convoy duties in the Baltic were not much easier. When the *Albemarle* arrived at Elsinore in November 1781, he found

> *about Fifty sail in the Roads waiting for Convoy, but upon information from the Consul here I find that there are now upon their Passage, and in Ten Days or a Fortnight there will arrive here, upwards of One Hundred Sail more.*

Even more were coming, but Nelson wrote to the Admiralty that he wanted to proceed, as waiting for the rest could delay the whole fleet in worsening weather conditions. He was already acting independently, taking initiative and writing directly to the Admiralty. He clearly realised that commanding a successful mission was about more than seamanship – little progress could be made without mastering the bureaucratic and political systems too.

North America

After this tedious convoy work he was sent to Quebec in mid-1782, again using his initiative to take action against privateers who were harassing merchant ships in the St Lawrence. Serving under Admiral Hood, based in New York, he made yet another useful connection – the young Prince William Henry, the future King William IV, then a midshipman on board Admiral Hood's flagship. This acquaintance gives us a rare glimpse of what Nelson, the still-young captain, looked like at this time. He came over as unconventional but conservative, the first of many contradictions in his make-up. Prince William Henry, observing Nelson's barge coming alongside, spotted

> *the merest boy of a captain I ever beheld; and his dress was worthy of attention. He had on a full lace uniform: his lank unpowdered hair was tied in a stiff hessian tail of an extraordinary length; the old-fashioned flaps of his waistcoat added to the general quaintness of his figure. There was something irresistably pleasing in his address and conversation; and an enthusiasm, when speaking on professional subjects, that showed he was no common being.*

If the outfit was designed to attract the opposite sex, it was hardly successful. On meeting the sophisticated Mary Simpson, 16-year-old daughter of the provost marshal of the garrison at Quebec, Nelson fell so much in love that he considered resigning his commission. His friends, including Alexander Davison – who became his prize agent, a strong supporter and willing creditor for much of Nelson's life – managed literally to drag him back to sea. Mary, who did not realise the catch she had missed, married very much later a more junior and much less distinguished naval officer. She was to be the first of many objects of Nelson's affections. He pursued possible marriage candidates and later mistresses in the same way that he managed many of his campaigns – with determination, passion and total commitment.

But total commitment was not always effective. In early 1783 he broke off from the squadron commanded by Lord Hood to intercept a French merchantman. The captured prize was worth about £20,000, but Lord Hood ruled that the money should be shared throughout the squadron because the action had taken place in sight of them all. Then in March Nelson led an attack by several ships on the French-held Turks island off the coast of Haiti. He ordered a frontal attack that was easily repulsed by the well-entrenched defenders. He had learnt that reconnaissance, planning and craftiness are as important as sheer bravado, but would not leave without firing the last shot. Before retreating Nelson ordered fellow officers, 'you are hereby required and directed to Anchor as near the Town as possible and to batter the Enemys Intrenchments... till they are totally destroy'd.'

Peace, France and the West Indies

Nelson was now 24, the American Wars of Independence had ended, and he had already gained a strong track record as an experienced and able officer. At home and restless, he decided to visit France. French was the language of the educated and aristocratic classes, and it might be the language of the next immediate enemy. He observed the countryside and peasantry with a slightly condescending manner, and fell in love with Bess Andrews, one of the daughters of an English clergyman's family with whom he was staying. But he had no money to propose marriage. Nelson, who saw everything in such a black-and-white way, implored his uncle William Suckling, brother of Maurice, to provide an allowance: 'The critical moment of my life is now arrived, that either I am to be happy or miserable – it depends solely on you.' But Bess turned him down, leaving him to return to England still with little money and the scantiest grasp of the French language.

However, in 1784 he secured a rare peacetime appointment for the next three years. In the *Boreas* he sailed again for the West Indies, this time to dabble in politics. It was not to be a happy experience, but it had some consolations. Nelson discovered that American ships were still trading among British islands in the West Indies. The Navigation Acts restricted trade to British colonies: only ships built, owned and crewed by Britain were allowed. In the interests of commerce (and the need to rebuild the economy after the devastations of the American War), the local authorities continued to allow trade with ships and merchants from the former American colonies – now newly independent America.

This technical breach was overlooked by most of the local customs offices; Nelson nevertheless impulsively insisted on pressing the implementation of the Navigation Acts, taking several ships and their cargoes as prizes. In the process he ran foul of powerful merchants and traders but also of his own admiral (Sir Richard Hughes, with whom he had clashed before) and the Governor of the Leeward Islands.

Nelson, angry and frustrated, couldn't understand why other people didn't see the importance of his rigid sense of duty to the letter of the law. He was beginning to build his reputation as a politically naïve troublemaker, spoiling for a fight and being more than a little self-righteous. This incident was to play a part in the subsequent long period of unemployment.

As always, Nelson nevertheless made some important and lasting alliances at this time. He was joined in his campaign by two other captains, the brothers William and Cuthbert Collingwood (the latter was to be a lifelong ally, commanding the second line at Trafalgar, of whom Nelson wrote that he was 'a very good Officer and an Amiable Character'); and he met a beautiful young widow who became his wife. Frances Herbert Nisbet (Fanny) and Nelson married on 11 March 1787 and two months later returned to England.

It was a difficult time, as the enforcement of the Navigation Acts left legal threats and costs. Not for the last time did the Admiralty worry about Nelson's over-zealous pursuit of what he saw as his duty. They did not confirm the promotions and appointments he had made as temporary senior officer in the Leeward Islands. It was a worrying sign. Nelson was put on half pay for the foreseeable future. Fanny had a little money, but the couple were not well off and they moved in with Nelson's father in Norfolk.

Unemployment

The worst thing that can happen to a born fighter is to have no cause for which to fight. Norfolk was quiet and boring compared with Nelson's life at sea. Shooting pheasants and rabbits was not much of a substitute and he was a dangerous huntsman, keeping his weapon fully cocked and firing from the hip at anything that moved. Both he and his wife missed the colourful West Indies.

Nelson was continually trying to get command of a ship, writing endless letters to anyone he could think of who might help him, and there were times when he considered volunteering for another navy, such as Russia's, then neutral. His growing desperation is revealed in a letter he wrote to his friend Cornwallis in October 1788, where he was willing to accept a subordinate position and promised to obey orders.

Although I am set down here in a Country life (And although Happily Married) I always shall as I have ever done be ready to step forth whenever Service requires or My friends may wish Me to serve. Fame says you are going out with a Command [as Commodore in the East Indies]. If in either Active Service or a Wish of Yours to accept of one under Your Command who Reveres and Esteems You, I am ready and willing to go forth and by a Strict adherence to your orders as My Superior.

Visits to London for job hunting were expensive. One journey, in July 1789, cost a total of nearly £21, including the post chaise hire from Burnham Thorpe for 130 miles and back, payment for turnpikes and for lodgings and victuals. This was a big dent in the budget for a young couple living off a few hundred pounds a year. The economy Nelson learned at this time was to be useful later in managing the fleet and dealing with suppliers. Like many able administrators he handled a budget as if it were his own household account (though he was never tight-fisted in either!).

Two of Nelson's brothers were in much less dramatic and more secure modes of employment, in naval administration (Maurice) and in the church (William), but these lacked the dare-devil appeal Nelson sought. He read widely in politics, history and literature and spent the time at home in reflection, learning and thinking, and preparing for battles to come. Five years of sustaining his vision in enforced inactivity took some doing, especially in the face of rejection, both real and imagined.

Going into a trading business would have been risky and not prestigious, and in any case he did not have the capital to get started. To enter politics even more money was needed, as well as influence, and he could do nothing about his less than aristocratic birth. Serving the navy as an agent was a possibility, but there was not enough action and it would have been too bureaucratic and routine. Other professions such as the arts and teaching were badly paid, and required a university education and a certain talent.

Besides, the navy continued to have strong attractions as a career. It was one of the few professions that did not require the purchase of apprenticeships or commissions. Free tuition had been provided to learn his trade, he had enjoyed opportunities for prize money (although he had not made much) and he had had a chance to see the world. Compared with the army, the navy was the senior service. It played a crucial role in defending merchant ships and would defend Britain if war broke out. The poor state of the army as a mostly volunteer operation rather than a standing force meant that regiments would be called up when needed, but not otherwise. By contrast, the navy was the largest and one of the most prestigious bodies in Britain, and was well run compared with other arms of government. The British navy was already much more efficient and a better fighting machine than any other naval force, and in the European fervour for empire war was bound to break out again, sooner rather than later.

So Nelson, the unemployed naval officer, visited relatives in London, and called repeatedly at the Navy Office and the Admiralty for a job. Following up his affairs from the West Indies and continuing to defend his legal position took up some months, and depressingly convinced him that his star was not in the ascendant. Returning to Norfolk had given him the chance to take his wife home and to call on relatives not seen for years, but the freezing weather, the lack of children of his own, and the feeling that he still had not really made it as a naval officer were all demoralising. He was accomplished in so many aspects of his profession and was devoted to it – but where was it getting him?

Then, with the outbreak of the French Revolution in 1793 and the likelihood of war, Nelson was able to write, 'after rain comes sunshine'.

Nelson may not have been the best seaman of his day: other officers had stronger reputations for brilliant seamanship. But he was good enough to pass muster, to gain the respect of seamen, fellow officers and the Admiralty. He was intensely ambitious, willing to make sacrifices to progress his career, and he knew how to work the system of patronage.

From his earliest days at sea as a captain's servant and a midshipman, command was something he wanted. Passing the examination as lieutenant and then being 'made post' as captain, all by the age of 21, were tangible proof of his professional ability. But captains and admirals concerned with promoting talented officers were also looking for management and leadership skills, and they seem to have had a shared view of what these were, although they were not specifically identified or formally measured. Certainly, the ability of a young officer to take command was recognised for its presence or absence fairly early on in his career.

Nelson's rapid promotion reflected his success at patronage, at gaining the invaluable support of his superiors, especially the captains who took him under their wing. Although the eighteenth-century navy was generally meritocratic, especially in times of war, 'influence' or 'interest' was extremely important. This was a crucial consideration for a young officer, and accounts for the many very capable seamen who did not progress beyond lieutenant.

Nelson never regarded himself as wanting in expert knowledge. He drew confidence from his commitment to the navy as a career, his personal courage, and his teamwork with his officers. The foundation of his leadership ability, valuable throughout his whole career, was his expert knowledge from 'learning the ropes', being a practical seaman.

Having a vocation for the navy was an essential part of the mixture. Being an expert leader can be limiting as it commits the leader in question to one area, in Nelson's case to active service at sea, on the front line; although this was very much his choice. He was best used by his superiors as the manager of a large fleet in hostile waters, making the most of his abilities as a manager, a networker, and an inspirer of officers and men, and exploiting the terror he created in the hearts of the enemy. Without knowledge of ships and how they operated, this would have been impossible.

Nelson communicated to others his profound sense of purposeful-ness, and they responded to the ideal he represented: that by excelling at their profession officers and men could become party to something far greater than themselves. By recognising 'vocation' as the ideal of every kind of work, they reached beyond what has in a modern and more pro-saic age been called 'self-actualisation', towards something best called, in Nelson's own dying words, 'duty', as in 'thank God, I have done my duty'.

Nelson's Way
Vocation

How can you develop and show a sense of vocation as Nelson did? This is not just being an expert at your job to gain respect, but seeing the job as a calling. To have a vocation is to have a deep inner commitment to do something, to be part of some greater purpose – not just to be the boss. Having a vocation is much more than being busy and making some money to survive – it is a pursuit in which you really believe.

For you as a leader, to be seen as having a vocation you need to show total commitment – to your profession (as a lawyer, teacher, research chemist), or your company (its brand, culture, identity) or your cus-tomers (patients, students, corporates). It can be difficult, but not impos-sible, to commit to all three at once. You show your commitment by what you prioritise and achieve.

Your colleagues will also be choosing the emphasis of their voca-tion. Ideally, they need to achieve results for their profession, organisa-tion and customers, as well as loving their job. Do you know where they stand? If they are more dedicated to their profession – being a really top pharmacist, for example – this may be at odds with some of the objec-tives of their pharmaceutical company, if research programmes con-flict with profit targets. If they want to please the customers, they may be discounting and over-delivering, and failing to maximise profit margins.

When you are hiring new people, which of the three areas of dedica-tion do you want? If it is loyalty to the organisation, you are looking for knowledge of and interest in that organisation's mission, values, achievements and traditions. For loyalty to a profession, it would be personal qualifications, skills and awards. For customers, it would be testimonials, repeat business, customer loyalty.

GE uses this concept as a matrix, balancing vocation against diligence – or commitment to the values of the company and achieving results. Ideally, it wants people to have both. Those who are diligent but have no sense of vocation undermine the organisation, because they are successful – and possibly admired – but cannot personally represent its values. Those who love the organisation but are weak on results may need more training or resources. Those without diligence or vocation don't belong at GE.

Leadership comments
Sir Jonathon Band

Sir Jonathon Band can be said to have emulated Nelson, joining the navy at 17 and rising through the ranks to Admiral, He is now Commander-in-Chief Fleet, Commander Allied Maritime Component Command Northwood. But, as he explains, 'If you decide to stay in the navy after your apprenticeship, you really have to have that feeling for Nelson.' Inevitably, anyone with a true vocation for a career in Britain's sea-based defences cannot avoid comparing himself (or now, herself) with Britain's most famous naval warrior.

Band makes the point that this comparison is simpler and easier for the navy, as heroes to emulate in the other services are more scattered. 'Nelson's legacy is one of the navy's greatest blessings, lending it a unified character 200 years later,' he points out. Everyone in the navy can look up to Nelson, and 'Trafalgar Day gives us a day in the year to get together as a firm; we are spared the army's regimental loyalties; and the RAF have looked for years to find a unifying event.'

In the navy ambitious officers – just like Nelson – see both their commitment to 'the firm' and their seafaring specialism as equal parts of their vocation: you need deep technical expertise to be a leader. And this is now even more complex than in Nelson's day. 'Every leader here has to be credible; you've got to be a professional, to know the business. As a captain, this is both technically and in the human sense. Getting the right mix of technology and people creates a very strong force,' Band explains. Nelson achieved a good balance here: 'We all use his stories, especially how he dealt with people.'

'These days you need a firm grasp of the technology at your disposal, to know what effect you are having on the operation, to be able to prioritise your actions in the light of the bigger picture and thus to have a good feel for the context.' Technology is a means to an end. 'You are really adding something as a leader if you can put a vocational sense of the impact of technology on the overall operation – as a calling, a service, not just a job to do,' Band insists.

Nelson knew that to rise to the top he had to gain diverse experiences when still young, and this is what Band focused on in his career. So during the 1970s he gained experience in ships in the Far East, he joined an exchange with the US Navy, he served in the West Indies and the South Atlantic, and he worked in fisheries protection around the UK coast, commanding a minesweeper. He gained operational-level experience in the Falklands campaign. He was promoted to Commander in 1983, after 16 years in the navy – not quite so rapid a promotion as Nelson, but without quite so many wars to speed things up.

Patrons and mentors were important to Band too. He acted as Flag Lieutenant to the Commander-in-Chief Fleet during the Falklands – and now occupies that position himself. Continually developing expert knowledge was also vital. Nelson did it by experience; Band was able to add attendance at training courses. Overcoming setbacks also proves your vocational commitment. Nelson overcame unemployment and substantial injuries; Band hung in there despite defence cuts and the considerable reduction in strength of Britain's armed forces in recent years, when others ducked out.

Band departed from Nelson's career track by moving out of a strictly operational and sea-going role and joining the Ministry of Defence – but in the navy, technical excellence is not role limiting, as it may be in other careers. And Band was able to move back and forth between land-based and sea-based jobs.

Band also promotes a sense of common intent in his colleagues, as Nelson did: 'Nelson's colleagues knew they were in his thoughts; they knew what he would have wanted. These days we refer to this as "mission command" and this is what we do – you share what you want to achieve and leave it up to the captains to decide how to do it as circumstances change.'

Everyone having the same sense of vocation brings them more closely together. As Band explains, 'It's people who win and lose campaigns. If you talk with them when there is time, they'll do anything for you in a fight. I say to the young captains, "Talk to your people – they all have financial worries, loves, hates, families, just like you."'

Vocation is expertise with feeling and Band, as Nelson did, tries to emphasise the feeling part. 'Know your people, treat them as individuals, talk to them when they are a bit scared,' he recommends. 'Nelson's ability to talk to his men in this way was unusual but not unique. Personnel issues can go wrong because someone didn't have the guts to say, "You've done that wrong." Are you prepared to tell a guy to his face what he's like, that he's got to sharpen up?' Band follows Nelson's path of combining vocation with diligence. It's not enough to be committed to your work; you must achieve results too.

To prove your sense of vocation you need to be good at all aspects of the job, and 'there is an element of hard work in everything worthwhile. British sailors, by the time of Trafalgar, were well trained and ready to fight for years, reflecting long-term dedication. And they were sustained for so long by Nelson, a charismatic leader with a strong sense of his calling. When it comes to someone to look up to, give me Nelson any day – a national hero who dies at his greatest hour. What stronger commitment can you show?'

Leadership lessons
Vocation

⚓ Do you have to be an expert in your field to be a leader? Not all organisations require it. Many leaders succeed through their generic skills, which are an expertise of their own. But a sense of vocation converts a job into something meaningful and worthwhile.

⚓ What is your vocation? Will becoming a leader of your organisation force you to compromise?

⚓ On the other hand, do you have a vocation to be a leader, and can you achieve this in your field without deep technical expertise?

⚓ If you want to be a leader where expertise is the route to respect, focus on gaining expert knowledge quickly and apply it for ideal ends. This will give you respect beyond the ordinary.

⚓ Search for patrons or mentors and build relationships to gain expert knowledge, using them to give you more opportunities to learn and as stepping-stones to increased influence.

⚓ To prove your dedication to your chosen profession (your vocation), don't give up if you face barriers and bleak times – they will always happen – and don't be diverted by outside interests. You have to be prepared to make sacrifices.

⚓ Keep using the expert knowledge of your specialism even if you are a leader and others can now do these expert jobs. It's a way of reducing risk in decision making, avoiding being ripped off, and continuing to bond with all levels of the organisation – you speak the same language.

⚓ If expert knowledge is respected in your organisation, then use it to select good people.

⚓ You can't be good at everything, so choose a specialism in which to excel within your area of vocation.

⚓ Expert knowledge has to be maintained – nothing stands still, so it has to be worked on all the time.

⚓ Realise the limitations of a vocation to a specialism – this may keep you to an operational role, and there's a long jump from there to higher ranks.

⚓ Vocation is expertise with feeling. Leadership relies on it!

3

COURAGE

Leading from the front, 1793–1798

'It was during this period that perhaps my personal
courage was more conspicuous than at any other part of
my life.'
Nelson

Nelson's bold move to leave the line of battle and opportunistically attack larger Spanish ships threatening to reunite with the rest of their fleet – bringing his ship the *Captain* alongside the *San Nicolas* and using it as a bridge to board the *San Josef.*

'Nelson boarding the San Josef *at the Battle of Cape St Vincent, 14th February, 1797' by George Jones, undated*

B Y MID-1797, THE WAR HAD BEEN IN PROGRESS FOR FIVE years and things were not looking good for Britain. The one great success was the Battle of Cape St Vincent. Rear-Admiral Sir Horatio Nelson, fresh from his triumph at that battle and delighted at his promotion and knighthood, was anxious for more success, and the country needed it. Now flying his flag in the *Theseus* and commanding the inshore squadron blockading the enemy in Cadiz, he tried to provoke them into action: come out and fight, he taunted them, in a highly proactive gesture of aggression. The Spanish had recently come into the war on the French side after being doubtful allies with England, and Nelson – egged on by his Commander-in-Chief, Earl St Vincent, formerly Sir John Jervis – thought they should pay the price.

With 26 ships at Cadiz and another 10 expected to join them from the Mediterranean, the Spanish outnumbered the British force, but had good reason to avoid battle. Their ships were in poor condition and manned by soldiers rather than seamen. Nelson's blockading squadron was only 10 strong, as other ships were away for water and provisions. Nelson insisted on a close blockade, so close that 'we are looking at the Ladies walking the walls and Mall and know of the ridicule they make of their Sea Officers'.

But despite the taunts of both the British and their own women, the Spanish would not come out, so Nelson started a more active bombardment, encouraged by the suddenly bullish Admiralty. It was risky, as there were 4,000 soldiers in Cadiz and impressive fortifications. The blockade was forcing the Spanish to draw on their reserves and weakened their ability to threaten Britain's ally, Portugal. Eventually they might be tempted out to protect the treasure ships expected from South America, but the Spanish sat still. 'What a despicable set of wretches they must be,' Nelson reflected.

Imprisoning the Cadiz fleet was not enough; Nelson and St Vincent wanted to destroy it. They fired shells directly into civilian quarters, 'to irritate the inhabitants' and 'make them force out their fleet'. They then planned a daring but foolhardy bomb vessel attack. On 3 June 1797, Nelson leaked a warning to the Spanish that the British bomb vessels would 'lay Cadiz in ashes'.

In the early hours of 4 June, directing operations from his barge, Nelson suddenly spotted several Spanish gunboats swarming out of the harbour. He ordered Captain Fremantle and 11 of his best men to join him and pull as hard as they could towards the oncoming Spaniards. The seamen raised a cry of 'Follow the admiral!' and made after him, joining a fierce hand-to-hand sword fight. A Spanish barge with 30 officers and men attacked Nelson's 13. It was a moment for outstanding personal courage, visible leadership and skilful swordsmanship.

Nelson knew that every time he led from the front he validated his leadership among the men. The risks he faced were even greater than theirs, as he was so prominent in the uniform of a significant officer. It was a desperate and bloody mêlée, with pistols flashing in the dark, cutlasses clashing, the assailants shouting and cursing. Nelson was proudly able to record that 'eighteen of the Spaniards being killed and several wounded, we succeeded in taking their commander'.

For all his courage, Nelson owed his life to his coxswain, John Sykes. As described by an eyewitness, the burly sailor kept close to his commander at all times, during this ferocious fight:

> *John Sykes was close to Nelson on his left hand, and he seemed more concerned for the Admiral's life than his own: he hardly ever struck a blow but to save his gallant officer. Twice he parried blows that must be fatal to Nelson, for Sykes was a man... who never knew what fear was, any more than his Admiral. It was cut, thrust, fire... the Spaniards fought like devils, and seemed resolved to win from the Admiral the lau-*

rels of his former victory; they appeared to know him, and directed their particular attack towards the officers.

Twice had Sykes saved him; and now he saw a blow descending which would have severed the head of Nelson. In that second of thought which a cool man possesses, Sykes saw that he could not ward the blow with his cutlass... he saw the danger; that moment expired, and Nelson would have been a corpse: but Sykes saved him – he interposed his own hand! We all saw it – we were witnesses to the gallant deed, and we gave in revenge one cheer and one tremendous rally... there was not one man left on board who was not either dead or wounded. 'Sykes,' said Nelson as he caught the gallant fellow in his arms, 'I cannot forget this.' But his wounded shipmate only looked him in the face, and smiled, as he said, 'Thank God, sir, you are safe.'

It was certainly unconventional and even arguably improper for such a senior officer to engage in small skirmishes in such a proactive way. Once committed it was kill or be killed. Exposed in this way he had to be protected and supported – and saved and rescued – by his seamen and brother officers. But this establishes camaraderie like no other: leading from the front is leading in the midst, and is the very essence of heroic leadership. He fought with them, he bled with them and he shared with them the 'rush' of a fight – he really was one of the lads!

The attack as a whole, although militarily of meagre results, became legendary through Nelson's display of courage. Otherwise the results were modest, the British capturing two Spanish boats and 121 prisoners, of whom 91 – those who lived – were handed back later in an exchange. Some civilians had been hurt or killed, including several priests in a monastery. 'That's no harm, they will never be missed,' said Nelson.

With the outbreak of war again in 1793, Nelson was seen as the courageous, battle-hungry, task-oriented, action-led expediter his overlords needed. For much of his life, although the Admiralty and his superior officers needed his strong following and reputation for success, and the fear he struck in enemy hearts, they found him hard to manage. Nelson was no loose cannon, because he always acted in the spirit of the navy and focused on defeating the French, but he was not exactly predictable. He became bored easily, especially in the early 1790s when he was desperate for action after five years of unemployment.

In the next five years, Nelson emerged as the courageous fighter and national hero, finally scoring the first substantial victory over Napoleon's forces, at Aboukir Bay, near the mouth of the River Nile in Egypt. This very active phase of his career shows how highly he valued visibility and setting an example – to say nothing of his own thirst for action.

With the appointment of Admiral Sir John Jervis as Commander-in-Chief of the Mediterranean fleet at the end of 1795, Nelson found a leader after his own heart, totally dedicated to the success of the navy. 'Of the fleets I ever saw, I never saw one in point of officers and men to our present one, and with such a commander-in-chief fit to lead them to glory,' enthused Nelson. Jervis was willing to recognise merit in his captains – and particularly in Nelson. He reflected after close observation of his maverick commodore, 'I never saw a man in our profession... who possessed the magic art of infusing the same spirit into others which inspired their own actions... all agree there is but one Nelson.'

During the 1790s France consolidated its control of the Mediterranean, which was more or less closed to British shipping. The garrisons on Corsica and Elba were evacuated, and Spain and the Italian states allied with France. Britain's only allies were suffering defeats in the German states. Repeated harvest failures at home brought shortages, starvation and the constant threat of rebellion. Only bad weather had prevented a French expedition landing in Ireland, from whence they had planned to invade England.

Nelson's 'dare to win' approach was pitched exactly right for a nation desperately in need of victories, cornered on all sides by the ambitious and brilliantly successful Napoleon, mustering troops only 22 miles away across the English Channel. This was an age of courage, an age of bravery. These were the last few years in which wars were fought between enemies who could literally see and often stab each other, with weapons that were powerful but inaccurate. It would be another 60 years until the American Civil War inaugurated the long-range rifle, forcing commanders on land to the back of the battlefield; meanwhile wars were still fought in much the same way as by the armies of the ancient world.

Away from the battlefield, Protestantism had brought a new sense of individualism and the ideological grounds for believing in a personal destiny sanctioned by God. The growth of a middle class and opportunities to create wealth through trade and industry quite apart from ownership of land reinforced the ideal of the self-made man. Romantic poetry and fiction celebrated the heroic soul and its unique vision, at last set free from the orthodoxies of mediaeval Catholicism. Most of all, though, England needed a hero with courage and bravery, and an age in which war was the norm rather than the exception produced Nelson.

In January 1793, aged 34, Nelson took command of the *Agamemnon*. It was a relatively small vessel – with 64 guns it had less fire power than a major flagship like the *Victory* and the most popular line-of-battle ships, the 74s – but Nelson was delighted with its speed and manoeuvrability.

The six years from 1793 to 1798 were years of conspicuous courage for Nelson. The episodes in which he was able to exhibit this courage in dramatic scenes of leading from the front were many and varied. It would be impossible to discuss them all, so here we will focus on a series of five well-known engagements, told as far as possible in his own words and in those of contemporaries: Corsica, the battle with the *Ça Ira*, the Battle of Cape St Vincent, Tenerife and the Battle of the Nile.

Corsica

After the fall of the French naval base of Toulon to revolutionary French armies and Britain's need for a new base in the western Mediterranean, Nelson's commanding officer, Lord Hood, sent him to Corsica, to the fortified towns of Bastia and Calvi. Bastia surrendered after a seven-week siege. Nelson then went on to attack Calvi, which fell after a six-week attack, and to make sure the powers that be got the message of his contribution clearly this time, he sent a racy and frank account of the siege – and of his personal bravery – to HRH the Duke of Clarence:

> *We landed about four miles to the Westward of Calvi on June 19th [1794]; on July 19th we were in full possession of every outpost of the enemy with very trifling loss. Our batteries were erected with impunity in situations which the enemy ought to have prevented.*
>
> *Had they kept even a moderate look-out, our loss of men must have been great, every battery being within reach of grape-shot from its opponent... we were then only 650 yards from the centre of the citadel, and they allowed us to erect very strong batteries... without firing a single shot or shell... [while negotiations were continuing] four small vessels got in, which gave them hope of more effectual relief, for they rejected our offer [of accepting their surrender] and our fire opened with all the effect we could expect... when the parapet was beaten down, and the houses in the citadel were either in ruins or in flames, the enemy hung out a white flag, and requested a suspension of hostilities for a few hours, to prepare terms.*

In a private letter home, Nelson admitted:

> *you may hear, therefore as it is all past I may tell you that on July 10th last a shot having struck our battery the splinters and stones from it struck me most severely on the face and breast. Although the blow was so severe as to occasion a great flow of blood from my head, yet I most fortunately escaped by only having my right eye nearly deprived of its sight. It was cut down, but is as far recovered as to be able to distinguish light from darkness, but as to all the purpose of its use it is gone. However, the blemish is nothing, not to be perceived unless told. The pupil is nearly the size of the blue part.*

Nelson did not wear the black, piratical eye patch of popular legend and made little of his injury, except when it was to come in useful later, in the famous blind-eye scene at Copenhagen. It was certainly one of the costs of leading from the front.

Fighting with his sailors and an army detachment in this territory that had passed from Italian to French hands, Nelson showed both courage and resilience:

> we have upward of a thousand sick out of two thousand, and others not much better than so many phantoms. We have lost many men from the season, very few from the enemy. I am here the reed among the oaks: all the prevailing disorders have attacked me, but I have not the strength for them to fasten upon. I bow before the storm, but the sturdy oak is laid low.

Despite his injuries and sufferings, Nelson was more concerned with gaining the all-important recognition. His greatest concern was

> what degree of credit may be given to my services I cannot say. General Stuart... is as far asunder as the other generals. They hate us sailors; we are too active for them. We accomplish our business sooner than they like. We throw them – both on sea and on shore – into the background.

After the sieges on Corsica Lord Hood wrote describing the action to the Admiralty and when Nelson saw that his contribution was overlooked in official dispatches, he wrote that Lord Hood

> wished to put me where I never was – in the rear. The whole operations of the siege were carried on through Lord Hood's letters to me. I was the mover of it – I was the cause of its success.

The Ça Ira *and the* Agamemnon

Having at last had a taste of command, Nelson's ambition and desire for action were almost uncontainable and his impatience was showing. His subsequent commander-in-chief, Admiral Hotham, irked him particularly.

Satisfied with modest gains in an engagement with a French flotilla off Toulon, Hotham drew Nelson's wrath when he called off the action. An attack on the 80-gun French *Ça Ira* led to the ship's capture (and the killing and wounding of 400 officers and men) by the smaller *Agamemnon*, but the rest of the fleet escaped. Nelson stormed on board the flagship, more angry at his commander-in-chief than at the enemy, frustrated that 'we have done nothing in comparison with what we might'. This disgust with his superior, bordering almost on mutiny, derived from his desire for action, but more significantly his desire for a result. It was not enough to engage in a fight and win – he was determined to commit his every effort and his forces to achieve the intended outcomes of the campaign. This in part explains his ruthlessness. He was not bloodthirsty, but he did not baulk at unremitting ferocity in pursuit of his ends. Courage was a matter of personal bravery, and it was also the courage of his convictions – to prosecute the cause that he believed to be right.

Nelson knew his own nature. His pent-up ambition was voiced in another letter home:

> *my disposition cannot bear tame and slow measures. Sure I am, had I commanded our fleet... either the whole French fleet would have graced my triumph, or I should have been in a confounded scrape. I went on board Admiral Hotham's ship as soon as our firing grew slack to propose leaving the crippled ships and pursuing the enemy; but he, much cooler than myself, said, 'we must be contented, we have done very well'. Now, had we taken ten sail, and allowed the eleventh to escape when it had been possible to have got at her, I could never have called it well done: we should have had such a day, as I believe the annals of England never produced.*

Cape St Vincent

The opportunity for the fleet action Nelson had sought for so long came, after months of searching, as the enemy was encountered by the small but fighting-fit British fleet of 15 ships commanded by Sir John Jervis, off Cape St Vincent on St Valentine's Day 1797. The captain of Jervis's flagship called out the numbers of the approaching Spanish vessels with increasing alarm.

'There are eight sail of the line, Sir John.'

'Very well, sir.'

'There are twenty sail of the line, Sir John.'

'Very well, sir.'

'There are twenty-five sail of the line, Sir John.'

'Very well, sir.'

'There are twenty-seven sail, Sir John.'

'Enough, sir, no more of that: the die is cast, and if there are fifty sail I will go through them.'

This was very much in the spirit of Nelson himself, who was probably reacting in the same way on board his own ship, pacing up and down with a mixture of excitement and trepidation.

As Jervis had insisted earlier, 'a victory is very essential to England at this moment'. He knew the fleet was ready for this action; he had told the First Lord of the Admiralty, 'Commodore Nelson and several of the captains of the line of battle ships and frigates under my command are of a temper that will work to anything.' And the men were ready for it too. As a veteran mariner at the battle recorded,

> *when everything was cleared, the ports open, the matches lighted, and guns run out, then we gave them three such cheers as are only to be heard on a British man-of-war. This intimidates the enemy more than a broadside, as they have often declared to me. It shows them all is right: and the men in the true spirit baying to be at them.*

Nelson could not have felt more at home than in such company.

As the battle began, the British fleet had succeeded in taking advantage of the separation of the Spanish fleet into two sections, and was concentrating on engaging one group at a time. The Spanish had suddenly seen an opportunity to reunite their split forces and made the necessary manoeuvre. Nelson, in his ship the *Captain*, was third from the rear of the line and saw the Spanish wearing their ships to rejoin the rest of their fleet, potentially turning the tide of the battle.

By leaving Jervis's carefully constructed line of battle, Nelson gambled on an unconventional tactical move, flying in the face of traditional naval procedure. This was a courageous move for many reasons – he knew it would mean that the weight of fire power from many ships would be directed at the *Captain* and also that he may aggravate his commander-in-chief – but with his focus on effect rather than form he took the initiative once again and placed himself in the front line, even though he had been placed near the rear.

Nelson made an order to put the helm hard over, left the British line and sailed straight at the much taller forest of Spanish masts and yards. As an observer wrote after the event:

> *Commodore Sir Horatio Nelson went clean about, and dashed in among the Spanish van, totally unsupported – conduct totally unprecedented, and only to be justified by the most complete success with which it was crowned.*

Another observer wrote that in executing this bold manoeuvre

> *the Commodore reached the sixth ship from the enemy's rear, which was the Spanish Admiral's own ship, the* Santissima Trinidad, *of 136 guns, a ship of four decks, and said to be the largest in the world. Notwithstanding the inequality of force, the Commodore instantly engaged the colossal opponent, and for a considerable time had to contend not only with her, but with her supporting ships, ahead and 'astern, of three decks each.*

As Nelson was joined by other British ships and delivered rapid and devastating broadsides, the Spanish Admiral began to give up the idea of reuniting with the rest of his force.

Nelson argued in letters written for the newspapers after the event that his efforts to prevent the unification of the Spanish fleet won the day. His ship the *Captain*

> *having passed the stern-most of the enemy's ships, consisting of seventeen sail of the line, and perceiving the Spanish fleet to bear up before the wind, evidently with the intention of... joining their separated division or flying from us. To prevent either of their schemes from taking effect, I ordered the ship to be wore... and was soon in close action with*

their van... I was immediately joined and most nobly supported by the Culloden, *Captain Troubridge.*

The *Captain*, a 74, was then being fired on by three first-rates. Nelson continued his description of the events:

At this time, the Captain *having lost her fore-topmast, not a sail, shroud, or rope standing, the wheel shot away, and incapable of further service or in chase, I directed Captain Miller, her commanding officer, to put the helm a-starboard, and calling for boarders, ordered them to board. A soldier having broke the upper quarter-gallery window [of the nearby* San Nicolas*] jumped in, followed by myself and others... having pushed on to the quarter deck, I found Captain Berry, late my first lieutenant, in possession of the poop, and the Spanish ensign hauling down. The next ship nearby, the first rate* San Josef *at this moment fired muskets and pistols from the Admiral's stern-gallery on us.*

I directed my brave fellows to then board this adjoining first rate which was done in a moment. When I got into her main-chains a Spanish officer without a sword came upon the quarter-deck rail, and said the ship had surrendered. On the quarter-deck of a Spanish first-rate, extravagant as the story may seem, did I receive the swords of the vanquished Spaniards, which I gave to William Fearney, one of my bargemen, who placed them, with the greatest sang-froid, under his arm... thus fell these ships. The Victory *passing saluted us with three cheers, as did every ship in the fleet.*

As Nelson continued:

there is a saying in the Fleet too flattering for me to omit telling – viz., 'Nelson's Patent Bridge for Boarding First Rates', alluding to my passing over an enemy's 80-gun ship to then board and take another, larger vessel.

Accounts of the battle differ. Some claim that other British ships from the front of the line had managed to fire a broadside into the *San Nicolas* before Nelson reached it, and the three ships that followed Nelson into the fray were not long in joining battle. The action was, in any case, an example of this fleet's readiness for pell-mell action and the courage it entails. Nelson's initiative exemplified this attitude: he led the attack even if the outcomes depended on a multitude of causes – and Admiral Jervis recognised and supported his initiative.

Nelson gained the Order of the Bath, and his promotion to Rear Admiral by seniority had already been gazetted. His exciting narrative of events, his strong teamwork skills and his ability to inspire and encourage fellow officers and seamen enabled him to shine in this first major fleet action. Undoubtedly his level of personal activity and courage, in leaving the line of battle and boarding the enemy ships, was an important part of his contribution to the success of this battle. His performance in this engagement validated his forward leadership style to himself and others.

Setbacks at Tenerife

However, Nelson's approach to leadership did not come without risk. Under the directions of Jervis (now created Earl St Vincent), Nelson and his comrades-in-arms attempted a night attack on Santa Cruz, Tenerife, with the aim of capturing rich Spanish treasure ships, homeward bound from America. Despite the failure of a previous attempt, Nelson would not give up on the idea. With his dramatic do-or-die tag-line 'tomorrow my head will probably be crowned with either laurel or cypress', he launched another courageous attack. He included this phrase in a letter to Jervis. It was the last he was to write with his right hand.

Nelson believed the harbour of Santa Cruz to be poorly defended and was convinced that a frontal assault was best. Leading a flotilla of small boats rowing several miles in bad weather, he drew his sword to step onto the harbour wall and received a direct hit that shattered his right arm. White-faced and bleeding heavily, he was laid in the bottom of the boat and rowed back to the *Theseus*. As a young midshipman on board wrote,

> *at half past ten the marines and seamen from the different ships put off and began to row towards the mole head, under the command of our*

brave Admiral. At one a.m. commenced one of the heaviest cannonading I ever was witness to from the town upon our boats, likewise a heavy fire of musketry, which continued without intermission for the space of four hours.

At two, Admiral Nelson returned on board, being dreadfully wounded in the right arm with grapeshot. Imagine my situation when I beheld our boat approach with him, whom has been a second father to me, his right arm dangling by his side. With a spirit that astonished everyone, he told the surgeon to get his instruments ready, for he knew that he must lose his arm, and the sooner it was off the better. He underwent the amputation with the same firmness and courage that have always marked his character.

This loss at Tenerife was an important aspect of his development as a leader and manager. It reduced, but did not entirely erase, his determination to lead from the front. From now on we see fewer examples of personal bravado on his part, but no lack of courage.

The kind of engagements in which he was involved after 1797 – the major fleet actions of the Nile, Copenhagen and Trafalgar – presented fewer opportunities for leading from the front. A ship of the line is much less mobile and manoeuvrable than an army battalion and an officer on horseback. Once aboard a ship in the middle of a major battle, Nelson faced a constraint familiar to all who like to lead from the front. Enveloped in immediate action, shrouded in smoke and noise, a front-line commander has little opportunity to influence the unfolding events of a large-scale battle. Personal courage must give way to the moral courage of conviction that characterises effective strategic command.

The tragic failure of Tenerife, of which Nelson was reminded every moment by excruciating pain in the stump of his arm, left him in the depths of depression. In an unsteady left-handed scrawl, he wrote to his commander-in-chief:

I am become a burthen to my friends and useless to my Country... a left-handed Admiral will never be considered useful... I hope you will be able to give me a frigate, to convey the remains of my carcase to England.

Jervis's encouragement ('mortals cannot command success,' he reassured) restored Nelson's confidence. After a difficult seven months of recovery at home, he rejoined the Mediterranean fleet, where he was to achieve possibly his greatest triumph, at Aboukir Bay at the mouth of the Nile on 1 August 1798.

The victory of the Nile

In early 1798, having recovered from the loss of his arm, Nelson joined the *Vanguard*, with Captain Edward Berry, and re-entered the Mediterranean, where the French were preparing a large expedition. He was chosen to lead the squadron as, the Admiralty agreed,

> *his acquaintance with that part of the world, as well as his activity and disposition, seem to qualify him in a peculiar manner for that service. The appearance of a British squadron in the Mediterranean is a condition on which the fate of Europe may at this moment be stated to depend.*

Nelson's squadron of 15 ships was captained by men he respected, with experience of major fleet actions, and he came to know them well over the two months of the campaign, discussing contingencies for every circumstance of battle and building up the team culture he saw as an important part of his leadership style. It was a frustrating search as Nelson and his captains fruitlessly hunted a massive French convoy, commanded by Napoleon himself. Acting on information from the Turkish governor, Nelson arrived off Alexandria for the second time, and suddenly realised there were many more vessels in port than had been there before and they were not Turkish or Egyptian. It was the French transports – but where were the ships of the line?

Anxiously Nelson and his squadron sailed eastwards along the coast and found the French at anchor in Aboukir Bay. It was already late and the sun was beginning to go down. The French captains were dining with their admiral. From the point of view of surprise, it was the perfect moment, but a night attack was almost universally considered too risky. The British had few recent charts of the bay, but knew it to be shallow.

The French were anchored and might have swung chains between the boats to prevent the British sailing between them and raking them fore and aft. Worst of all, a night attack risked 'friendly fire'. Knowing all this, and that the French would know it too, Nelson ordered an immediate attack in the sailing order in which they arrived.

As Captain Berry of the *Vanguard* described:

> *the utmost joy seemed to animate every breast on board the squadron... the Admiral himself had the highest opinion of, and placed the firmest reliance on, the valour and conduct of every captain... It had been his practice during the cruise, whenever the weather and circumstances would permit, to have his captains on board the* Vanguard, *where he would fully develop to them his own ideas of the different and best modes of attack, and such plans as he proposed to execute upon falling in with the enemy, whatever their position or situation might be, by day or by night. With the masterly ideas of their Admiral, therefore, on the subject of naval tactics, every one of the captains of his squadron was most thoroughly acquainted. Upon surveying the situation of the enemy, they could ascertain with precision what were the ideas and intentions of their commander, without the aid of further instructions; by which means signals became almost unnecessary, much time was saved, and the attention of every captain could almost undistractedly be paid to the conduct of his ship...*
>
> *As all the officers of our squadron were totally unacquainted with Aboukir Bay, each ship kept sounding as she stood in. The enemy appeared to be moored in a strong and compact line of battle, close in with the shore, their line describing an obtuse angle in its form, flanked by numerous gun-boats, four frigates, and a battery of guns and mortars on a nearby island... The situation of the enemy seemed to secure to them the most decided advantages, as they had nothing to attend to but their artillery, in their superior skill in the use of which the French so much prided themselves.*
>
> *The position of the enemy presented the most formidable obstacles; but the Admiral viewed these with the eye of a seaman determined on attack, and it instantly struck his eager and penetrating mind, that where there was room for an enemy's ship to swing, there was room for one of ours to anchor. No further signal was necessary than those*

already made. The Admiral's designs were as fully known to his squadron as was his determination to conquer, or perish in the attempt.

So this was the scene: the French ships, 13 in number, were moored close to the shore, stretched in a line of nearly two miles, with four more nearer the shoreline. The 15 British ships approached in a scattered formation. The French captains interrupted their dinner with Admiral Bueys and hurried back to their own ships.

Nelson's flagship, the *Vanguard*, was not at the head of the line as they approached, and he was able to observe events until he engaged directly with *Le Spartiate*. Troubridge on the *Culloden* was first in, but ran aground on a sandbank. He was followed by Captain Foley of the *Goliath*, who spotted that the French were anchored only by their bows and must therefore have enough deep water to swing. Acting on his own initiative Foley was the first to sail between the French fleet and the shore, followed by three other ships, carefully sounding the depths as they progressed. As his midshipman reported,

> *it was agreed there was room to pass between the enemy ship and her anchor, the danger being the ship was close to the edge of the shoal... I heard Foley say he should not be surprised to find the Frenchman unprepared for action on the inner side; and as we passed her bow I saw he was right. Her lower deck ports were not run out, and there was lumber, such as bags and boxes, on the upper deck ports, which I reported with no small pleasure. We first fired a broadside into the bow. Not a shot could miss at this distance.*

Nelson was thus able to concentrate his forces on the head of the French line – the windward end, meaning it would be hard for the other French ships to put on sail and come to the relief of their comrades. The British ships, several sailing between the French ships and the shore and firing on their unprotected and unarmed side, attacked their enemy from left and right in a devastating pincer movement. Each British ship anchored close to their appointed enemy and pounded them relentlessly, one by one.

Samuel Hood, the captain of the *Zealous*, told his story:

I commenced such a well-directed fire into Le Guerrier's *bow within pistol shot a little after 6pm, that her foremast went by the board in about seven minutes, just as the sun was closing the horizon; on which the whole squadron gave three cheers... the French later admitted that the enthusiastic cheers were very disheartening to them... and in ten minutes more her main and mizzen masts went; at this time also went the mainmast of the second ship,* Le Conquérant. *I could not get* Le Guerrier's *commander to strike for three hours, though I hailed him twenty times, and seeing he was totally cut up and only firing a stern gun now and then.*

The approaching night made the battle dangerous for both sides. Nelson tried to help the British ships identify each other by a system of lanterns swung from the mizzen peak, but many ships were dismasted and without colours and much chaos ensued, while the British captains did their best to secure prizes and prevent unnecessary loss of life.

For the French, the lowest point in the disaster was the explosion of *L'Orient*, their 120-gun flagship. As a young midshipman recalled:

the conflagration soon began to rage with dreadful fury... the brave Brueys, the French commander-in-chief, having lost both his legs, was seated with tourniquets on the stumps, in an armchair facing his enemy, and giving directions for extinguishing the fire, when a cannon ball put an end to his gallant life, by nearly cutting him in two.

Both fleets waited for the inevitable explosion.

Nelson, forgetful of his own wounds [a head wound that was to cause headaches and dizziness years later] hearing from his captain of the expected fate of his rival Admiral, came on deck and ordered every boat to be dispatched to save the crew... the cold, clear, placid light of the moon formed a striking contrast with that of the burning ship and enabled the lines of the hostile fleets to be clearly distinguished. Every moment the dreadful explosion was expected – the least noise could now be heard, where the din of war before raged with such uncontrollable violence – till at last an awful and terrific glare of light blinding the very sight showed L'Orient *blowing up, with an astounding crash, paralyzing all around her, by which near a thousand brave spirits were hastened into eternity.*

As Nelson became sure of victory, Captain Berry reported:

the first consideration that struck his mind was concern for the danger of so many lives, to save as many as possible. A boat, the only one still seaworthy, was instantly dispatched from the Vanguard, *and other ships that were in a position to do so immediately followed the example; by which means the lives of about seventy Frenchmen were saved.*

Soon after the burning of *L'Orient*, Nelson called for his secretary to begin writing his dispatch to Earl St Vincent. At the sight of Nelson with a bloodied bandage covering most of his head, the secretary was too overcome to write. Impatiently pushing up his bandage, Nelson started drafting his report, sent a day after the battle and arriving in London at the Admiralty more than two months later:

Almighty God has blessed His Majesty's arms in the late battle, by a great victory over the fleet of the enemy, who I attacked at sunset on the 1st of August, off the mouth of the Nile. The enemy were moored in a strong line of battle for defending the entrance to the Bay of Shoals flanked by numerous gun-boats, four frigates and a battery of guns and mortars on an island... but nothing could withstand the squadron your Lordship did me the honour to place under my command. Their high state of discipline is well known to you, and with the judgment of the captains, together with their valour, and that of the officers and men of every description, it was absolutely irresistible.

Could anything from my pen add to the character of the captains, I would write it with pleasure, but that is impossible... the support and assistance I have received from Captain Berry cannot be sufficiently expressed. I was wounded in the head, and obliged to be carried off the deck: but the Service suffered no loss by that event: Captain Berry was fully equal to the important work then going on, and to him I must beg leave to refer you for any information relative to this victory. He will present you with the flag of the second in command, that of the Commander in Chief being burnt in L'Orient.

The Battle of the Nile catapulted Nelson to stardom. As described by Sir William Hamilton, the British Ambassador in Naples, 'the glorious victory of the first of August is like the Church of St Peter's in Rome. It strikes you at first sight from its magnitude, but the more you examine its dimensions and details the more wonderful it appears.' With a knighthood and recognition as a brilliant, if maverick, sea officer, the success at the Nile was an essential step on the trail of glory that culminated in Trafalgar. It was to be Nelson's first independently commanded fleet action, and was also a product of his success in building up those important relationships with his captains. If the Battle of St Vincent was the climax of Nelson leading from the front, the Nile saw the rise to prominence of the 'band of brothers', the group of captains that formed an essential ingredient in future battles.

This period, culminating in the victory of the Nile, secured the Nelson legend. His iconic status rested on his trade-mark style of leading from the front in a series of dramatic engagements, exhibiting his personal bravery and acting as a magnet in inspiring others. His personal courage was many times tested and not found to be wanting. The engagements described are just a selection of some of the more famous incidents; there were dozens more, and many hundreds of pages could be (and have been) filled with descriptions of them.

With the huge success at the Nile Nelson gained a greater degree of confidence and assertiveness. It confirmed his aggressive approach and strengthened his position at the Admiralty. The role of a supportive superior officer was key, freeing Nelson from the yoke of an admiral whose authority he could not respect. On behalf of himself and his brother officers, he described St Vincent as 'our father, under whose fostering care we have been led to fame'.

Nelson's way of leading from the front was not just bravado, it took things forward. He wanted action and progress and was impatient with people sitting around waiting for things to happen. Daily life in the late eighteenth century would have been affected by much that was beyond the control of ordinary people: the weather, the economy, wars and God. Although Nelson believed in God, or Providence, he also believed in taking charge. He would willingly accept responsibility whatever the risk, seeing every battle as having one of two outcomes: 'Westminster Abbey or Glorious Victory!'

This simplistic, black-and-white view – typical of the 'fighting from the front' approach – was at odds with the more measured, balanced view of political leaders, less carried away with the glory of the whole thing. Thus the Admiralty often held a different opinion, that a success was less dramatic or a failure less spectacular. Not there at the scene, they may not have shared the excitement of battle and were looking instead at the cost and political results. Nelson's perspective was much more immediate and could be less strategic. And because of his escalating fame, and his detailed and well-written accounts, his interpretation has tended to gain more attention.

These years of the mid-1790s showed the ongoing development of Nelson as commander, maintaining the hierarchy and systems of the navy but building outstanding support from his seamen and officers through his concern for their morale, welfare and other needs. It strengthened his power base, increasing in all the dimensions of formal and informal power. But Nelson would be the first to admit that his effectiveness rested on the very solid foundation of a large and successful organisation with a strong track record – the navy. He had strengthened his position of respect through his expert knowledge of (and commitment to) his profession, reinforced by experience in combat. He had built up a good reputation as a commander of immense personal courage, taking anything the enemy could give. Now, in the years after the Battle of the Nile, this commitment was to be tested in a unique and unexpected way.

Nelson's Way
Courage

How can you, as a leader, develop courage? It could be mental or moral courage, not necessarily the more obvious Nelson-style physical courage. Is your organisation too large and complex for your courage and confidence to be visible to all? You can practise 'quiet leadership' from behind the scenes and still show moral courage, doing what you think is right. How can you encourage others to discover their courage in their own way and overcome their fears? How can you find courageous people to work for you?

Courage is mental, moral or physical strength to confront fear and withstand danger. It is not about blind bravado, but about purposefully overcoming difficulties and barriers, being brave at heart. It is having pluck, fortitude and confidence, and being resolute. It is sticking to what you believe in.

To be seen as courageous, you need to have the courage of your convictions. It may mean commitment to targets and objectives, despite problems standing in the way. It can mean making tough decisions: to pull out of a profitable market where the company is ethically compromised, to downsize when you have to, to enforce unpopular regulations.

There are drawbacks to being courageous. Over-confidence, denying problems and refusing to admit mistakes may appear to be courageous but could just be pig-headed obstinacy. However, being afraid to stand up for what you believe because of the fear of losing approval is a real failure of courage.

Colleagues and subordinates will be courageous in an atmosphere of trust, where they can see that their leader is resolute in his or her objectives, and if their own sense of conviction to the cause is encouraged. Different people will show different forms of courage – jumping into a river to save someone from drowning, giving an interview to the press on live television, whistle-blowing on unethical activities or standing up for others who they feel are being abused. Evidence of courage is to be found in most businesses wherever people take risks for what they believe to be right.

Leadership comments
Henry Mintzberg

Always prepared to go against established thinking, management professor Henry Mintzberg recognises courage as crucial to leadership: 'Nobody can be a leader without courage because by definition leaders break away from the crowd, from what is known and accepted. Nelson did this. Other admirals were behind the scenes, but Nelson was out there, with his wounds on display. But leaders don't have a monopoly on courage. Lots of people are courageous, but as a leader you have to demonstrate it for people to respond to it. This is not to say that you have to be in the spotlight all the time: modesty is a virtue too, a sign of real heroism, and very effective.'

Mintzberg has also taken risks, been outspoken and had the courage to be slightly maverick – and he has been visible about it. The Cleghorn Professor of Management at McGill University in Canada, he is a renowned scholar, and is especially known for being an innovator in management education and development. In the 1970s he went against the grain of management research by basing his work on observations of what managers actually do (rather than theoretical notions about what they 'ought' to be doing – planning, controlling and so forth). Then a few years later he did the same with strategy, pointing out that strategy actually emerges from a mass of small innovations in response to unfolding events. What we often call strategy is an attempt to see patterns in this mass of activity.

He considers that Nelson's brand of courage was also shown in his 'deep visceral understanding' of the navy; he lived and breathed it, 'like Gandhi lived and breathed India'. Nelson was passionate about his work, as we shall see in the next chapter: 'Of course he had contradictory passions, and like most of us he struggled to find a balance. Anyone who has just one passion is dull – passionate people can commit totally to more than one thing.'

Mintzberg points out that Nelson maintained other people's trust, mainly because he was honest with them: 'It would be difficult to find anyone as revered as Nelson who didn't have that trust. It's about honesty. This kind of moral courage was really more important in the long run than physical courage, though that too is a kind of honesty in action.'

Certainly, one of the most attractive things about Nelson is his authenticity. No one could accuse Nelson of being too modest, but his high visibility was functional – people knew what he stood for. It was obvious what he was about, and his weaknesses were not hidden away. He always had the courage of his convictions, even when he was wrong.

Mintzberg considers that Nelson represented courage because he did what he thought was right in an instinctive way: 'The actual meaning of heroism is about taking risks and doing decent things.' Nelson laid himself on the line – he wasn't detached and distant, and he had a strong sense of responsibility. He was a manager as well as a leader – as all leaders should be – and was getting on with the job on a daily basis, and everyone knew it.

Nelson lived in an era where physical courage was needed to operate and live from day to day. Mental and moral courage were less obvious, but just as inspirational in the long run. 'Inspiration is a chemical thing,' Mintzberg maintains. 'There is a certain chemistry that works in the right conditions.' Nelson's courage and authenticity inspired people at the time; his example has inspired others more broadly since then, but he probably could not have arisen as a hero in any other context.

Leadership lessons
Courage

- Courage can be mental and moral as well as physical. As a leader you are always visible, even if no one can see you – they will have an image of you and they know if you have courage or not.
- Some situations require more visibility than others – especially in operational roles – but there is no hiding place, even if you choose to be behind the scenes.
- If you want to be a courageous leader, you'll never make a name for yourself without taking risks and huge responsibility.
- People have to know what you stand for – you can't be courageous without a cause.
- In the middle of the action, things will look different than from behind the scenes. Don't expect others to see things the same way as

you do – and your perspective may not always be accurate. Are you sure you can see the wood for the trees?

⚓ Being at the front you are showing your courage, but you are most exposed if things go wrong, and you need to ask yourself whether this way is the best use of your leadership role.

⚓ If you are at the front, show moral and mental courage as absolute confidence in a positive outcome – others are looking towards you to set an example.

⚓ Having the courage to be creatively insubordinate is easier when you've done it a few times, especially if you've built a reputation for being successful.

⚓ But being a maverick is similar to being a loose cannon – you will not always get away with it, and not everyone will share your enthusiasm. Courage can be seen as over-confidence.

⚓ Even out of the limelight all leaders need moral courage above all!

4

PASSION

Public life and private life, 1798–1801

'I am writing opposite Lady Hamilton, therefore you will
not be surprised at the glorious jumble of this letter, was
your Lordship in my place I much doubt if you could write
so well, our hearts and our hands must be all in a flutter.
Naples is a dangerous place, and we must keep clear of it.'

Nelson

A pastel portrait of Emma Hamilton (part of a pair with a portrait of Nelson) painted on their overland journey from Naples to England. His favourite picture, it hung in his cabin at sea and he called it his 'guardian angel', bringing him both luck and victory.

'Lady Emma Hamilton' by Johann Schmidt, 1800.

A S NELSON GUIDED HIS BATTLE-SCARRED SHIPS NORTH towards Naples in early September 1798, he could have had little idea of the reception awaiting him. It was a month after the annihilation of the French fleet at the Battle of the Nile; he was still nursing his injuries, with headaches and fever brought on by the stress. He knew he had achieved a fabulous victory, but he was not prepared for this gushing letter from Emma, Lady Hamilton, the young wife of the British Ambassador, whom he had met only once, five years before:

> *My dear, dear Sir how shall I begin what shall I say to you – tis impossible I can write for since last monday I am delerious with joy and assure you I have a fevour caus'd by agitation and pleasure. Good God what a victory – never never has their been any thing half so glorious so compleat. I fainted when I heard the joyfull news and fell on my side and am hurt but what of that – I should feil it a glory to die in such a cause – no I would not like to die till I see and embrace the victor of the Nile. How shall I describe the transports of the Maria Carolina [the Queen of Naples] – tis not possible - she fainted cried kiss'd her Husband her children walked frantic with pleasure about the room cried kiss'd and embraced every person near her exclaiming oh brave nelson oh God bless and protect our Brave deliverer, oh nelson nelson what do we not owe to you oh victor saviour of itali.*

The letter continues in the same vein for another three pages, about the rejoicing, the 3,000 lamps of illuminations, the excitement of the Neapolitans, 'not a french dog may show his face', 'all the english vied with each other in celebrating this most gallant and ever memerable victory'. Emma sent him fan mail, letters from the Queen of Naples, described her dress with Nelson's anchors embroidered all over it, invited him to stay at the Embassy, and declared: 'I pitty all those who were not in the Battle. I would have been rather an english powder monkey or a swab in that great victory than an emperor out of it.' She was suddenly his greatest fan.

Sir William Hamilton, the Ambassador, added his more phlegmatic but similarly enthusiastic note:

> *History ancient or modern does not record an action that does more honour to the Heroes that gained the Victory than the late one of the first of August. You have now made yourself, My Dear Nelson, Immortal. God be praised! And may you live long to enjoy the sweet Satisfaction of having added such Glory to our Country and most probably put an end to the Confusion and Misery in which all Europe would soon have been involved. You may well conceive, my dear Sir, how happy Emma and I are in the reflection that it is you, Nelson, our bosom Friend, that has done such wondrous good in having humbled these proud robbers and vain boasters. A pleasant apartment is ready for you in my House, and Emma is looking out for the softest pillows to repose the few wearied limbs you have left.*

Captains Thomas Troubridge and Alexander Ball were the first of the Nile commanders to arrive at Naples, and out went dozens of boats to meet them, including the barges of the King of Naples and the Hamiltons. When Sir William reached Ball's ship the *Alexander*, he pointed out the royal barge and shouted: 'My lads! That is the king, whom you have saved, with his family and kingdom!'

'Very glad of it, sir – very glad of it,' came the reply. The next day was the anniversary of the King's coronation, and a perfect time for the hero Nelson to arrive.

The quayside and sea front were thronged with a heaving mass of Neapolitans from the early morning, and the bay was filled with 500 boats, including those of the Hamiltons and the royal family again, with their sea-borne bands playing. Every vessel was waving flags, all moving towards the dark hulk of a battle-scarred warship, the *Vanguard*. Nelson, standing on his quarter-deck in his best frock coat with his Star of the Order of the Bath, was moving the stump of his right arm, his 'fin', as a sign of irritability. He had given two orders to the fleet that morning, a 21-gun salute to the King and 'the Ships of the Squadron at this place are to use all possible dispatch in victualling and fitting for sea and report to me the moment they are ready'.

At that point, Nelson wanted nothing more than to be away from the place as soon as possible.

During the Battle of the Nile Nelson was wounded again with a painful laceration to his forehead. It caused him constant headaches, possibly impairing his vision, and some suggest that it affected his judgement. Now he, his ships and his men were exhausted. His first major independent command, months of fruitless searching, a battle lasting over 22 hours and finally the stunning victory were almost too much for him.

Naples was then the second largest city in Europe, after Paris, and was a thriving, cosmopolitan centre of culture. The threat of French invasion had been lifted. The city opened its arms to Nelson, and he fell exhausted and relieved into them – in the person of Emma Hamilton. She loved his fighting spirit, shared his sense of adventure, thrived on the adoring crowds and led the gratitude of Naples towards the man who had – temporarily – saved them from Napoleon.

There had been a number of previous women in Nelson's life. There were several young ladies he wanted to marry before he met Frances Nisbet, who became his wife. Then a succession of mistresses in a series of ports cheered his campaigns. One such was Adelaide Correglia, an opera singer in Leghorn, who received letters from him in his bad schoolboy French in 1796.

Nelson did seem to differentiate between 'respectable' ladies and those less so (Emma being a nice combination of the two), but overall showed a lack of experience in dealing with women, not surprising after the death of his mother and separation from his family at such a young age. And as a sailor, he spent most of his life at sea. Since 1793 he had been home only for seven months' convalescence after the loss of his arm.

By the time of the Nile campaign Nelson was already lukewarm about his marriage. Much of the excitement had gone after his long period of unemployment, and Fanny had begun to fuss over his health and exposure to danger in a way that irritated him. They had no children of their own, though Nelson had taken his stepson Josiah to sea and ensured his rapid promotion. But Josiah was a disappointment both as an officer and a companion. Nelson enjoyed praise and adoration and, although his wife was loving and devoted, it was not her style to flatter him. Yet her behaviour was always exemplary and probably the worst thing she did, as far as Nelson was concerned, was to stand in the way of him marrying Emma.

Nelson also had limited experience of the life of the aristocracy and gentry in smart society in London, and did not much care for what he heard about it. He had spent the major part of his life overseas and found varying moral standards everywhere he went. The fact that he already realised that Naples was 'a dangerous place' is a hint about his appreciation of a completely different outlook there, somewhere he was to describe as full of 'fiddlers and poets, whores and scoundrels'. But with this backdrop it was certainly easier to indulge in an adulterous affair. It was an intoxicating place, far from the conventions of his home, his wife and fine society.

Nelson came to Naples to refit and repair his ships after the battle, and – as we have seen – did not originally intend to stay there very long. But the ships made slow progress, Nelson himself was sick with fever and he still had to keep up the blockade of Alexandria to prevent the French transports from escaping. The reception from the Neapolitan crowds, and the Hamiltons themselves, was so much warmer than he expected, and before he knew what he was doing, Nelson had moved into the Pallazzo Sessa, the British Embassy, and was being sucked into life at court.

Emma's own history was well known in Naples and she was widely seen as having improved her position in life considerably in becoming the wife of the British Ambassador. She was born of poor parents from the Wirral in Cheshire, and had moved to London to make her fortune after the early death of her father. Fêted as a great beauty, she was wild and untamed, without social graces. After a series of aristocratic lovers (including one by whom she bore a child) she was picked up by the Honourable Charles Greville and established as his mistress, aged 17, with her mother as his housekeeper, in Paddington Green. Here she met the artist George Romney, who painted at least two dozen studies of her in various poses during her years in London, establishing his reputation with the 'Divine Lady'.

William Hamilton left England in 1764 for a career in the diplomatic service in Naples. Knighted in 1772, he was a much-respected ambassador and keen art collector. His first wife died childless in 1782, and he was on leave in London in 1784 when, at the house of nephew Charles Greville, he met Emma and invited her to Naples. By now Greville wanted to marry an heiress and needed both money and respectability, so he passed Emma to his uncle, who coincidentally settled his estate on Greville.

Arriving in Naples aged only 21, Emma at first believed that Greville would come for her, but eventually settled comfortably into high-society life. As an unmarried woman she could not be officially presented at court. Sir William adored her beauty, charming company and having her youthful energy around the place – perhaps as a more exciting item in his art collection – and wanted her to join in his life at court. Briefly back in England in 1791, when he was 61 and she was 26, they married. From the beginning he would have a fear of being cuckolded. Contemporary satirist John Wolcott wrote:

O Knight of Naples, is it come to pass,
That thou hast left the gods of stone and brass,
To wed a deity of flesh and blood?
O lock the temple with thy strongest key,
For fear thy diety, a comely She,
Should one day ramble, in a frolic mood!

Naples was a wild and exciting place, well suited to the young Emma. She presented posed 'Attitudes' in Greek costume, she sang, and she was accepted at court. Queen Maria Carolina was the sister of Queen Marie Antoinette in France – they were Habsburgs married to Bourbons – and her brother Leopold was Emperor of Austria. When Leopold died and the new emperor was too young to rule, the Convention in Paris took the opportunity to declare war on Austria. Naples then became closer to Britain and gained protection from the British fleet. In return, Naples would supply troops to help the British cause in the Mediterranean.

Before the Nile...

Nelson had first arrived in Naples in September 1793 and was presented to King Ferdinand (although the Queen was more effectively the ruler) and met Sir William. Nelson negotiated the sending of 6,000 Neapolitan troops to Toulon, in support of a British garrison fending off a concerted French siege (in which a young artillery officer, Napoleon Bonaparte, distinguished himself). He also met Emma, who visited the *Agamemnon*, but Nelson left in a hurry, as French warships had suddenly been sighted off Sardinia. Meanwhile the Neapolitan troops in Toulon were easily defeated, and Nelson was not to return for five years.

Emma became an established part of the diplomatic and social life of Naples. She was so beautiful and pure looking that she was, apparently, mistaken by local Neapolitans for a reincarnation of the Virgin Mary.

Then in early 1794 Lord Hood ordered his attacks on Bastia on the island of Corsica, firing shells imported from Naples. They were 'but good for nothing,' said a captain who fired them. The court in Naples was plunged into mourning for the guillotined Marie Antoinette, sister of the Queen. A Jacobin plot was discovered, Vesuvius erupted, and visitors poured into Naples, attracted by its reputation for fashion and libertine values. Emma became increasingly close to the Queen, introducing her to visitors and translating for her, speaking fluent Italian interspersed with English in her Cheshire accent.

Meanwhile the alliance against France was disintegrating, and Charles IV of Spain wrote to his brother Ferdinand in Naples that Spain would join France and help it invade England. Maria Carolina stole the letter, gave it to Emma, and she copied it to the British Government. Emma's role in acting between the Governments of Naples and England was later to be part of her claim to fame, or at least a claim to her pension. It was also a service she offered to Nelson, who used this as a way of justifying their relationship; Emma was a 'heroine' and useful in the cause against the French.

But 1796 was disastrous for the allies. The French army conquered Holland, Belgium, Savoy and up to the Rhine, and everyone knew that Naples would be next. After occupying Milan, the French headed south. As a result of the treaty between France and Spain, Charles IV was to declare war on England, and Naples signed an armistice of neutrality with France. Sir John Jervis, Nelson's commander-in-chief, then abandoned the Mediterranean. There were no bases left for British ships, so it was impossible to sustain a presence.

By 1797 Sir William and Emma wanted to go home on leave again, but it was clearly impossible, with the Mediterranean a complete war zone.

The Austrians had withdrawn from Lombardy, and with the British leaving the Mediterranean, the influence of Naples was dramatically undermined. Napoleon was progressively moving down Italy and had occupied Rome. The pro-French Marquis de Gallo had been installed in Naples to keep an eye on the Hamiltons and the royal family. The Neapolitans begged Jervis (now Earl St Vincent) for assistance. He decided to re-enter the Mediterranean to support a new coalition against France, and Nelson was put in command of a detachment from the fleet.

St Vincent now needed to win a signal victory to improve morale and boost anti-French efforts across Europe. Nelson, thus charged, left Cadiz in May 1798. Off Toulon in early June, he was joined by a total of thirteen 74-gun ships, and by a group of officers who were to become his 'band of brothers'. As St Vincent wrote to Nelson:

I am sure your heart will bleed, when I tell you, that the lovely Queen of Naples is in the deepest affliction and distress, and has called upon me personally to fly to her succour. Happy you! Who have that lot.

In the process, any port not letting him land for water and provisions should be seen as hostile. Nelson, rushing around all over the

Mediterranean, sent Troubridge to Naples with three questions: Where was the enemy? Would Naples send frigates to help Nelson's efforts? And were the ports of Naples and Sicily open to the British fleet? Sir William Hamilton was trying to get the answers, but Naples was officially neutral and just a few ships were allowed in at any one time, not a whole fleet. Naples was afraid of a rupture with France, especially since the French had taken Malta and left Naples heavily exposed.

Nelson's greatest concern was that his ships and seamen should be fed and watered, and so Emma arrived on the scene again, claiming that it was she who obtained an order from the Queen to the governors of the ports of the Kingdom of Naples and Sicily enabling Nelson to victual his fleet in Syracuse. Troubridge was also able to get a written order to the same effect, and in any case Nelson was prepared to breeze in and try his luck. After being in pursuit of the French for two months without stopping – and there was nowhere to stop – the call at Syracuse was a lifesaver. Nelson acknowledged Emma's contribution:

> *The British fleet under my command could never have returned the second time to Egypt, had not Lady Hamilton's influence with the Queen of Naples caused letters to be wrote to the governor of Syracuse, that he was to encourage the fleet being supplied with everything, should they put into any port in Sicily. We put into Syracuse, and received every supply; went to Egypt, and destroyed the French fleet.*

Emma was to play this card in the future, arguing that she contributed a key factor to the victory of the Nile and thus deserved a pension in her own right. She annotated Nelson's letters on such matters to try to strengthen her case. For example, when Nelson was critical about the failure of Naples to rise up against the French occupation of Rome soon after the Nile (in a letter dated 13 August 1798 he asked, 'Why will not Naples act with vigour?'), she wrote on the back, 'In consequence of this note we made Naples act with vigour' then signed 'Emma Hamilton'. Of course, Naples did not act with the vigour that Nelson required, but both of them could argue that it was out of their hands.

...and immediately after

The parties, celebrations and illuminations that greeted the conquering hero and his fleet as he arrived in Naples were replicated in Britain. Stardom and hero worship took off on a massive scale, not only around Nelson but in letters from home. This was from the usually restrained wife of Earl Spencer, the First Lord of the Admiralty:

> *Joy, joy, joy to you brave, gallant, immortalised Nelson! May the great God, whose cause you so valiantly support, protect and bless you... this moment the guns are firing, illuminations are preparing, your gallant name is echoed from street to street, and every Briton feels his obligation to you.*

Nelson realised the danger of all the adulation going to his head, writing to Lord Spencer that 'if God knows my heart, it is amongst the most humble of the creation, full of thankfulness and gratitude', but to his father that 'I am placed by Providence in that situation that all my caution will be necessary to prevent Vanity from shewing itself superior to my gratitude and thankfulness.'

Three days after arriving at the Palazzo Sessa, with Emma bathing his head wound, giving him asses' milk and gazing at him angelically and full of hero worship, he wrote home to his wife:

> *She is one of the very best women in the world. How few could have made the turn she has. She is an honour to her sex and a proof that even reputation may be regained, but I own it requires a great soul. Her kindness with Sir William to me is more than I can express. I am in their house.*

If this were not enough to worry Fanny, she must have been upset by the references to her son, Josiah, whom she had not seen for nearly six years:

> *Her Ladyship if Josiah was to stay would make something of him and with all his bluntness. I am sure he likes Lady Hamilton more than any female. She would fashion him in 6 months in spite of himself.*

Josiah, meanwhile, had got drunk at Nelson's 40th birthday celebrations, angry at the attentions his stepfather was paying to Emma, and had to be taken out by Troubridge, who was also less than enamoured with the situation. Nelson was still thinking of leaving Naples at the first opportunity: he was expected back in England, and Sir William was thinking of retiring. Nelson's agent Alexander Davison was also trying to persuade him to come home: 'your object now ought to be that of contributing to the Tranquility and Comfort of your Inestimable Wife.'

At that point, in late 1798, Nelson seems to have believed himself to be the centre of the world for his wife, his father and his friends. He wrote to Fanny:

> *the Grand Signior has ordered me a rich jewel if it was worth a million my pleasure will be to see it in your possession. My pride is being your husband, the son of my dear father and in having Sir William and Lady Hamilton for my friends. While those approve of my conduct I shall not feel or regard the envy of thousands.*

In the coming months the situation was to change somewhat.

St Vincent, Nelson's commander-in-chief, could see the relationship beginning. 'Pray, do not let your fascinating Neapolitan Dames approach too near him; for he is flesh and blood, and cannot resist their temptations,' he wrote to Emma. 'I thank God that your health is restored and that the luscious Neapolitan dames have not impaired it,' he wrote to Nelson.

Meanwhile the luscious Emma ran around the Embassy, with her lovely girlish face and full woman's body, wearing thin muslin dresses with no drawers, stays or petticoat – they were unfashionable and uncomfortable. Many aristocratic visitors saw her as coarse and vulgar, but Nelson never did. She could speak French and Italian fluently, sing and play the piano. She had loved Charles Greville and Sir William, and she adored Nelson. He was vulnerable, dependent, sick, wounded and, if not handsome, was melancholy and sensitive. Above all, he was a hero and, in her romantic notions, she wanted to be Britannia.

At the same time Sir William was inspired by Nelson, infected by his patriotic zeal, and he loved having the admiral around, with frequent visits from his gallant sea captains. Nelson admired the intelligent, civilised and entertaining old gentleman, who was always kind and hospitable. And so it continued.

Political forays

Many commentators, both contemporary and modern, agree that Nelson's involvement in Neapolitan politics was probably not a good idea. It seems that his growing infatuation with Emma Hamilton was causing him to stay longer in Naples, and that under her influence he was getting out of his depth in the death throes of a corrupt administration under attack from a common enemy. Meanwhile, the French had occupied almost all of Italy. In trying to help out the Hamiltons and the Neapolitan royals (and securing Britain's bases in the Mediterranean, he argued) Nelson inspired the King of Naples to attempt to become the liberator of the whole country. King Ferdinand must declare war on Napoleon and his new republics and march on Rome. This appealed to the King and, by that point, Naples was the only city-state of the whole Italian peninsula that was not yet occupied by the French.

In October 1798 Nelson's argument for war was reinforced by General Mack, sent by the Austrians to command the Neapolitan army. Nelson was not impressed by the soldier: 'General Mack cannot move without five carriages. I have formed my opinion and heartily pray I may be mistaken.' Queen Maria Carolina (described by Napoleon as 'the only man in Naples') was also anxious for action. An army of 30,000 made ready, supported by Nelson's fleet, which sailed to capture Leghorn in order to cut off the French lines of communication. Nelson feared that the Austrians would fail to support the Neapolitans and that Mack would be routed. As he expected, the offensive turned into a disaster. The idea had been good but the execution collapsed, and the French were provoked into attack.

With the fall of the city of Naples now imminent, Nelson rescued the Neapolitan royal family, all their treasures and other refugees from the English colony on board the *Vanguard*. After a terrible voyage, in which all were seasick, the Neapolitan royals set up in their second kingdom of Palermo. Nelson's dabbling in politics, egged on by Emma Hamilton as the intimate confidante of the Queen, was beginning to cause consternation among the overlords at home in England.

The first signs of official displeasure at Nelson's continuing stay in Naples came with the appointment of the flamboyant Commodore Sir Sydney Smith to the Levant with orders to command the navy in that area, acting independently of Nelson. In the eastern Mediterranean Nelson had to follow his orders, which filled him with irritation and disgust. Nelson hated Palermo but could not drag himself away from Emma, and Fanny was threatening to come out and visit him.

Naples fell to the French in early 1799. The commercial middle classes and minor nobility supported the French, but they were opposed by the Church, especially in the form of Cardinal Fabrizio Ruffo, who hoped and plotted for a restoration.

Nelson showed a contrasting side of his nature after the short-lived Republic of Naples fell to the monarchist Ruffo. Having been sent to Naples by King Ferdinand to enforce the rebels' surrender to Ruffo, who had successfully stirred up royalist support among the rural masses, Nelson was convinced that the rebels should be executed rather than being helped back to France, as they had been promised. He believed there should be no armistice or treaty with the rebels, agreeing with the Queen and opposing Ruffo's more moderate line. Nelson took a hard-edged, ruthless and perhaps simplistic view. The Jacobins believed themselves protected by the truce and embarked to evacuate, but Nelson's men captured them in their boats and a series of executions followed.

One of the rebels was Admiral Prince Caracciolo, at one time Commodore of the Neapolitan navy. He had fled with King Ferdinand from Naples to Palermo, and subsequently returned to the mainland, changing his allegiance and agreeing to defend the new Parthenopian Republic against the British fleet. He was captured on attempting to escape and court-martialled by Nelson with no witnesses and no defence counsel. Turning down his application for a gentleman's and an officer's death by firing squad, Nelson hanged him from the yardarm. This one incident especially cast a pall over Nelson's record, and particularly highlighted his political naïveté. His actions were condoned by the Admiralty but criticised in the House of Commons as an unnecessary and degrading horror of the war.

Much of the criticism of Nelson at this point was levelled at his support of the corrupt Bourbons, whom he saw as allies against the French revolutionaries. He was seen as putting his own interests – himself, the Neapolitan royal family and the Hamiltons – above those of the Admiralty and Britain's longer-term political objectives. Nelson argued that he was just trying to defeat the French in any way he could, but his superiors considered that he showed a distinct lack of political judgement. Was it the head injury, was it love, or was he just a tactician well out of his depth in political strategy?

Becoming lovers

Nelson and Emma were growing increasingly intimate, and were lovers by the end of 1799. This was after 18 months of close contact, and recently discovered letters show that this was much later than previously thought. By January 1800, confident of a safe passage for his letters, Nelson was making explicit sexual references in his messages to her. Their relationship was overwhelming for Nelson who, at 42, was still practically a virgin (there is no evidence that his wife or any of his mistresses excited him like this). He wrote to Emma from sea:

> *In one of my dreams, I thought I was at a large table, you was not present, sitting between a Princess who I detest and another, they both tried to seduce me and the first wanted to take those liberties with me which no woman in this world but yourself ever did.*

Later in the dream, he imagined that Emma said, 'I love nothing but you my Nelson. I kissed you fervently and we enjoy'd the height of love. No love is like mine toward you.'

Recall to England

Lord Keith had replaced Earl St Vincent as commander-in-chief in the Mediterranean at a time of considerable anxiety for Britain. The French still held Malta and had broken through the British blockades of Egypt and Toulon. Keith thought that an attack on Minorca was imminent, and ordered Nelson there. He refused to go, saying there was more danger to Naples at this particular time. It was just as well that Nelson was right: disobedience would otherwise have been combined with a huge misjudgement. It was, for a time, passed over but not forgotten. Nelson regained some prestige from the capture of the only two French ships that escaped from the Nile, *Le Généraux* and *Le Guillaume Tell*.

However, Nelson received an icy letter from the Admiralty asking him not to stay at Palermo any longer. He was recalled to England, and so was Sir William Hamilton, so there was no longer any reason to stay.

Travelling overland across Europe, Nelson was fêted in many cities such as Vienna, Hamburg and Dresden. In company with the Hamiltons, he went to the opera, met civic dignitaries, waved to crowds and had his portrait painted. Back in England, especially in Yarmouth among his kinsmen and with the general public in the many cities they visited, he was as popular as ever, but many noticed the incongruity of the hero and the strange couple from Naples.

Nelson's friends and family had to get used to the idea. He was very open with them about the whole affair. They all had to make a choice between accepting Emma or remaining loyal to Fanny, and gradually most came to accept the situation, settling into friendship with Emma, at least as the only way to get to Nelson. Two of Horatio's three sisters became quite intimate with her and even Nelson's father – the respectable parson – came round to the idea, though he remained close to Fanny too. Nelson attended church with both the Hamiltons and his family, asking for prayers and blessings for them, as the increasingly large Emma sat in their pews, six months' pregnant with Nelson's child. Clearly he thought his God would have got used to the idea as well.

Nelson's brother officers and even his superiors were expected to share in his adoration of Emma, and even at sea he invited them to help him celebrate her birthday. He wrote to his old friend Captain Fremantle, 'If you don't come here on Sunday to celebrate the birthday of Santa Emma, Damn me if I ever forgive you.'

Nevertheless, despite his great victory at the Nile and his first appearance back in England after several years, Nelson was snubbed by the King and had major difficulties with the Lords of the Admiralty. His superiors were concerned about the poor judgement he showed in his involvement in Neapolitan politics, and it was even suggested by Lord Keith that Lady Hamilton was directing the fleet.

Realising that the only thing was to eat humble pie and accept whatever he was offered to return to active service, Nelson bowed to the requirements of the Admiralty and accepted being a second-in-command to Admiral Sir Hyde Parker in the expedition against the Danes. The incidents in Naples and his long absence from duty made any attempt to play politics among his superiors fraught with problems. He was clearly torn between love and duty: 'nothing could alleviate such a separation but the call of our Country,' he wrote to Emma.

Finally splitting up with his more conventional but respectable wife, Nelson openly settled with his mistress. Their daughter Horatia was born in late January 1801. By any standards, this was a most unconventional situation. Emma's husband was still with them and the *ménage à trois*, which might have been acceptable in Naples, was certainly not normal in England. Nelson defiantly affirmed their relationship in public, prompting thousands of column inches in the gossip pages of the newspapers.

Emma also took substantial risks and suffered a backlash in the press. She had won respectability and had distanced herself from her early life through marrying the Ambassador to Naples, and all this was lost when she took up with Nelson. The story of their affair has always been one-sided, as Nelson meticulously burned all her letters to him while she kept all of his, so some commentators have accused her of not really loving him as much as he did her. She never publicly admitted to being the mother of their child, although Nelson ultimately did not conceal his paternity. She sent him into paroxysms of jealousy when she hinted she was seeing the Prince of Wales, known for his amorous adventures, while Nelson was stuck at sea patrolling the frozen Baltic for months on end. He remained fiercely loyal, promising never to sleep on land when away from her, leading to an unnecessarily lonely existence for a highly sociable man: 'I have been faithful to my word never to partake of any amusement or to sleep on shore.'

During the brief peace between March 1802 and May 1803, particularly after Sir William's death in April 1803, they enjoyed time together at home and touring the West Country, but as soon as war was inevitable Nelson felt the pull of duty and left for the Mediterranean.

Emma did not spend time on his ships and Nelson did not approve of captains having wives with them at sea. Neither would he let her travel out to his theatre of operations while he was back at sea. Towards the end of his life, his sense of duty increased as impending battle approached. He had asked for leave in October 1804, having been at sea for over a year, but received approval only on Christmas Day that year, such was the difficulty of communicating with the Admiralty. He tried to placate Emma by explaining that 'my anxiety to fall in with the Enemy has been very great indeed and to satisfy you beyond contradiction of my intentions I send you a copy of my letter to the Board of Admiralty and I am sure you will approve, my beloved Emma'.

He wanted her to share his pride that he was out fighting rather than being with her: 'longing as I do to be with you yet I am sure under the circumstances in which I am placed you would be the first to say my Nelson try & get at those french fellows and come home with Glory to your Emma... don't I say my own love what you would say.' As he insisted, 'you are always upper most in my thoughts day or night Calm or full wind.'

Writing from Portsmouth on his way to the *Victory* on 14 September 1805, he wrote that he was 'overwhelmed with business since my arrival but you are never for one moment absent from my thoughts'. She had to content herself with that. So she lived for the time he came ashore, and their last 25 days together in August and September 1805 were blissfully happy.

In this pivotal phase of his life, after his first great independently won victory, the culmination of five years' active service and having survived several serious wounds, Nelson was physically and emotionally vulnerable. He found it very difficult to strike a balance between love and duty, and arguably did not achieve a successful *modus vivendi* until his relationship with Emma settled down to a form of cosy domesticity in his final few years.

There is no doubt that Nelson allowed his fixation with Emma to determine his tactics in the Mediterranean. Lord Minto, latterly

Ambassador in Vienna, described him as like a baby in her presence. He put caring for the Neapolitan royal family above almost any other aspect of his mission; and he became hopelessly mired in doomed attempts to restore the old order in the Kingdom of the Two Sicilies. Back in England he and she were figures of ribald popular fun – yet when they toured the country they were met by cheering crowds who seemed quite unabashed by their hero keeping company with his mistress and her husband. Some would say he allowed his better nature to be ruled by erotic infatuation; but perhaps it is impossible to separate the lover who acts on his feelings from the impetuous and courageous warrior who leads every charge onto the enemy's decks. He had passion for everything he did.

Sea officers knew a good deal about easy virtue and were not for the most part censorious men, but they were genuinely shocked by such a fundamental failure of duty and doubly so because it was their greatest hero who had fallen. If Nelson's fellow officers were shocked, this was nothing compared with the reaction of polite society in London. The impact on Nelson's family, and especially his wronged wife, was a further consideration that it seemed he was ignoring, although he did go through enormous personal tortures at the time, pacing the streets of London all night wracked with guilt.

Many of his more protective fellow officers saw Emma as a scheming adulteress who led him astray. Why did he allow his private life to impinge on his responsibilities as much as it did in 1798–1801? Was it inexperience, bad advice, lack of thought about the outcome, belief that he was such a hero that he could get away with it, or because he was so much in love? Maybe the last explanation is the most convincing.

Nelson was a workaholic who embraced responsibility. He was ambitious to rise to the top of his profession and personally cared about every ship, officer and seaman in his fleet. His success at the Nile jettisoned him to stardom and he enjoyed – or suffered – the public attention of celebrity. His life was no longer his; he was a public icon.

He was unconventional in many ways, in risk taking, in his participative leadership style, in his eye for detail. He was also unconventional in his choice of lover, a woman married to his close friend, a former prostitute and now the wife of a diplomat, seen by many as coarse and vulgar.

Nelson was carried away by his love for Emma, who became an extraordinary source of inspiration to him, so much so that for once in his life his passion for action and duty was over-ridden by his desire to be with her. For two years, the balance of his passions fell towards love rather than duty. He followed his heart and he compromised the professional status he had worked so hard to establish. But in the process, he became involved with a woman who responded to his need for hero worship, adoration, inspiration, sexual release and a child of his own. He certainly felt the relationship was blessed – he repeatedly avowed the purity of their love, for this is what it felt like to him; as self-evidently right as were his opinions about the French and about war.

Nelson continued to feel a tension between love and duty and he wrote passionately to Emma, often two or three times a day. As he saw it, indulging himself with her was the ultimate reward for victory. He wrote in June 1805, 'therefore only pray for my success and my laurels I shall with pleasure lay at your feet and a sweet kiss will be ample reward for all your Nelson's hard fag.' By then, many of his superiors had come to accept her existence, though the couple were seldom received in polite society together. The fact that she was ignored on his death shows what they really thought of her and the whole affair.

Nelson's Way
Passion

Passion is an intense, driving, uncontrollable feeling, an outbreak of anger, of ardent affection, of love. It is the object of strong liking, devotion or interest, and of strong sexual desire. It means expressing feelings. A passionate person has zeal, fury, will, vehemence in what they do, and may be tormented by the need to achieve their goals.

If you are passionate about your work, you will be enthusiastic in your chosen focus – achieving the goals of your company, building your professional practice, serving your customers. You need to be aware of the challenges: people may think your passion is fake, or that you are obsessed. The boundary between passion and obsession is not always clear. Passion is incompatible with balance and challenges established priorities.

Being expressively passionate does not suit all personalities. In the eyes of others, passion for work may inspire but passion for a lover arouse envy or ridicule.

It's hard to imagine a great leader without the capacity for passion. Don't be embarrassed about being enthusiastic.

What if your passion elicits no response from others? Then you need to work hard on your colleagues and subordinates and convince them of your sincerity. You need to create an environment where passion is rewarded, not scorned. Passionate people can be identified by the things they care about, their enthusiasms and their energy. It all needs to be channelled in the right direction. Being 'passionate about food', having a 'passion for fashion', being 'passionate about quality' can make customers think that you care, not a bad thing for which to be known.

Leadership comments
Danica Purg

In the late 1980s Eastern Europe was in turmoil and its future was uncertain. One of the outstanding people who came to the fore at this time of upheaval was Dr Danica Purg, who founded and still directs the Bled School of Management in Slovenia, the first business school in the region. Being so innovative and determined took a great deal of passion. By directing her emotional energy to a cause and managing conflicting passions, Purg was exploiting one of Nelson's most important attributes.

'I always wanted to be a forerunner. When I was five years old I wanted to change things. I don't like compromises. I take a position where I can lead,' she insists – just like Nelson – 'or I won't do it.' Purg also showed Nelson's impatience with incompetent superiors: 'My first job was working in the government. I saw my so-called leaders around me, not knowing how to motivate people, lacking vision, and I said to myself I'd be a real leader.'

Her passion is infectious: 'Friends often ask me to talk to their children to make them enthusiastic. At school I did teaching to earn some money. I felt I had the power of persuasion.' She needed it. 'I did not have the skills when I started [the management school], but I had vision and commitment. I wanted to succeed, that my dream should become reality – that management should overcome its negative image of the communist period. In the process I managed to bring together business and management educators from all the Eastern European nations, who had many historical reasons not to cooperate. We faced the almost impossible task of bridging the gap between East and West. I still have to fight like crazy for the image of my school.' She has always been very active: 'Behind a good horse is a lot of dust,' she quotes.

Like Nelson she had a dream, fought for it and gained it – for herself and for her organisation. 'All my dreams have come true, and more,' Purg reflects, 'and I am getting new ideas all the time, this profession is enriching for me.'

Achieving a balance is important for Purg, and she strives to achieve this for her students of business and management, as well as for herself. 'I am convinced that we must educate managers in the arts, so our school is an art gallery and all our courses include contact with the arts. I see myself as a multidimensional manager – a manager and a cultured person. Art inspires people, and makes them more creative; it is provoking and makes you more reflective. Managers are often too much in routine. More than 31,000 managers have been through this school. I see how responsible they are and how much they can do for society, and we can't let them do this as one-dimensional people.' This multidimensional and reflective approach was also a strength of Nelson's, in his personality, his relationships, his letters, the way he thought through the challenges he faced, which made him a cut above the able and competent captains he led.

Leaders always face the issue of balancing work and love, and Purg is the same as Nelson in that 'my work became my love'. Luckily for her, her partner understands this, 'and we have arranged our life in such a way that I can work. He understands a lot about my work, and pushed me into it, saying, "Slovenia needs management, you should do this – it's a real challenge." I have good friends whom I need, who relax and liberate me from the problems. But if I had children it would be terribly difficult with this tempo. I have intensive fun: I go to the theatre, to concerts, to art shows – this is very important.'

Balancing leadership and management is essential too: 'A manager can be successful only if he or she is a leader. Everyone should have vision, and if organisations expected it we'd have a better society. Members of your team should share in your vision and have a vision of their own too. Mine follow me because they think that I am really doing the things I speak about – I put ideas into practice, and have successes.' Nelson attracted his following for the same reason. 'But you have to have patience. Often I see I am not communicating enough where we are going or why. Of all the virtues, the most important for me is honesty, being straightforward and honest in every respect.' Passion can only be convincing if it is real and sincere.

Leadership lessons
Passion

- Passion and obsession are not the same but they're not far apart – one may disperse energy too widely, the other focus it too narrowly. Real leadership requires passion.
- Where is your emotional energy going – to your job, your team members at work or your private life? Make sure it is aimed at where you want to go.
- Appreciate that the constant exercise of leadership, and the expectations of others, can give you an unrealistic sense of power – and can have repercussions on relationships at work and at home (and in between!).
- Acknowledge when you might be at your most vulnerable to work/life imbalance, such as at times of stress, when passions are conflicting.
- Being passionate often means being unconventional. This can be a plus and is a common characteristic of a charismatic leader. But getting away with it can depend on the importance of your contribution, the culture of your organisation and the support of your superiors.
- Sometimes there's a real conflict between the demands of the job and your relationships. If balance isn't possible, you just have to make a choice.
- You can't be passionate about everything – sometimes passion is not appropriate.

⚓ Make sure your passion is real and comes over as sincere. Beware of cynics, who may see it as naïve and simplistic.

⚓ Remember that feeling strongly is not the same as being wise. Understanding yourself – your own reactions to success and failure, to praise and criticism – is the only way to ensure you are more than a straw in the wind. Harnessing your passions is not giving up real feelings, it is directing them for ideal purposes.

⚓ Take into account your partner's views on your leadership style – he or she may see things that others can't tell you.

5

LOYALTY

The band of brothers, 1801–1803

'We few, we happy few, we band of brothers;
For he today that sheds his blood with me
Shall be my brother; be he ne'er so vile,
This day shall gentle his condition.
And gentlemen in England, now abed,
Shall think themselves accursed they were not here;
And hold their manhoods cheap whiles any speaks
That fought with us upon Saint Crispin's day.'
Shakespeare, Henry V *(IV. iii. 60–67)*

'I had the happiness to command a Band of Brothers.'
Nelson

This celebratory engraving shows miniatures of 14 captains and Nelson, with images of palm trees, the Sphinx, forts and ships. 'Victory is not a name strong enough for such a scene,' Nelson reflected of the enemy's annihilation.

'Victors of the Nile' by William Bromley & John Landseer (engravers) after Sir Robert Smirke (artist), 1803.

I T WAS THE NIGHT OF 1 APRIL 1801. NELSON'S FLAGSHIP WAS moored just outside the approaches to Copenhagen. Next day the British fleet would do battle with the Danes, so he – as was his frequent custom – invited his captains to dinner on board the *Elephant*. These events were much enjoyed, providing close fellowship, stimulating conversation, a chance to discuss tactics and ideas with the approachable and enthusiastic admiral, good wine and food; better than on their own ships. But this night was different. It was a pre-battle dinner, for which Nelson was famous.

He was calm and confident, drinking a toast to victory on the morrow. It was a briefing, as well as a convivial dinner and pep talk. His flag captain was Thomas Foley, who had led the way round the French line on the inshore side at the Nile, one of the 'band of brothers' *par excellence*. Thomas Hardy, a staunch supporter who had volunteered to stay with his chief after many adventures together, missed the dinner itself, so concerned was he with laying buoys to act as markers for the next day. After a final round of conferring with his captains – they had been discussing how to deal with every eventuality for the last three months – Nelson dictated the final orders, which were copied by a team of clerks.

Nelson had chosen 12 lighter and faster ships from the fleet and had, that night, safely passed the Danish capital of Copenhagen and anchored to the south, leaving the commander-in-chief, Admiral Sir Hyde Parker, to the north with the remainder of the ships. With the collapse of diplomatic negotiations, the decision had been made to bombard Copenhagen, in an attempt to break up the 'Armed Neutrality of the North', comprising Denmark, Norway, Sweden and Prussia, that

Tsar Paul of Russia had revived at Napoleon's instigation. The Danes were not the hated French, but they were the enemy nonetheless.

The 'band of brothers' as battle approached included Foley and other Nile veterans: Sir Thomas Troubridge, Sir Thomas Thompson and Thomas Fremantle. Rear Admiral Thomas Graves was well known to Nelson, as was Captain George Murray. But many of the others were in Nelson's squadron for the first time. By now they had formed a bond with their leader. Nelson had emerged as effective commander of the squadron not through bullying or toadying but because Admiral Parker acknowledged, late in the day, that he was the man for the job.

He produced the ideas and plans, reduced apparently complex problems to their bare essentials by his grasp of the strategic and tactical situation. These ideas were shared and worked out with the captains, and they bought in to Nelson's sense of urgency, which Parker had failed to generate.

Dinner was normally taken by officers on board ships in the early afternoons, but this day, on the *Elephant*, it was delayed. As soon as the ship had anchored ready for battle the next day, Nelson invited Admiral Graves, his second-in-command, and other old friends to dinner. Foley, Fremantle, Hardy, Captain Inman of the *Desire*, Colonel Stewart and Lieutenant-Colonel Hutchinson of the Marines, and Captain Edward Riou were invited – the last named the only naval officer present not previously known to Nelson. He was invited because Nelson was quick to appreciate his agile mind and superb seamanship, and before the night was out he was to prove the quality of his brain.

Nelson had spotted Riou's talent earlier that day. Colonel Stewart had reported the movement of Nelson's fleet through a difficult channel to reach their anchorage, mentioning that

> *Captain Riou showed the greatest ability in ascertaining the course of the channel this forenoon, and worked his frigate through it in a most masterly style. She, on one occasion, touched the rocky shore on the island of Saltholm side, and by his presence of mind, and rapidity of giving her a press of sail fairly pushed her over a shoal... Lord Nelson was in raptures with this able officer.*

This was how Nelson created his 'brothers' – by observing strong potential and rewarding it by inviting the newly spotted talent to join the chosen few. In these last few days, Nelson had seen for himself the ability of his team to work together. As Stewart again recorded, Nelson had his division under sail

> with astonishing alacrity, and anchored them all without damage before dark in the new roadstead. The whole thing was done with a correctness and at the same time with a rapidity which could never have been exceeded.

So dinner that night was, in the words of Colonel Stewart again,

> an important one. As soon as the fleet was at anchor the gallant Nelson sat down to table with a large party of his comrades in arms. He was in the highest spirits, and drank to a leading wind, and to the success of the ensuing day. Every man left with feelings of admiration for their great leader, and with anxious impatience to follow him into the approaching battle.

Nelson, Foley and Riou stayed on to finalise the details of the plan of attack. As Stewart described,

> Lord Nelson was so much exhausted while dictating his instructions that it was recommended to him by us all and, indeed, insisted upon by his old servant, Allen, who assumed much command on these occasions, that he should go to his cot. It was placed on the floor, but from it he still continued to dictate... he was every half hour calling to his clerks to hasten their work, the wind becoming fair.

Hardy, in a small boat taking soundings and laying buoys around the hulks in the channels, returned to the *Elephant* at 11 p.m. Nelson's orders were succinct, giving as much detail as was required but no more, and the rest would be left to their initiative. Imparting his orders to the captains was done in such a way that even comparative strangers were enthused with his vivacity. This was an attitude rather than a method: the attitude that while even one enemy ship remained afloat and still flying its own colours, the job was not finished. They all got the message. Up at 6, Nelson hoisted the signal to weigh at 9.30, and 'the shout with which it was received throughout the Division was heard a considerable distance.'

An admiral was charged to fulfil a strategic mission, but had a good deal of autonomy on how to actually complete the task. He often controlled a varied flotilla of ships scattered around a large area, with no way to communicate once ships were out of sight of each other. Admirals needed to trust their subordinates, and captains had to trust each other to deliver on their promises. If a couple of ships sailed off to take on supplies, they could be gone for weeks, while their fellow captains depended on them returning successfully to a pre-arranged rendezvous. Yet along the way any ship might encounter an enemy, be engaged in battle, win (or lose) prizes, or be required to make significant policy decisions about future supplies, trading arrangements, credit and so forth.

For captains in a fleet, loyalty to the cause and to each other was far more than a matter of personal motivation: it was an absolutely crucial element in the operational capability of a fleet. If this was true in the ceaseless tasks of blockading ports, harassing enemy ships, policing trade and enforcing the terms of treaties with subject governments, it was even more essential in battle.

Firing a broadside created so much smoke and carnage that it would be almost impossible to see the enemy, let alone other ships. This was one reason it was so important to aim well for the first broadside: gunners were firing more or less blind after that. Signaling between ships was unreliable – especially once the masts were shot away – and sending messages in smaller boats was intrinsically hazardous and time consuming. So long as ships were fighting one to one, the advantage was clearly with the side that could fire fastest and sustain its effort for longest – and at this the British were acknowledged leaders. However, if two ships could lay either side of one, or could sail behind one and rake the length of its decks, victory was almost certain.

Nelson's tactics – developed from many forebears and especially from French manuals on naval tactics published in the 1780s – were always to concentrate his force on a limited area of an opponent's line, and thus to destroy the ships in this area before reinforcements could arrive. This depended on superior seamanship as well as gunnery, and on each captain responding to the exigencies of the collective action. Nelson himself, and many of his trusted captains, would hurl themselves in to the fray confident that their fellows would follow if support were needed.

There was one other important motive for loyalty among the captains. In the strict line of command characterising relations in the navy, the captain held paramount authority and was liable to the isolation and loneliness inherent to this position. Some formed close bonds of trust and friendship with professionals outside the direct line of command – Nelson relied on his chaplain and intelligence officer, Rev. Dr Alexander Scott; Captain Thomas Fremantle took his young wife Betsey with him, especially in the early days of their marriage; Cuthbert Collingwood kept a dog. But most importantly, captains needed the company of other captains – just as CEOs in modern organisations find a sense of support and understanding in the company of other CEOs, even if they are from quite different industries and market situations.

Thus loyalty bound the captains to each other in a common intent and mutual dependence. Although no leader could ignore the need for loyalty, there were significant differences in interpretation. While Nelson did all he could to build a sense of loyalty to the mission and to one another (albeit clothed in the language of patriotism and duty to the monarch), other admirals – Sir John Jervis, for example – laid more emphasis on loyalty to the hierarchy of command and to the central position of the admiral himself.

In a highly selective way, we have chosen only 12 of the most outstanding 'brothers' who were closest to Nelson, from a potentially much longer list of peers and subordinates whose lives were touched by him.

The origin of the 'band of brothers', 1795–1798

It began with Nelson's first independent command in 1795, managing a squadron of frigates cooperating with the Austrian army along the Riviera, under Admiral Hotham. The first recruit was Thomas Fremantle. Also joining the navy at 12, he had served in the West Indies and the Mediterranean, and was with Nelson at Bastia. During the taking of the *Ça Ira*, in the frigate *Inconstant*, he had taken the initiative to attack the French, inflicting heavy damage on the 80-gun ship while dodging out of range himself. From Buckinghamshire, Fremantle was short, stocky and round-faced with fiery black eyes, good-natured and lively. Smart and efficient, he ran a spotless ship 'in the most officer-like manner' and was widely popular. Rescuing an English family evacuated from Florence to Leghorn, he fell in love with and married their 17-year-old daughter, Betsey, who wrote detailed diary entries about their life.

Fremantle joined Nelson in his ill-fated expedition to Tenerife, this time in the *Seahorse*. Fremantle was also wounded, not so seriously as Nelson. Lying in the bottom of the boat in extreme pain after his arm had been shattered by grapeshot, Nelson was first rowed back to the *Seahorse* as the nearest ship. Knowing that Fremantle's young wife was aboard, Nelson declared he would rather die than 'alarm Mrs. Fremantle by her seeing me in this state when I can give her no tidings of her husband'. Fremantle recovered from his wounds after a painful crossing to Cadiz, and Nelson, in one of his first left-handed letters, wrote 'God bless you and Fremantle' to Betsey. All the brother officers came on board to wish her husband a speedy recovery. He received a gratuity of a year's pay and a pension of £200 a year. Nelson received a pension of £1,000 at the same time, but he had lost his eye as well as his arm. On leave, Betsey gave birth to a son, their first child, and the Fremantles were visited by Nelson in London.

Foley, a captain at the Nile and later to be Nelson's flag captain at Copenhagen, was a Welshman from a modest family who had owned their lands since the fourteenth century. His forebears had fought in the English Civil War and had sailed with Anson around the world. He had joined the navy at 13 and served with another friend of Nelson's, Prince William Henry. He was present at the Battle of the Saints, during Hood's pursuit of the French in 1794, and served under Hotham. Tall at over six feet, his height was on a par with that of Hardy, Nelson's flag captain at Trafalgar, and Foley towered over many of his superiors including, of course, Nelson, who was not unusually short at 5'6". With eager blue eyes and risqué humour, he made up for his lack of social graces with fine seamanship. One of his midshipmen was the son of the Viceroy of Corsica, young George Elliot, who served with him for five years 'without one unhappy day... his kindness only increased as years rolled out', an unexpected tribute in a service known for brutality and discomfort.

Foley was given the job of taking on a ship from a previous captain described as 'an imbecile, totally incompetent' and Foley 'soon restored her to order'. The unfortunate 'imbecile' then took command of Foley's previous ship, and 'was so feeble that the very first night he received the ship, her company took the command from him and have been in a state of licentiousness ever since'. It was not that easy to command a ship, and good captains, loyal to an admiral, were to be highly valued – as with management talent throughout the ages.

Another 'brother' dating from these early days was Benjamin Hallowell, also involved in the capture of the *Ça Ira*. A Canadian, Hallowell was known for his bizarre sense of humour. He presented Nelson with a coffin carved of wood from the mainmast of *L'Orient*, the flagship of the French at the Nile, and Nelson was delighted at the originality of this souvenir. He kept a much-admired musical band on board his ship, entertaining all the ships in company. Nelson described him as having 'indefatigable zeal, activity and ability'. On the fall of Corsica, Hallowell, described as 'of gigantic frame and vast personal strength', was given command of Nelson's old frigate *Lowestoffe*, and also served with Jervis off Toulon.

Hallowell, resembling a prizefighter, was kindly and humorous, generous and thoughtful, intelligent, blunt and entertaining. He was once court-martialled for the loss of his ship running ashore in a gale while he was detained on shore, but honourably acquitted. Off Cape St Vincent, he was on the quarterdeck of the *Victory* when Jervis's flag captain was announcing the number of Spanish ships looming up on the horizon. When Jervis declared that however many Spaniards there were he would fight them, Hallowell slapped his admiral on the back and exclaimed, 'That's right! And, by God, we'll give them a damned good licking!'

Sir Edward Berry, who commanded Nelson's beloved *Agamemnon* at Trafalgar, was the same ship's new first lieutenant in 1796. He was later Nelson's companion at a levee with the King in 1798, when Nelson was recovering from the amputation of his arm. 'You have lost your right arm!' remarked the King. 'But not my right hand, your Majesty,' Nelson replied. 'May I present Captain Edward Berry?' Berry was one of seven children, five of them girls, of a London merchant who died leaving a young widow badly off. He had also been educated in Norwich and had volunteered for the navy. He was immediately promoted to lieutenant for gallantry in boarding an enemy ship in 1794 and distinguished himself at the Glorious First of June.

Good-looking, slim, with fair hair and bright blue eyes, Berry was by personality very much in the Nelson mould: brave to the point of foolhardiness and uncontrollably impulsive. Lacking Nelson's judgement and intellect and sometimes unreliable, he was nevertheless a great fighter and was first over the side when Nelson called for boarders at the Battle of Cape St Vincent, and was on the poop hauling down the Spanish colours of the *San Nicolas*, crossing on 'Nelson's patent bridge' to the *San Josef*. On leave with Nelson in late 1797, Berry was summoned by his chief to be his next flag captain, and they sailed in the *Foudroyant* in early 1798. Berry had married in the meantime and his wife, separated soon after their nuptials, was comforted by Lady Nelson.

Thomas Masterman Hardy was lieutenant on board the *Minerve* frigate when Nelson was sent by Jervis to help evacuate Elba. Hardy, from Dorset, was descended from a Channel Islands family, then small country landowners. With six sisters and two brothers, 'having expressed a determination to go to sea almost as soon as he could speak', Hardy always had his pet dog with him and became known for his excellence in seamanship and navigation. He was at Toulon, with Hotham, and with Nelson off Genoa. Hardy suffered as a prisoner of war when his prize was recaptured off Cartagena in late 1796, but was luckily exchanged and liberated soon after by Nelson. Tall, weighty and with broad shoulders, ponderous and placid, unimaginative, blunt and a little dull, Hardy was the complete antithesis of Nelson. But the two men felt perfectly comfortable together, and indeed Hardy was to be the last of the 'brothers' to see Nelson alive and kiss him farewell.

When Nelson moved his flag to the *Captain* before the Battle of St Vincent, his new flag captain was Ralph Willett Miller, a New Englander from America then aged 35 who had joined the navy at 14. Serving in every action fought by Admirals Barrington, Rodney, Hood and Graves, Miller had been wounded three times and had assisted at the evacuation of Toulon. Meeting Nelson for the first time on Corsica, he was talent-spotted by Jervis, and Nelson saw him as amicable, quick and imaginative – but with more judgement and common sense than Berry. Novel and creative and with an interest in painting and drawing, Miller managed the beleaguered *Captain* while Nelson and Berry went storming off in boarding parties, and accompanied Nelson when he shifted his flag to the *Theseus*. Miller was with Nelson off Tenerife and survived the ordeal.

Returning to England, Nelson visited the Miller family and told them Miller was well, expressing his great regard for his captain. Miller was hugely relieved and grateful, telling Nelson he had 'completely saved the torment of all those anxious fears to which the tenderness of a female bosom is so liable'. Miller was subsequently killed in action soon after the Nile, off Acre. Nelson raised a subscription but mostly paid out of his own pocket for Miller's memorial, near his own in St Paul's Cathedral.

Thomas Troubridge, an experienced and highly capable 'brother', had met Nelson when they were midshipmen in the West Indies. A year older than Nelson, he was of humble parentage, his father being a baker in London, and he had risen slowly in the ranks. Also talent-spotted by Jervis as having uncommon abilities and with potential to command a whole fleet, Troubridge and Nelson became Jervis's most reliable deputies in these years. They were very much alike, with quick tempers, vivid imaginations, passionate, excitable, moody, and single-minded in their hatred of the French. Once a prisoner of war, Troubridge's unrelenting invectives against his captors ended only when the ship in which he was held captive was recaptured by the British. Troubridge was seen as more ruthless than Nelson, regarding his crew with a patrician condescension, summed up in his comment, 'When ever I see a fellow look as if he was thinking, I say that's mutiny.'

The leading ship in the British line at St Vincent, Troubridge's *Culloden* dominated the early part of the battle. Pouring a double-shotted broadside into a huge enemy three-decker, Jervis exclaimed,

'Look at Troubridge! He tacks his ship to battle as if the eyes of all England were upon him; and would to God they were.' Troubridge was the first to rush to support Nelson's initiative at the battle, and was singled out for special praise in Jervis's dispatches.

Afterwards, he visited Nelson at home in Norfolk, and together they hatched the plot for their attack on a Spanish treasure ship at Santa Cruz, Tenerife – a somewhat less successful venture. Troubridge was hand-picked by Nelson to accompany him, but made a disastrous miscalculation. Landing on a beach and hoping to tackle the fort from the rear, the party ran into heavily fortified valleys impossible to cross, and had to re-embark. Miller was 'very much dissatisfied' and Troubridge 'almost dead with fatigue'. Troubridge had gone back to ask Nelson's permission to attempt this landing, and Nelson later took responsibility for the action, defending the conduct of his subordinates against the threat of court-martial.

Nelson led the next attack on Santa Cruz himself, also disastrously. This time Troubridge made it into the city and, with amazing sangfroid given his small, battered force, demanded a truce. His fellow captain Samuel Hood, carrying the message, was asked by the Governor to allow him one hour for an answer. Hood, caught up in the cool-headed bluff, said he could only have five minutes before the British would open fire again. The Governor, confident in his position, allowed the British a more or less honorable way out. He gave them a good dinner, presented his colours, gave them food and wine for their journey, allowed them to purchase supplies and even gave them the dispatches of their defeat to carry to the Court of Spain. It was all very civilised – Nelson sent back a cask of English ale and a cheese. But the British had lost 280 men, with many badly wounded, including several 'brothers'.

Cuthbert Collingwood, second-in-command under Nelson at Trafalgar and afterwards assuming leadership of the Mediterranean fleets as his successor, commanded the *Excellent* at Cape St Vincent, where he was also a strong supporter of Nelson's *Captain*. In Nelson's words, he 'gallantly pushed up with every sail set to save his old friend and messmate' and came so closely between the *Captain* and the enemy *San Nicolas* that 'you could not put a bodkin between us'. Collingwood was also highly commended by Jervis.

Samuel Hood was also very much a 'brother'. The speed of his repairs to his ship after St Vincent 'would have exhausted an ordinary mind' and, with Troubridge and Hallowell (and, of course, Nelson), was described by Jervis as abounding 'in resources and very great characters; they will achieve important services to their country while I sleep with my fathers'. Hood was appointed to the *Zealous* when its previous captain had got the ship 'in a most undisciplined state, the people incessantly drunk'; Hood soon had them in order. He was selected by Nelson to join him at Santa Cruz and, as we have seen, distinguished himself with Troubridge.

From a distinguished naval family (his brother Alexander Hood was a captain, and his cousin was Admiral Hood, under whom Nelson served in 1794), he served off Halifax with Prince William Henry. It was a wild time with 'fair drinking' and the Prince, who just as well brought his own claret, gave 23 bumpers without stopping. Twenty dinner guests drank 63 bottles, and Hood was probably relieved when the Prince went on a cruise. On his return 'we drank 28 bumper toasts'. Hood then attended the Prince's father on his summer trip to Weymouth. The honour of providing dinner for his sovereign put Hood £700 in the red, the equivalent of almost a year's salary.

Hood was also of great height (he had his hair dressed through the skylight of his cabin), loose-limbed and with a kindly but authoritarian expression. Seen as not very polished in manners, he was unaffected and natural, loved being at sea and excelled at astronomy, geography and knowledge of shipbuilding.

Another of the early 'brothers' was Sir James Saumarez, a Channel Islander who captained the Orion at St Vincent, where two Spanish first rates struck their colours to him. At Cadiz in April, Nelson handed over command of the inshore squadron to Saumarez. Like Hood, he came from a distinguished naval family. Captain Philip Saumarez had been Anson's first lieutenant, and had introduced the first standard naval officer's uniform. Captain Thomas Saumarez had won an action off Lundy Island in the West Country the year Nelson was born. Serving at the Battle of the Saints, James Saumarez commanded a ship of the line at 25, and was knighted for capturing a French frigate. An excellent navigator, he was frequently able to get his ship out of trouble with his strong seamanship.

By contrast with many of the other 'brothers', Saumarez was formal, uptight and seemed inflexible. Nelson found him one of the most difficult to work with, seeing him as 'aloof' – but he still chose him for Trafalgar. Saumarez's crews were Guernsey volunteers, not a pressed man among them, and they adored him. But Jervis left him out of dispatches and, rather than complaining as Nelson did, he kept his feelings bottled up and festering. He was unforgiving: he was told off by Hyde Parker and then refused his invitation to dinner. However, Saumarez was not averse to a little social banter: he wagered £100 against peace with France, winning the bet with Sir John Jervis. Saumarez and Ball helped substantially in getting Nelson's *Vanguard* ready for service in May 1798, and led a division in the search for the French across the Mediterranean.

The band of brothers in action – the Nile

When Nelson sailed from Cadiz at the end of April 1798, he was joined by Troubridge, Miller, Hood and Collingwood, who took part in the long chase and action that locked the fraternity together forever: the Battle of the Nile.

Sir Alexander Ball, eventually to become a Rear Admiral, served with Nelson at the Nile and became the first British governor of Malta. A close friend of Nelson for many years, Ball came from an old Gloucestershire family, joining the navy at 12 after reading *Robinson Crusoe*. He served with Rodney at the Battle of the Saints, and joined the fleet for the Mediterranean at Gibraltar, meeting Betsey and Fremantle there. He looked more like a university professor than a sea captain, with a high forehead, thoughtful expression and reflective eyes, and had literary friends like Coleridge. He lacked Nelson's insights, Troubridge's seamanship and Hood's natural leadership skills, but he was more stable and calm than the others, and somewhat more rational than the more instinctive Hardy, Foley and Hallowell.

Ball was able to win over the loyalty of his men through enlisting their reason and conscience. If, for example, he needed to punish a seaman, he would ask him if he had indeed committed the act, if he knew it was against the Articles of War, and if he had tried to avoid it. Thus he allowed few needless punishments and his air of reasonableness was extremely effective. He was adored by the populace as Governor of Malta, giving them their first taste of independence and self-determination. Many hung his picture next to that of the Virgin and Child on their walls. This was still to come.

When the fleet arrived in Naples in June 1798, Troubridge and Hardy went ashore to find the whereabouts of the French and negotiate the purchasing of supplies. The Ambassador, Sir William Hamilton, remarked of the former, 'he went straight to the point, and we did more business in half an hour than we should have done in a week in the usual official way'. After two hours they re-embarked. Hardy and Hood were sent to Alexandria to snoop around. By now, after months of searching, Nelson felt he ought to send Earl St Vincent a long letter of apology for having missed the French, sending it to Ball first for his comments. His 'brother' and friend insightfully replied;

> *I felt a regret that your too anxious zeal should make you start an idea that you are not perfectly satisfied with your own conduct. I should recommend a friend never to begin a defence of his conduct before he is accused of error.*

Nelson clearly needed the help and advice of his brother officers as much as they needed him.

The 'brothers' bonded during this long and painful chase, and they were elated when the French fleet was discovered. Saumarez had just finished dinner with his officers when they heard the news, drank a quick bumper to their success and rushed on deck. Nelson's signals were mostly the very general ones they were waiting for, 'form line of battle as convenient'. The competitive Foley shot ahead of Hood to lead the line, taking the initiative to go between the French ships and the shore, where they were unprepared, as he had guessed. The 'brothers' excelled themselves in this action and, like Nelson, Hood, Miller, Saumarez and Ball were slightly wounded. Poor Troubridge, who had played a dominant part at the Battle of Cape St Vincent, was stuck on the shoals and was desperately frustrated watching the action from afar.

Saumarez followed Hood inside the line, then Miller, all three ships cheering as they went, the British seamen laughing at the pathetic attempts of the French to cheer back. Nelson followed them with the rest of the fleet, both inside and outside the enemy's line. Ball and Hallowell followed up as reinforcements. The cannonade causing the explosion of *L'Orient* came from Ball's ship. Subsequently a naked young man wearing only a cocked hat came aboard Hallowell's ship, explaining that he was the first lieutenant of *L'Orient*, and raised his hat to prove he was an officer!

After the battle, immediately recognised as of vast strategic importance and greeted with massive acclaim, Nelson was generous with his praise in dispatches. He acknowledged that they solved immediate problems of tactics themselves, they were all brilliant fighting seamen, and they were of one mind with Nelson. As Lord Howe, a veteran admiral and talent-spotter, observed, the battle 'stood unparalleled and singular in this instance that every captain distinguished himself'. As Saumarez said, 'greater unanimity never existed in any squadron'.

Nelson's captains presented him with a sword and asked him to sit for his portrait, for the newly formed Egyptian Club, established to commemorate the battle. As Nelson acknowledged in explaining why he had decided to attack the French immediately, 'my prompt decision was the natural consequence of having such captains under my command... that in the Battle the conduct of every officer was equal'.

In a letter of September 1798, Nelson wrote:

> *we were, and are, & I trust ever will be a band of Brothers, never do I believe did every individual in a fleet before exert themselves to their Utmost, were I to praise one more than another I should reproach myself I could not tell where to begin.*

Copenhagen

After the Nile the band of brothers dispersed, Nelson's infatuation with Emma Hamilton and his deep entanglements with Neapolitan politics left little room for masculine camaraderie. Two years later, however, key members of the team did reconvene for the campaign to the Baltic. Nelson had been sent as second-in-command to Admiral Sir Hyde Parker, an aged and indecisive commander who had gained his rank largely by surviving long enough to inherit it through seniority. Pleased to be in active service again, and away from juggling the needs of wife and mistress in the full glare of a very public life, Nelson warmed once again to the company of seafaring men heading for a fight.

Troubridge was now a naval commissioner at the Admiralty, and Nelson complained to him that Admiral Parker would neither take him into his confidence nor listen to his advice. Nelson, knowing he was being punished for his indescretions in Naples, was given a tough job. Even his ship was uncomfortable (he had moved to the 74-gun *St George* from the *San Josef* – one of his prizes from St Vincent – for the sake of a shallower draft with which to navigate the approaches to Copenhagen). The only compensation was his captains, many of whom were by now old friends he could depend on, especially Foley, Hardy and Fremantle. As the last-named wrote to Betsey, 'Nelson is just the same man I ever knew him, and shows me every attention and kindness possible.'

Relations between Britain and Denmark became strained with a series of impromptu British attacks on merchantmen, apparently to prevent trade with the French, but doubtless also motivated by prize money. Britain sent in the Baltic fleet to assert its right to control all maritime commerce. With the possibility of battle, Nelson had the chance to retrieve the reputation that many – including the 'brothers' – thought he had thrown away in the Mediterranean.

Six hundred troops had embarked with the fleet, under the command of Colonel Stewart, who observed Nelson very closely.

The Vice Admiral soon became impatient with what he saw as the indolence of his superior, and took few pains to hide it. We entered Yarmouth Roads on March 6 or 7... Sir Hyde was on shore, and I remember that Lord Nelson regretted this. He reported his arrival, and his intention of waiting on him the next morning. We breakfasted that morning, as usual, soon after six o'clock, for we were always up before daylight. We went on shore, so as to be at Sir Hyde's door by eight o'clock, Lord Nelson choosing to be amusingly exact to that hour, which he considered a very late one for business. Lord Nelson's plan would to have been to have proceeded with the utmost dispatch... to the mouth of Copenhagen Harbour; then and there to have insisted on amity or war, and have brought the objects of negotiation to a speedy decision... by the rapidity of his proceedings he hoped to anticipate the formidable preparations for defence which the Danes had scarcely thought of at that early season. The delay in Yarmouth Roads did not accord with his views... every delay, however trifling, gave cause for regret, and favoured the views of the Northern Coalition.

Ever the pragmatist – some would say Machiavellian – Nelson set about winning the confidence of his admiral. Some of his junior officers sent him a fine turbot caught off the Dogger Bank, which Nelson promptly sent to Parker, with his compliments. The gesture worked and the superior officer began to confide in him. Nelson, however, knew the role he was expected to play and the fact that he was Britain's star fighter. As he remarked, 'Now we are sure of fighting, I am sent for. When it was a joke, I was kept in the background.'

Nelson wrote to his superior officer a pointed letter, that not a moment should be lost in attacking the enemy.

They will every day and hour be stronger; we shall never be so good a match for them as at this moment. The only consideration in my mind is how to get at them with the least risk to our ships... In the event of a failure of negotiation, you might instantly attack, and there should scarcely be a doubt but that the Danish fleet would be destroyed, and the capital made so hot that Denmark would listen to reason and its true interest. Now the Danish government seems hostile to us in the greatest possible degree... on your decision depends whether our country shall be degraded in the eyes of Europe, or whether she shall rear her head higher than ever.

How best to honour our country and abate the pride of her enemies, by defeating their schemes, must be the subject of your deepest considerations as commander in chief.

Nelson, 20 years younger and still an advocate of aggressive action in preference to negotiated peace, impressed his own point of view on his commander. 'The mode I call taking the bull by the horns, especially avoiding support from the Swedes,' he explained. He offered alternative plans, but there was no doubt about his own choice: 'I am of the opinion that the boldest measures are the safest.' Stewart, one of the few soldiers Nelson seems to have liked, concurred. Nelson was impatient for action, especially as the Danes were showing more evidence of hostility and were preparing their defence in earnest.

The fleet advanced first towards the castle of Elsinore, 20 miles from Copenhagen. The city's defences seemed much more forbidding than anyone had expected, but Nelson was all for attacking without delay. Parker hesitated, wanting to go by the Sound, and Fremantle voiced Nelson's frustrations: 'I should say the Danes are exceedingly alarmed but delay gives them courage and they will by degrees make Copenhagen so strong that it may resist the attack of our fleet.'

Nelson, having checked out the enemy defences, suggested that Parker in the main fleet should approach the well-fortified Three Crowns Battery from the north, and he would take the King's channel from the south. Stewart observed:

> *Nelson and his party carried out reconnaissance work around the nearby channels on board a frigate: Lord Nelson was struck with admiration at the superior discipline and seamanship that were observable on board the frigate and took pains to tell them so, much to their delight.*
>
> *The Commander-in-Chief, with sound discretion, and in a handsome manner, not only left everything to Lord Nelson for this detached service, but gave two more line of battle ships than he demanded... the energy of Lord Nelson's character was remarked... Lord Nelson kept pacing the cabin, mortified at everything which savoured either of alarm or irresolution. Applied to the possibility of the Swedes joining the action, he sharply observed, 'the more numerous the better' and of the Russians, 'I wish there were twice as many; the easier the victory... Close with a Frenchman, but outmanoeuvre a Russian.'*

These orders, agreed among all the officers and bearing a close resemblance to those used at the Nile, were carried out with enthusiasm but suffered early setbacks, with ships coming under heavy fire before being able to fire back and running into the shoals, at least three running aground.

Stewart reported that

an instance of Lord Nelson's presence of mind now occurred, with his decision to suddenly change the order of sailing and prevent more ships going aground. The British ships were then all engaged with the enemy within the next hour, advancing carefully into the unknown shoals... Lord Nelson was at this time walking the quarter-deck, sometimes much animated, and at others heroically fine in his observations. A shot through the mainmast knocked a few splinters about us. 'It is warm work, and this day may be the last for any of us at a moment... but mark you, I would not be elsewhere for thousands.'

Four miles away, Parker was convinced that the battle was progressing disastrously and ordered the signal to retreat. According to Stewart,

the historic moment of insubordination came when the signal, no. 39, for leaving off action, was made... he did not appear to notice it... the Lieutenant asked if he should repeat it... Lord Nelson answered, 'no, acknowledge it' asking 'is no. 16, for close action, still hoisted?', exclaiming 'mind you keep it so'. He now walked the deck considerably agitated, which was always known by his moving the stump of his right arm. 'Leave off action! Now damn me if I do! You know I only have one eye – I have a right to be blind sometimes' and then, with an archness peculiar to his character, putting the glass to his blind eye, he exclaimed, 'I really do not see the signal'.

Nelson, aware that Danish resistance was weakening and that a withdrawal now would have led to huge loss of life and ships, made the decision to overrule his commander. It was a gamble, but it paid off. An hour after the signal, most of the Danish ships had ceased firing and, securing its prizes, the British fleet was endeavouring to save as many of the enemy crew in the water as it could. After another half hour, appalled by the loss of life with the continued firing of the shore batteries, Nelson sent a letter of truce on shore, addressed to the Crown Prince:

to the Brothers of Englishmen, the Danes. Lord Nelson has directions to spare Denmark, when no longer resisting; but if the firing is continued on the part of Denmark, Lord Nelson will be obliged to set on fire all the floating-batteries he has taken, without having the power of saving the brave Danes who have defended them.

By 3 o'clock, half an hour after receiving the letter, many other Danish ships had struck their colours and the Danes returned the flag of truce, suspending the fire from the batteries. It is just as well Nelson stopped when he did, as the British ships were badly damaged and not in a position to carry on attacking the enemy's line, where several ships were still firing. It was not at all clear what was going on, and Foley and Fremantle suggested that the navigational difficulties were too great to attempt closer engagements.

Nelson was depressed by the carnage. The 12 British ships had captured, burned or sank 12 of 18 moored Danish ships, despite the added challenge of the shore batteries and the Danes fighting on home ground. But the losses were tremendous – the British lost 254 men killed, including his new protégé, Captain Riou, and 689 wounded (more than at the Nile) and the Danes slightly more. Nelson's second-in-command confided:

I am told the battle of the Nile was nothing to this. Considering the disadvantages of navigation, the approach of the enemy, their vast numbers of guns and mortars on both land and sea, I do not think there was ever a bolder attack... it was worthy of our gallant Hero of the Nile. Nothing can exceed his spirit. Sir Hyde made the signal to discontinue the action before we had been at it two hours, supposing our ships would all be destroyed... but Nelson was right to refuse it, for if we had discontinued the action before the enemy struck, we should have all got aground and been destroyed.

Nelson took the risk that his insubordination would be forgiven by his less daring superior. 'Well!' he had exclaimed, 'I have fought contrary to orders, and I shall perhaps be hanged: never mind, let them.' The Battle of Copenhagen in 1801 thus introduced the phrase 'to turn a blind eye' into common parlance. It was a tough battle, adding to Nelson's prestige and enhancing his growing reputation for creative initiative and intolerance of less go-getting superiors. The Admiralty got the message and it was the last time he was appointed as a second-in-command. In his own words,

> the glorious 2nd of April was a day when the greatest dangers of navigation were overcome, and the Danish force (which they thought impregnable) totally taken or destroyed by the consummate skill of the commanders and by the undaunted bravery of as gallant a band as ever defended the rights of this country.

Entering Copenhagen to begin armistice negotiations, Nelson chose to walk to the palace rather than take the heavily guarded carriage on offer. This was an extraordinary choice, given that he had just commanded the massacre of many hundreds of Danes within sight of the city. According to Danish informants he was looked on with a mixture of awe and hatred; but his own account sounds more than a little delusional, perhaps understandably after days of fighting and lack of sleep. He claimed he was received 'with cheers and viva Nelson'. Nonetheless, he seems to have maintained a fine sense of realism in his negotiations, pointing out that while the Danes were great friends of the British, the palace would burn well – during the cease-fire Nelson repositioned his mortars to cover the main batteries of the city defences. Hardy was with Nelson during several rounds of negotiation, commenting, 'I will venture to say His Royal Highness never had so much plain trooth spoken to him in his life.'

Under the terms of the armistice, hostilities would cease for 14 weeks, Denmark would suspend its part in the coalition, open its ports to the British fleet for trade and leave its ships unharmed. Nelson took Foley and Fremantle with him to complete the negotiations. Ball, in the Mediterranean, wrote to Nelson, 'this last brilliant occasion has proved to the world that you possess the abilities of a statesman as well as the qualities of a great hero.'

Ironically, the battle need never have been fought, as Tsar Paul had been assassinated and the Armed Neutrality broken up a few days before. The news reached the Danes during the negotiations, and their stance may have been more influenced by this than Nelson's skilful negotiations.

After the battle

The battle of Copenhagen, for all the lukewarm reception it received in England, added to Nelson's prestige. He was made a Viscount, and Hyde Parker was ordered to hand over his command to his more illustrious deputy.

In rebuilding his reputation after Naples, Nelson once again converted the consequences of his actions to the best advantage. He was energetic, risk-taking and building his stardom, for himself and his brother officers. His diplomatic achievements, however temporary in impact, brought him new respect. Finally, the relationships he enjoyed with his cadre of senior captains played a key part in his success. This was now his standard way of operating.

Nelson suffered his usual post-battle depression, and was keen to go home to see Emma and his daughter. His captains, as always, were a great source of comfort. As he wrote to Ball, 'All the fleet are so kind to me that I should be a wretch not to cheer up. Foley has put me under a regimen of milk at four in the morning. Hardy is as good as ever.'

Nelson kept busy before his recall. He rose at four and usually by eight had written enough letters to handle the immediate business of the fleet. At five, his hour for breakfast, he invited the young officers of the middle watch. As Colonel Stewart remarked, 'a midshipman or two were always of the party, and at table with them he would enter into their boyish jokes and be the most youthful of the party.' To dinner he invited the captains and ship's officers in rotation, including, in one case, Troubridge's young son, also Tom, who was 'too polite by half and "my lords" him too much, and tells him you [Troubridge senior] were never so polite.'

Another happy duty was congratulating Sir Thomas Graves, made a baronet in the King's birthday honours list and whom Nelson personally dubbed knight in the name of the King on the quarterdeck of the *St George*.

After Copenhagen, back in England, Nelson was visibly more confident moving around Whitehall and among the merchants of the City.
He made his maiden speech – somewhat dull and humourless – in the
House of Lords, to some acclaim because as a hero, he was back in
favour politically. After a brief period of commanding naval forces in the
English Channel, he was given command of the Mediterranean, probably his favourite battleground and one of the most decisive in the war
against Napoleon.

Nelson was proud of leading his captains, consulting and sharing with
them his ideas and plans, depending on them for support and friendship
– and expected them to be as dedicated and daring as he always was,
and be always there for him. This was in contrast with many more autocratic leaders of the navy in his era, and a generally much less demo-
cratic operating context. Mindful of the high levels of expertise,
experience and commitment of his brother officers, Nelson actively
wanted and needed their inputs. The whole situation benefited from his
ability to quickly build strong relationships with his peers, for mostly
they were similar to their chief in age and experience, and only his position as their commander set him apart. Some he knew well; others he
knew slightly; some not at all; but his trust and companionship were
infectious.

Nelson's style of leadership involved creating a close-knit group of
carefully chosen followers, and he tried to make it inclusive rather than
exclusive. Although the 'band of brothers' quote was probably a *post hoc*
description, he was describing a real sense of camaraderie and shared
mindset – principally a forward-leaning propensity for action and an
eagerness for a fight. There was little new in terms of his tactics, which
were essentially to get in close and fight it out fast and furious. This
needed courage, stamina and trust that your fellows will join in too –
hence the need for comradeship at such a high level. It is almost a gang
culture.

In such a form of participatory leadership, some measure of idolatry
is often required, but then there can be room for initiative and empower-

ment, as long as it supports the cause. If a member's loyalty was in question, he could be shafted. Turncoats would never be tolerated. It went without saying that the band of brothers were completely dedicated to each other – 'all for one and one for all' could have been their motto. This is entirely different to a more naked autocracy where fear and dependency unite the members and commit them to a plan.

Nelson felt comfortable in the mode of participatory leader, given his ability to form strong relationships with his captains and make sound judgements of their abilities. His attention was lapped up by these careworn and often lonely men. His quick intelligence, his insight into a person's doubts and uncertainties, and his tendency to speak forthrightly all added to the sense of trustworthy integrity. The ability to weave a sense of shared loyalty is a function of personal magnetism, sociability and zeal – it is not something that can be attained by simply asserting 'we are a team'. It is also helped by having a common enemy, a tangible threat and a technical need for interdependence. Nelson genuinely wanted to be a team player, and his natural personality suited this choice.

However, this does not mean that the personalities of the band of brothers were subsumed to Nelson's. They were all very different men and, although able and competent, respected Nelson's leadership. This was partly because of his reputation for seeking out enemies and bringing them to battle, and hence the possibility of winning prize money. It was also because they respected the Admiralty and its choices and decisions. But finally, the captains respected his leadership for his own qualities and personality, and his drive to take ultimate responsibility. Nelson saw no contradiction with the exceptional status he claimed for himself within the team: teamwork did not imply compromise, consensus or mediocrity; loyalty meant being there for your mates, not agreeing with them all the time, nor expecting them to follow like sheep. He recognised openly that the band of brothers enabled him to achieve his greatest victories.

Nelson's Way
Loyalty

Loyalty means unswerving allegiance to a person, to a country or a cause, and being faithful. A loyal leader – and follower – is observant, dutiful, pays homage, gives consent, and shows readiness, willingness and eagerness to serve. A loyal leader has a sense of devotion, obligation, commitment, responsibility and accountability for his or her followers, and meets these obligations.

To be a loyal team player as a leader, you and your team need to know what the other members are thinking and have empathy with them. As their leader you need to delegate large and complex tasks and monitor loosely, trusting in your team's ability to do the job. They need to understand your 'big picture' perspective and to be clear about objectives. Praise their contributions openly and often. In a trusting environment, any mistakes made can be addressed and solutions supported. This is not closing ranks and covering up, but sharing and helping, being of one mind.

But of course it can be overdone. Blind loyalty drives out independent thought, creativity and initiative and can be self-destructive of any kind of team. Personal loyalties within a team can produce cliques and cronyism. Even effective teams can develop greater loyalty to each other and their subculture than to the organisation as a whole.

Evidence of a successful group working together at the top of the organisation can mean more committed teamwork throughout. It helps to hire team players in the first place, who acknowledge the contribution of others, who talk about how a good boss has helped and encouraged them, who say 'we' and 'us' rather than 'me' all the time. These people are rugby players rather than marathon runners; they play doubles in tennis rather than singles.

Teamwork in organisations is shown by colleagues helping each other's customers when there is a problem and volunteering to other units when they have a crisis. It is shown in an absence of blame and recrimination when things go wrong, but taking responsibility for any failure jointly. It's a bellboy recommending guests to the hotel restaurant rather than taking commission from one along the road. It's a manager taking over a subordinate's job when a customer complains, and not complaining about the subordinate back to the customer. It is at the heart of seamless service everywhere, such as between bank branches and consulting firm offices.

Leadership comments
Sir John Harvey-Jones

'Nelson was the founder of participative leadership,' insists Sir John Harvey-Jones, a widely respected and internationally recognised business leader known for his keen interest in motivation and teamwork. 'My own leadership style has been based very much on Nelson. He has been a lifelong hero of mine.'

'When I changed my career from the navy to industry the lessons seemed even more applicable,' Harvey-Jones says. 'While a leader has to provide the framework, he has to give away the leadership when actually going into battle, so to speak.'

He adds, 'People will do what they themselves are committed to. Getting commitment is a matter of talking and reasoning until everyone is totally clear what the objective is. Endless detailed command is enormously expensive and ineffective because it switches people off. People need head room if they are to contribute, and they can only do this if they understand what the whole enterprise is about. Leadership is about getting people to buy into the same ideal. Thus Nelson communicated ruthlessly, explained everything, then trusted his people to get on with it.'

Harvey-Jones feels that there was much scope for the leadership lessons he learned from Nelson at the beginning of his career. 'In the public sector, I soon realised that there is so little trust, people are checked on, micro-managed all the time – the antithesis of what Nelson believed in. Trust is contagious. If you meet people who trust their leader, the leader benefits. Trust is something that is communicated immediately – you can instantly see if people trust their leader.'

'Leadership has to be by personal example, believing in it totally, and exemplifying it,' he points out, describing how Nelson walked the talk, led from the front, and didn't expect men to do things that he wasn't prepared to do himself. 'It's no good banging on about communication if you don't listen. If you don't care, this communicates immediately. Leadership has to be felt as much as understood. The presentation of your ideas has to be a seamless whole, and reflected in even your tiniest actions. Anything that is false rings as clear as a bell. You have to believe in your ideas and demonstrate them with action.'

Harvey-Jones points out that loyalty is not easy to build: 'It takes a lot of courage to trust the people you lead, but it's not something you can command. Nelson won the loyalty he enjoyed. Loyalty is something you give your people, you share with them, and you'll get it back in return. If you don't give it there is no way on earth you'll get it back.'

'Like Nelson's captains, you must be constantly aware of the value your colleagues will put on your actions. If one of his captains faced choices about an engagement he would be overwhelmingly aware of the interpretations his colleagues would put on it,' he explains. 'People seldom believe the things they hear others say – they believe the actions they take. Courage comes into it: it is sometimes more courageous to run away than to stay and fight because of the public opprobrium which you must bear yourself.' You can't win every time. As a leader you never harm yourself by apologising if you've got it wrong. What worries your people is if you appear to not know that you've got it wrong.

Leadership lessons
Loyalty

- ⚓ If you want to be a participative leader and a team player, you have to create loyalty and trust. Being autocratic is quicker and easier but risks catastrophic failure.
- ⚓ As a participative leader, be *primus inter pares* – first among equals – admired and respected, but still promoting loyalty to the team.
- ⚓ Invest in getting to know your immediate subordinates and inner circle and help them to know each other, so they know what others are thinking and how they will act. They will be competitive but loyal and need one another's support too.
- ⚓ Let them know that your success depends on them. Give them the clear message that you're all in it together, sharing your plans and ideas – the whole is greater than the sum of the parts.

⚓ Create trust and honesty between all your team members and yourself, handling mistakes and failures in a supportive and positive way.

⚓ Link achievement to belonging. Some organisations form a 'club' for high achievers, creating loyalty to a shared task and sense of excellence. Carng for the work is at the heart of it.

⚓ Take team members with you to the most important and high-profile events, as a reward and for their exposure and development.

⚓ Make sure they are a team and not a clique. Members of a clique invest more in their own togetherness than in the work they must do together.

⚓ Use common interests to overcome differences in background, social status, nationality and personality.

⚓ Be a rallying point, offer guidance and decision making, while encouraging them to contribute, facilitating but not dominating discussions.

⚓ Look after their interests, their families, their promotion prospects and all chances for improvement.

⚓ Resolve differences and falling out between team members by listening and encouraging disputants to see the issues from the other's perspective.

⚓ Listen to their advice, consult them on your own problems, be human and vulnerable, offer real affection and enjoy receiving it in return – it's lonely at the top!

6

DILIGENCE

Running a tight ship, 1803–1805

'They were dull, weary, endless months, those months of watching and waiting of the big ships before the French arsenals. Purposeless they seemed to many, but they saved England. The world has never seen a more impressive demonstration of sea power upon its history. Those far-distant, storm-beaten ships, upon which the Grand Army never looked, stood between it and the dominion of the world.'

Admiral Mahan

Nelson explaining the 'Nelson Touch' to his captains, aiming to break the enemy line in two places, cutting off the rear and centre divisions from the forward (van) division. It was designed to achieve complete victory in one day.

'England expects every man to do his duty. Lord Nelson explaining to the Officers the Plan of Attack previous to the Battle of Trafalgar, and Position of the Combined Forces of France and Spain' by William Marshall Craig (artist), James Goodby (engraver), 9 January 1806.

O N 12 MAY 1801 NELSON WROTE TO HIS IMMEDIATE subordinate on blockade duty in the Baltic, Sir Thomas Graves, 'how does the Keen air of Russia agree with you... the Russian fleet of 43 Sail of the Line is moor'd about 10 Miles below Cronstadt... I have sent about Fresh beef but there are no Vegetables as yet thought of in this Country.'

This time to the Admiralty, on 12 August 1804 Nelson wrote about the *Gibraltar*, that

the very bad state of the ship's Hull... [makes it] proper [for her] to proceed to England, it being considered impossible to put the Gibraltar in a state even to rejoin me for the purpose of taking convoy from Malta... [I am] well aware that the Gibraltar's state made it dangerous for her to perform any service.

In another dispatch, written on 13 September 1805 again to the Admiralty, Nelson requested a pension for the widow of the late physician of the Mediterranean fleet, especially because 'I much fear that His Death was principally owing to his going to Messina for the purpose of buying lemon Juice for the fleet at Home which is likely to be obtained at 1/6 per gallon instead of 8 or 9 shillings.'

Writing on 6 April 1805 to the Bishop of London about his Chaplain whom he had 'poached', Nelson wonders if

the Rev. Mr Scott has got into any scrape with Your Lordship I much fear that I have been the innocent cause of it... Mr Scott is I will venture to say one of the most learned Men of the Age and of great

Observation of Men and manners. He is My Confidential private Foreign Secretary which on this station where so many languages are to be corresponded in is a place of very great importance... His health is very much improved by the fine Climate... I beg leave to recommend Mr Scott as a Gentleman who would do honor to any kindness Your Lordship may be pleased to Shew him.

These four letters, of which these are only short extracts, help to explain why Nelson was able to keep his fleet afloat and in fine fighting fettle for years. He cared about detail, one of the fundamentals of being a good manager. First of all, he knew what was going on and passed information around his subordinates. Secondly, he knew where and how to get food supplies. Thirdly, he was concerned about the state of his ships and their need for repairs. Fourthly, he knew about costs and the importance of making economies where possible. And fifthly, he recognised good staff when he saw them and looked after them. He managed all this with a remarkably small 'head office' team – between brief moments of heroic courage, he was a remarkably engaged manager!

Nelson faced the challenge of keeping a large number of ships victualled, repaired and armed as they blockaded and chased the enemy for months at a time, in challenging weather conditions and without easy access to friendly ports. To add to these challenges, the Admiralty had instituted major cutbacks and across-the-board economies as part of one of those restructuring exercises favoured by the top brass, but which caused havoc for operations – ironically under the leadership of Admiral the Earl of St Vincent.

The responsible bodies back in Britain were the Victualling Board and its sister organisations the Navy Board, the Sick and Hurt Board, and the Transport Board. These reported to the Board of Admiralty, which in turn reported to the Secretary of State, an appointee of the King and Cabinet. Communication with suppliers around the world was difficult enough, so much depended on the individual managers in each station and their relationships with the local commanders. Feeding and supplying a navy was already challenging in peacetime, when numbers were relatively low, supply ships relatively safe, and local markets readily available. But it was a completely different matter in a major war, and by 1810 the British Navy had reached a high point of over 1,000 ships and 140,000 men. More than half the British navy operated in distant waters, and the logistics of organising its victualling was immense.

During the early years of the nineteenth century, the only methods of preserving food were to dry it, salt it or pickle it. Canning had not been invented. The packaging materials then available were wooden casks and cloth bags. Thus the rations had to last, and the Victualling Board focused on ship's biscuit or 'hard tack', salt beef, dried peas and oatmeal, with some butter and cheese. It was washed down with a gallon of beer per man per day; this sounds a lot, although it was not the British gallon we know today but a 'wine measure' of five-sixths of a gallon, and the beer itself was 'small' or weak beer of 2–3 per cent proof. Britain was too far away from most ships on active duty to supply fresh meat and vegetables, so captains and admirals had to rely on their connections in ports throughout their stations to supply their needs, and the navy allowed a certain amount of substitution for the basic rations.

With a caring and competent admiral (such as Nelson) naval crews could be better off than land-bound civilian workers and merchant navy seamen, for whom there were no official victualling scales. A good naval manager would not rely on the Victualling Board's offerings to ensure morale and health. By themselves, these provisions supplied bulk, carbohydrates, proteins and calories; but they were very low on vitamins, and scurvy was a constant threat to sailors' health. There was already mounting evidence that scurvy resulted from a deficiency of fresh fruit and vegetables, now identified as containing Vitamin C.

Another management challenge was identifying the location of the enemy fleet. The only way to gain naval intelligence was to maintain a string of contacts throughout one's station, to intercept neutral and friendly shipping whenever they were encountered, to call regularly into ports and interview the well-informed, and to send frigates on ahead to see what was happening. Maintaining information networks required constant attention, much of it dependent on personal relationships built up over the years.

Looking after the ships (maintaining the 'plant') was another night-mare. The copper plating of ships' bottoms only partially reduced the growth of barnacles and seaweed. With few friendly ports, repairs could take months. And this was all in the context of a major crackdown on expenses. The war was costing Britain a fortune, and there was consid-erable pressure to reduce public expenditure – taxes were as unpopular as ever, and political capital could be made by politicians promising cuts.

Part of the admiral's job was, of course, working with immediate subordinates, in this context the captains. He was also active in manag-ing the rank and file – seamen and marines. Looking after their individ-ual needs was a substantial job. As we shall see, managing 'patronage' – arranging positions and promotions for his own protégés and those of fellow officers, friends and relatives – represented 15 per cent of Nelson's correspondence.

Nelson's objective as commander-in-chief of the Mediterranean squadron was to keep the enemy contained and ideally lure them into battle. He argued with those who said he was 'blockading' – he was not trying to keep the enemy in port; on the contrary, he wanted them to come out and fight. But he knew he could be forced to wait months and even years, and he had to be ready, in tip-top fighting order, whenever they chose to sail.

In May 1803, with the collapse of the so-called Peace of Amiens, Britain was once more at war with France, and the Admiralty appointed Nelson to take charge of the largest and most crucial theatre of war. His long experience in the region, his extensive network of political contacts and perhaps also his growing political and diplomatic skills made him an obvious choice, apart from his popularity and fame. (Ironically, the immediate cause of the war was Napoleon's insistence that Britain should give up control of Malta. Nelson's maiden speech in the Lords had been to argue that the island was inconsequential to Britain's inter-ests; he now wrote a powerful *tour d'horizon* on Mediterranean strategy, placing Malta at the centre.) All his administrative skills would also be called for, in what must be one of the most extraordinary feats of man-agerial persistence.

The key to understanding Nelson is thus appreciating not just his energy and focus and his achievements, but that he was well organised and structured, he spent a lot of time planning and thinking, and paid great attention to detail. Many observers have considered Nelson impatient and irritable when subjected to bureaucracy, and this is indeed true. But there was another side to him: the hours of slog at his desk and the careful and extended negotiations with suppliers to keep the fleet in great shape for when the day came. In this respect, in terms of the emphasis on administration, communication and organisational skills, Nelson was a very modern manager.

One recently discovered letter from Nelson to his second-in-command, Sir Richard Bickerton, in January 1804 shows the range of his managerial issues. Within 600 words he discusses the movements of the fleet's transports – 'my stray flock', one 'gone to Malta being short of bread which has surprised me'; Captain Keats's diplomatic mission to Algiers; the organisation of various convoys; the latest intelligence about the French fleet in Toulon; the work needed on certain ships – 'the *Niger* wants some refit and to be freed from Rats'; and he throws in a complaint about his bosses – 'what can I do, I have not the ships, the Admiralty gives me none.' There was also a shortage of men to contend with and seamen were recruited throughout the Mediterranean. Nelson would accept anyone 'who was not French'.

A war of attrition

By 1803 Britain was expecting a long war. Napoleon still harboured a plan to make a direct attack on the English and, more immediately, posed a threat to trade. The seas were the transport infrastructure of trade, and crucial to the continuing success of the emerging miracle of the industrial revolution. With trade came wealth, and the ability to fight a sustained war with the French superpower. So control of the seas was not simply a matter of containing the French fleet; allies and vassals of France who might threaten the trade routes had to be thwarted by diplomatic or military means. Frequent negotiations of alliances – and the fortunes of the land wars – created a constantly shifting political landscape.

Nelson could exert influence on all this. Blockaded ports suffered from shortages and damage to their trade. As he wrote:

> *it will make the inhabitants severely feel the baneful effects of French fraternity, and in the case of a co-operation with some of the continental powers, will make them ready to throw off the French yoke.*

Many politicians and military leaders hoped that the French would actually try to invade Britain, confident that they could be soundly beaten. If all his army was at sea, in the perilous flat-bottomed boats he had had built, Napoleon would be completely exposed to the British fleet. Then a decisive action could take place, which would bring the war to an end.

The French considered that they needed control of the Channel for long enough (as little as six hours was mooted by Napoleon) to ferry the *grande armée* of 120,000 to the beaches of southern England. From there, they would march on London, burn the city and proceed to destroy the naval dockyards and stores at Portsmouth and Plymouth. They thought this would take a further three weeks. While the army was mustered and training at Boulogne (another masterpiece of military administration) Napoleon could do nothing until the various squadrons of his navy could combine to wrest control of the Channel from the British – in one frustrated letter he thought that even 24 hours would be enough. Hence the intense British focus on keeping Napoleon's fleets dispersed and relatively powerless – and the public attention on the undramatic business of blockading Brest, Ferrol and Toulon.

The Mediterranean command was already very familiar to Nelson and undoubtedly his favourite. He hated the cold of the Baltic and found the Channel too small and confining, and in any case Cornwallis was doing a fine job in the latter. But in the Mediterranean he had significant strategic challenges, with Genoa, Leghorn and Corsica back in French hands, and Minorca controlled by Spain. Only Gibraltar and Malta were British, and they were far away from his main blockading area of Toulon. Naples was neutral, and Nelson's strong connections there meant he could access supplies when needed, although not much went on without the French knowing about it.

Nelson managed the entire Naples–Gibraltar–Toulon triangle, trying to lure the French out to do battle or, if not, keep them bottled up in harbour. The biggest danger was the potential of the French fleet to escape to the Atlantic. In January 1805 the fleet at Rochefort broke through the British blockade, and two weeks later the Toulon fleet slipped past Nelson's frigates at night. Nelson was desperate and, thinking they were heading for Egypt, set off after them. It was two weeks before he heard that gales had blown the French back to port, their inexperience at sea doing more to contain them than the British blockade. Nelson wrote to Collingwood:

> *Bonaparte has often made the boast that our fleet would be worn out by keeping the sea and that his would be kept in order... by staying in port; but now he finds, I fancy, if Emperors hear truth, that his fleet suffers more in a night than ours in a year.*

On his defeat and capture in 1815, and on the voyage to St Helena on the *Bellerophon*, Napoleon's constant curse was that the British navy had subverted his great dream. And this was not just because of the dramatic battles and capture and destruction of his own ships. It was just as much the constant blockades, the ubiquitous presence of the British squadrons, their ability to be at sea without cessation, which tied up his ships and men so he could not move them where he wanted.

The fleet

In 1803 Nelson had nine ships and four frigates, with two smaller craft stationed off Toulon, two frigates outside Gibraltar, and two sloops just inside the straits. He operated another frigate off Barcelona, with three ships of the line moving around several different stations. Initially he kept one at Naples and one off Algiers, mostly to keep in with valuable allies. He operated further ships escorting convoys, and there were always vessels in dock undergoing repairs and ships carrying dispatches between Malta, Naples and Gibraltar. Manned by over 5,000 men, this was the operation he had to keep at sea indefinitely. Supplies came from England, but more immediately from ports in the Mediterranean, from the few harbours open for business, and from the few suppliers willing to compromise their allegiance to France by selling goods to Nelson.

Such was the need to keep a close eye on the French that Nelson could ill afford to let any ships give up their blockade duties for refits, however necessary. Even the newest and best-maintained ships would begin suffering after six continuous months at sea. As Collingwood remarked, there was 'nothing but a copper sheet between us and eternity'. Several of Nelson's ships needed to go into dock for major repairs, and one of the best places to shelter was at Malta. But it was too far away – travel and repairs could take a ship out of service for two months – and Nelson was afraid of missing the French. So only ships in the worst condition were sent, one by one and, if possible, their repair trips were combined with convoy duties, for which Nelson never had enough resources. By contrast, the Spanish were known for splendid, huge ships that always impressed Nelson (he asked if he could have the captured *San Josef* as his flagship, given the choice), although he maintained that they lacked the quality of men to man them, and officers to lead them.

The challenge for Nelson was to keep his small and busy force in service, needing rope, canvas and timber as basic supplies. He was warned that, because of the naval cutbacks, he would have few reinforcements, few replacements for his oldest and most blockade-weary ships, and only limited quantities of dockyard stores.

At the high point of Nelson's Mediterranean command in early 1805 he managed a fleet of 40 ships, which were constantly on the move. He monitored their movements and the information they obtained (and helped them with their needs) through an elaborate system of rendezvous points, where captains could collect and leave reports, all referred to by code in case they fell into the wrong hands. To keep all this going, he dictated at least two dozen general orders per day, and wrote at least ten personal letters by hand.

Much of Nelson's everyday experience in more than half his life at sea was of continuous blockade duties (or, as he would have put it, waiting just over the horizon for the enemy to come out and then to pounce on them). At Naples and Malta, during the years 1798–1800, he had kept his ships seaworthy and ready to fight across the whole length of the Mediterranean.

He already knew the bad effect of a long blockade without good provisioning from his first major command, the *Agamemnon*, in 1794. He had then spent 15 months at sea in the northern Mediterranean without a break, fighting ashore as well as by sea. The 90 sick men on board represented up to around a quarter of his crew at that point. Supplies were often late and there were no friendly ports except Leghorn, where the ships went to recover. It took months for the ship's company to get well again. No wonder Nelson believed in prevention rather than cure.

Administrative staff

Nelson was also helped enormously by his small but competent staff, including the Rev. Dr Alexander Scott, an experienced intelligence officer and a great linguist, whom Nelson 'borrowed' from the Bishop of London. Proficient in French, Spanish and Italian (some of these languages self-taught out of textbooks while at sea), Scott wrote and translated letters for Nelson and searched for scraps of information wherever he could find them, as well as acting as Nelson's chaplain. They became very close. Dr Scott's accounts of Nelson's last hours, with the detailed notes of the surgeon, together with his letters describing his overwhelming sense of grief at Nelson's death, suggest the high esteem he felt based on years of working together.

Sometimes Nelson had to obtain extra translating help. Before Scott joined him he hired a

> *gentleman proper to go with Captain Troubridge to the Bay of Naples... having performed the fatiguing office he undertook in a manner as to give the greatest satisfaction to Captain Troubridge... I really think that fifty pounds is not more than a proper reward for his Zeal and Indefatigable attention.*

It might be thought that hiring (and suggesting the pay for) a translator for a captain was not the job of an admiral. But Nelson, with his zeal for micromanagement, was probably the person most able to do it, and he got around to it!

Another Scott, John Scott, was kept constantly writing as Nelson's secretary, and focused mostly on trying to get essential supplies. Nelson's immediate staff also included Captain Hardy, one of the band of brothers and flag captain, and one of his closest confidants.

The Captain of the Fleet George Murray, who handled fleet administration, was also invaluable to his chief, who would rather keep this vacancy open than fill it with anyone else. Nelson's personal steward William Chevalier and servant Gaetano Spedillo made up the rest of the team, and none of them was to leave the flagship for two years. Sometimes Nelson did not leave his own cabin for days. With all his letter writing and reading, together with the perusal of intercepted mail, Nelson maintained a more complex and far-flung network of intelligence-gathering mechanisms than any of his contemporaries.

Autonomy in decision making

Another reason Nelson liked the Mediterranean was that he could run his own show. He knew the port governors and had better contacts than anyone throughout the area. Contact with the Admiralty was infrequent and he rarely got news from England. Paris newspapers could be had from Spain – they were only 10–14 days old – and the able linguist Dr Scott was on hand to translate them.

Thus Nelson had to make decisions on the spot, and had a good deal of autonomy in many diplomatic as well as naval matters. With the reduction in available allies again, this was just as well. He was in good personal standing with Turkey, wearing honours bestowed on him by the Sultan following the Battle of the Nile.

If Nelson wanted autonomy for himself, he also wanted to be able to give it to others. He delegated duties to competent men and let them get on with it (as he had done when sending Troubridge to Naples before the Nile, and as he was to do with Blackwood in managing the frigates at Trafalgar). He explained goals and tasks clearly, and then did not interfere. He always supported his officers when they showed initiative. If things went wrong he defended them. He admired bold and decisive action in others as much as he followed this policy himself. He would rather mistakes were made occasionally than his men succumb to vacillation and inactivity.

Supplies and logistics

The immense operational area of the Mediterranean produced massive supply problems, with ships and men needing water, provisions, stores, and munitions, of up to 200 tons in a frigate and more than 400 tons in a ship of the line. Each ship was manned by between 200 and 800 seamen who needed to be fed every day.

Obtaining supplies was difficult, delivering them was problematic, and there was also a need to prevent rip-offs by suppliers. A trusted officer was posted at every point of delivery to check that the exact quantities were delivered and had arrived in good order. There were some dishonest transport captains as well as suppliers. At any point in the supply chain the vegetables, cattle, timber, stores and munitions could be interfered with and cheaper items substituted.

Nelson was appalled at the lack of patriotism and blatant profiteering that could influence suppliers from his own country to send poor-quality, substandard, rancid provisions to his fighting men. Suppliers from other countries were similarly unreliable, although Nelson could then exert direct pressure on the diplomats with whom he was friendly at each port. It all demanded constant vigilance, and the sort of attention to detail that became Nelson's obsession in the build-up to the Trafalgar campaign. He even wrote one letter complaining about the quality of rope supplied. No detail was too small.

Recent research suggests that Nelson's navy was fed rather better than might be implied by stories of rotten meat and weevily biscuits. But it was tough living on salted provisions for six months at a time, with indigestible meat and biscuits, rancid cheese and soggy oatmeal, washed down with rum and green, slimy water. The beer would have been consumed fairly soon after leaving home, and could turn sour in days if not properly stored. Freshly slaughtered bullock, fresh eggs, vegetables and fruit, wine and beer could make all the difference.

There were officially listed substitutes, which were the only ones for which the Admiralty would pay. These included a pint of wine, or half a pint of spirits, as equal to a gallon of beer. Four pounds of flour were equal to four pounds of salt beef. Four pounds of fresh beef were equal to four pounds of salt beef. One pound of rice was equal to a pound of bread. Sugar and molasses could also be substitutes. Nowhere are fresh fruit or fresh vegetables mentioned, so these would seem to be extras that Nelson insisted on and sought out. In a letter dated December 1804, in repatriating a captured Spanish merchant ship, Nelson admits: 'nineteen baskets of Macaroni has been the only thing taken out of her and if the owner will come off to the fleet I will direct his being paid.'

One of the reasons Nelson had to spend so much time with all this detail was that the bureaucratic system required his signature on all non-standard purchases. The captain and purser (the officer on board ship responsible for the handling of provisions and the accounting, who also sold small extra items to the crew) had to obtain written purchase orders from the commander-in-chief, unless based in a theatre of war where these were not available. It would seem that Nelson, who sometimes did not hear from the Admiralty for months at a time, approved thousands of purchase requests and put these as a high priority. Onions were a favourite counter to scurvy, and when he discovered a new supply of oranges he ordered 30,000 in one go! Nelson was also a great believer in fresh meat, and this meant bringing aboard live cattle (and fodder, to keep the animals alive).

His favourite ports included a group of small islands off Sardinia, which became a popular watering point. Here he could get timber, firewood, food and water – and was happy to give gifts of silverware to the local church. Sometimes having to make night journeys and provision by the light of the moon, Nelson and his ships would land in Agincourt Sound, at the Maddalena Islands. This was a secure and secret base, with onions, beef and sheep in good supply. Nelson even managed to source some food from the Barbary coast, not too far from Toulon. Tunis became another target and, using his contacts in the Francophone Arab world, he continued to make sure that the vital supplies came through.

Nelson had met several doctors in England and shared their view that citrus fruits were the best way to combat scurvy. Many also thought that salted provisions caused scurvy; although this was subsequently disproved, clearly a higher proportion of fresh food was the answer. Nelson believed in preventive health, it being much easier to keep the fleet healthy than try to cure them. He set up a naval hospital at Malta, but this was not the main focus of his healthcare policy. It says much for Nelson's efforts that after five months at sea there was not one man reported sick in the entire fleet. By January 1805, after over 18 months at sea, there was only one man in the sick bay of the *Victory*'s entire ship's company of 840 men.

Naval intelligence

Another management challenge Nelson faced was knowing what was going on, when letters took weeks or months, when newspapers were full of rumour and were mostly propaganda instruments, and especially when the enemy was at sea. With none of the modern technology of surveillance, it all depended on word of mouth and relationships. For example, he had maintained a long relationship with the British consul in Madrid, John Hunter, and his colleague James Duff in Cadiz. The latter had known Nelson for 27 years, through war and peace. A Quaker merchant in Barcelona, Edward Gayner, was also a close friend. They relayed a constant stream of information to Nelson and felt that this was a key part of doing their job. They would, of course, help other admirals, but Nelson held a special place in their regard. The importance of gaining this intelligence may be seen in his letters, in which he constantly asks for news and, when receiving it, passes it around. Sometimes it was false, for reasons of ignorance or deliberate misinformation. It was very hard to tell.

Despite his efforts, the enemy escaped twice. The first time, in January 1805 while Nelson was at Sardinia, it caused him great anxiety: 'consider how anxious I must be for information on the Enemy and one moments delay may enable them to accomplish their object.' He set up a system of moving his fleet from rendezvous to rendezvous, sending the frigates out for information, systematically eliminating every place the enemy may have gone. He sent a note listing all the rendezvous points, which each captain had to read and sign, its cover grubby and crumpled with constant handling.

In the first breakout the enemy returned to port, but the second breakout in April 1805 was more worrying and could have had even more dire consequences. Nelson had no idea where they had gone. It took him a month to gather enough information to give him the confidence to set off across the Atlantic to the West Indies, their presumed destination. Nelson's anxiety and tension mounted. But this was no wild goose chase – he had carefully thought through every eventuality and meticulously covered his ground, and rightly predicted the enemy's return and destination at Ferrol. He was snapping so closely at the heels of the French that Villeneuve, the French admiral, was unable to fulfil Napoleon's orders to concentrate the fleets in the West Indies – he gave up and came back to port, ultimately to Cadiz.

In assessing Nelson's all-round ability, Cuthbert Collingwood appreciated the importance of his organisational skills; it was not just his personality and luck. After Trafalgar, after the immediate shock of personal loss, Collingwood reflected that

> *he possessed the zeal of an enthusiast, directed by talents which Nature had very bountifully bestowed upon him, and everything seemed, as if by enchantment, to prosper under his direction. But it was the effect of system, and nice combination, not of chance. We must endeavour to follow his example, but it is the lot of very few to attain his perfection.*

Nelson's ability to manage his fleet was proven when he suddenly had to chase the French fleet across the Atlantic and back. They were supplied, trained, healthy and in high morale – a miracle of diligent management and fine seamanship. By contrast the French, who had been holed up in port where they should have had access to constant supplies, lacked the opportunity to train and develop. The British fleet effectively controlled their movements.

Nelson's ships waited for 22 months for the French – joined by the Spanish – to come out for battle. In an unparalleled feat of management, victualling, logistics and supply, Nelson's ships were in as good shape at the end as they were at the start of the blockade. St Vincent appreciated the widespread material deficiencies the fleet suffered and was impressed at Nelson's grasp of the everyday, humdrum detail needed for his painstaking administration of the fleet. Nelson's dedication and enormous capacity for routine, nit-picking problems did not obscure his ability to find creative solutions when needed.

Nelson's officers and men stayed in good shape through his ability to inspire them, through the promise of prize money, through the excitement of skirmishes and battles, by the provision of victuals and working conditions that were the best possible in the circumstances, by ensuring that the tools to do their jobs (naval stores and munitions) were supplied, and by trying to maximise the opportunity to go to battle, through diligent collection of naval intelligence.

Stepping back from the particulars, we can see that Nelson was good at planning, organising, influencing and controlling. His objectives – on which his plans were based – were quite broad-brush and given by the Admiralty: to keep the French Mediterranean fleet from combining with their counterparts in the Channel and the Atlantic, and bring them to battle.

No wonder Nelson longed for battle after such a wait. He wanted conclusion and culmination, but always had to live with the French tendency to adopt an avoiding strategy – they knew as well as Nelson did that if he brought them to battle he would beat them decisively.

Nelson's diligence – his ability to be a manager – was as much part of his success as the exciting and dramatic battles he fought, although much less memorable. He showed an impressive attention to detail and was effectively task oriented, unusual in such a relationship-oriented leader.

As we discuss below, a sharp distinction is sometimes drawn between leadership and management. However real this is in practice, Nelson was superb at both. But for all the initiative he showed, he was not what we would call an entrepreneur. He spent his life in the ordered world of the navy, and even when unemployed for five years he expended most of his energy trying to get another naval posting, although there were tremendous opportunities in trade and commerce. He was a company man through and through.

Nelson's Way
Diligence

Leaders should temper their enthusiasm for action with a capacity for routine administrative work. They need to resolve the tension between the two and appreciate the interdependence of leading and managing, of the big picture and detail. Leaders are all-rounders, handling the glamorous and unglamorous aspects of the job, with respect for both and nurturing the dual talents of vision and caring. They should also encourage such diligence in others. Not for nothing were two ships of Nelson's era called *Indefatigable* and *Zealous*.

Diligence is showing steady application and effort, being industrious, painstaking, persevering and studious. It means paying attention to action, to carrying out the business that needs to be done, to practising, to bustle, busyness, energy, enterprise and hustle. Diligence is about keeping going, being expeditious, assiduous, hardworking and dynamic. It is focus on detail – ardently, vehemently and tirelessly. It is being unsparing, relentless and strenuous.

Being diligent as a leader is being prepared to make sure that everyone's job is being done. The challenge here is not to be too nosy, micromanaging and interfering, for that would conflict with the team spirit and inspiration you are also trying to achieve. But you need to be sure only to delegate jobs that need doing.

If your tendency is to be more of a leader than a manager, you will rely on your colleagues and subordinates to be especially diligent. You'll be looking for people with an eye for detail, who are dedicated, hardworking and leave no stone unturned. They will be patient at research, painstaking at numbers, persistent at finishing the job, good at presentation, careful with accuracy.

Some businesses are built on diligence – they are in the background, behind the scenes, for example outsourced services such as accountants, lawyers or consultants. They are helping you to achieve what needs to be done, but leaving you to be heroic and to take the credit. Quiet diligence is good, but not great. A leader with an understanding of all the little details yet able to put them together in a compelling vision can be very powerful.

Leadership comments
Sir David Omand

Nelson is best known for his visionary and inspirational leadership, but we have seen how in reality he also had to be a manager, concerned with administration and resource allocation. He may be predominantly associated with the glamour of leadership, but most of the time he was busy being diligent with the hard work of management, and this was vital to his success.

There are few who appreciate Nelson's dual role more than Sir David Omand, who has held many senior positions in the British Civil Service, retiring as Security and Intelligence Co-ordinator and Permanent Secretary in the Cabinet Office in the spring of 2005. He served as Permanent Head of the Home Office and of GCHQ, and as Principal Private Secretary to the Secretary of State for Defence during the Falklands War. In the Ministry of Defence his experience spanned two defence reviews and six secretaries of state. Heading the government's response to terrorism between 2001 and 2004, Omand worked closely with ministers in governments headed by Thatcher, Major and Blair, especially concerned with planning and implementing reforms and with the delicate task of allocating scarce resources.

We have seen how Nelson laboured to keep his fleet supplied and motivated for long periods under unrelenting pressure. 'Anyone who has worked in a front-line public-sector organisation will recognise the struggle,' Omand reflects. 'We face lack of resources, unexpected crises, changing priorities and complex webs of professional and personal relationships. Holding all this together places unremitting demands on managers at all levels.' As well as being a diligent administrator, you have to be a leader at the same time: 'You have to give each participant a reason why they should align themselves to you.'

Omand's job 'has been to sustain the administration of government and of the public sector, to respond to "events" and "crises", and to lead the implementation of policies determined by politicians'. He is diffident about making a distinction between leaders and managers, and stresses the need for leadership in administration. 'It would be an oversimplification to talk about politicians as the leaders, and civil servants as the managers; nor is it a corporate model, politicians as chairmen and civil servants as CEOs,' he suggests. There are more grey areas, more over-laps. 'Leadership is provided by the Minister and the Senior Permanent Official, who formulate the policy together. Then the Official has to lead the organisation to deliver it, to be the senior commander. Nelson was a manager delivering government policy, but he had to be a leader to influence his followers to support it, and relate to those formulating the policy.'

Omand points to four key elements in the relationship between lead-ers and managers, and these were issues that Nelson faced in his daily work. First, there has to be trust. Those executing the policy need to be trusted 'to know the job and to act on things that need doing; and trusted to have integrity in dealing with people and information. In a successful organisation people will not be frightened to take well-managed risks. But sometimes things will not work out or mistakes will be made. The test of a good commander is if there is a rapid team effort to get back on track and insist on hard lessons being learned without fears down the line that those responsible are about to be scapegoated. Wise executives and commanders understand this and by their actions make it clear that they are running a tight ship but not a 'blame cul-ture'. And when it comes to strategy, those at the top have to be trusted to balance compassionately the overriding priority that has to be given to achievement of the aim with the interests or survival of those in the organisation. These are issues that Nelson would be familiar with, run-ning a fleet of ships, each with their own management problems and subcultures, and commanding them in battle.'

Secondly, the leaders had to have clear intentions, and leave opera-tional heads to do what is necessary in their own spheres. 'This is now called Mission Command and is a direct legacy of Nelson and his gener-ation of commanders,' Omand considers, echoing the comments of Admiral Sir Jonathon Band and Sir John Harvey-Jones. 'In the Gulf, for example, the military commanders would agree that a long screwdriver was not applied from London – there should be no micromanagement from the centre.'

There is often a conflict between this style of leadership and the demands of political accountability as ministers may be called on at any moment to provide detailed justification of individual decisions or actions and statistics on performance to Parliament. 'In the early years of the Blair government we over-emphasised targets, but now there is a growing recognition that setting large numbers of micro-targets is not the best way to drive up performance – it is far more effective to set big-scale strategies and leave the departments and agencies to work out the operational and tactical implications for themselves,' Omand explains. 'Again, this is Nelson-style Mission Command in action – empowerment of managers.'

Omand adds that when he was running the National Counter-Terrorism Strategy he formulated for the Prime Minister and Cabinet to agree to a strategic goal to reduce the risk from terrorism and divided the work up under strategic campaigns of the '4 Ps' of Prevention, Pursuit, Protection and Preparation. 'Then different departments and agencies could get on and optimise their own circumstances. This is like passing a strong magnetic field over iron filings and they line up. My aim was to set a strong strategic field so all the agencies could align themselves to it.'

Thirdly, Omand emphasises the role of responsibility on both sides. The leader has to 'shoulder the burden of responsibility for the organisation as a whole, which is something the heads of departments – the managers – can't do. The boss has to stand up for the organisation, absorb quite a lot of the pain of untoward events, and make sure Government ministers are aware of all that they are asking of the system.' Thus it is so crucial to articulate a strategic purpose and show the team that they have a contribution to make. 'What you are seeking is the highest common factor, not the lowest common denominator,' Omand insists. 'Nelson took on board the responsibility of a leader with the knowledge of how the system worked as a manager.'

Fourthly, Omand suggests that 'both leaders and managers must appreciate the risks involved, which can be from outside events – you can't do much to stop them, but you can be prepared to respond; risks which can be inherent in the activity, such as fighting wars; and self-imposed risks, changes you implement, such as new ways of doing things. There are always unexpected consequences of change and it's too easy to find yourself launching a new initiative just to cope with the effects of the previous one. The leader must consider if the system can cope, and allow it to adapt to the changes.' Nelson effectively knew the risks and implications of his actions because he was so engaged in the everyday life of his fleet.

'The armed forces need the politicians to justify and account for the results of an operation, but not to actually lead it; but the politicians often want to offer advice about how to put a policy into effect. This is where Nelson had the advantage: communication was so slow that he just got on with policy and implementation, though he also had to delegate responsibility to his captains,' Omand reflects. 'As in Nelson's case, we have to be diligent in both functional and operational areas. In the case of the former, we need ready access to expert advice, whether legal, scientific or from other professions; and in the latter, people who could combine deep understanding of the technology with experience of what happens when you change the way you use it.'

'Nelson had to be quite an all-rounder,' he adds, 'both a visionary leader providing innovative tactics to achieve the strategies of the government, and a diligent and hard-working administrator, knowing how to implement these tactics. He had to win the policy makers' trust, which he did through his record of delivering successful engagements with the enemy, so he could get on and do it. This is the way it should be.'

Leadership lessons
Diligence

- ⚓ Diligent managers who can't lead are dull and unexciting, while heroic leaders who can't manage are out of control. If you plan to concentrate on one or the other you'll need a partnership with a colleague or the team.
- ⚓ Deep understanding of how your organisation works enables you to 'feel the pulse' and be engaged in managing it. Without this you risk shallow heroics that add little value to anyone.
- ⚓ If you are more interested in people than things and can't do both easily, others around you will have to handle the things, and vice versa.
- ⚓ Identify the boundaries of your autonomy as both a leader and a manager – where do you have freedom to act, and where must you

conform to guidelines? How rapid are lines of communication to your superiors? How urgent is the situation? What can you get away with?

⚓ In your areas of freedom to act, focus on maximising the ability of your team to be successful, in terms of resources and tools to do the job, and provide them with opportunities for achievement – help them to be diligent too.

⚓ Make good use of the four functions of management. First, planning. Be clear on what you want to achieve and keep it rooted in reality. Share your goals with your team, seek their inputs and obtain their buy-in, allocate resources as effectively and economically as you can. Stay alert to opportunities suggested by unexpected events and innovations.

⚓ Second, organising. Develop a clear understanding of the system as a whole, keeping your focus on key value-adding processes and adapting to changing customer, supplier and market conditions, making use of talented people. Capitalising on unexpected opportunties requires constant effort.

⚓ Third, leading. Identify talent, build teams and design reporting relationships that suit your objectives. Keep communicating.

⚓ Fourth, controlling. Evaluate how well you are achieving your goals, monitor performance and take corrective action if needed. Choose key performance indicators and keep improving on the results, but remember these are only indicators – diligence means being so engaged in the organisation that you know what's happening before the indicators show it.

⚓ Appreciate that if you want to be a colourful leader, you nevertheless have to be prepared for tedious and dull grunt work as well as the glamorous stuff, unless you are lucky enough to find someone really good to do it for you. If you go this route, remember that while you get the glory, they get the power!

7

INSPIRATION

Winning hearts on the lower deck, 1805

'Success attend Admiral Nelson! God bless Captain Miller!
We are happy and comfortable, and will shed every drop of
blood in our veins so that the name of the *Theseus* shall be
immortalised as high as the *Captain*'s.'
Note dropped on the quarterdeck, signed by the Ship's Company

ADMIRAL NELSON recreating with his Brave Tars after the GLORIOUS BATTLE of the NILE

Nelson, slightly wounded and wearing a head bandage, celebrating with his men
on board the *Vanguard*. Nelson's involvement with and consideration for his men
marked him as a great and much-loved leader.
*'Admiral Nelson Recreating with his Brave Tars after the Glorious Battle of the Nile'
by Thomas Rowlandson, undated.*

ON 24 MAY 1797 NELSON, THEN ONE OF THE MOST JUNIOR flag officers in the navy, was given command of the Mediterranean inshore squadron, hoisting his flag on the *Theseus*, a ship described by St Vincent – the Commander-in-Chief – as 'an abomination'.

Among the crew were sailors recently involved in the mutinies at Spithead and the Nore. The discontent of the seamen, based on over 100 years without a pay rise, and with poor conditions and what they saw as excessively harsh discipline, had erupted at a moment of particular vulnerability for the Admiralty. The Spithead mutineers gained their demands and returned to their duties. The sailors at the Nore anchorage mutinied but met an unyielding response from the Admiralty. St Vincent, then cruising off Cadiz, took a tough stance towards disobedience of any kind; having found four men guilty of mutiny on the *St George* (they were protesting against the hanging of two men accused of 'unnatural acts'), he gave the order for them to be hanged immediately.

It was a Sunday, and St Vincent's second-in-command, Admiral Sir Charles Thompson, objected to the punishment being carried out on the sabbath. But the sentence was executed immediately. Nelson approved – the clarity of such swift justice appealed to him, and it brought into generous relief the occasions on which he chose to be lenient.

On board the *Theseus*, Nelson was joining a ship's crew renowned for their robust independence. Although sympathetic to St Vincent's tough line, he believed it was more important to emphasise the job in hand. A high level of activity would keep the men busy and their minds off discontent. First, to combat the boredom of blockading Cadiz Nelson devised frequent night attacks on the harbour; retaliation from the

Spanish would surely unite his men in defence. Secondly, he pointed to the strength of the enemy, up to 40 ships of the line when the British had only 20, and the need to be constantly ready for battle. Thirdly, his demonstrations of personal courage – which always appealed to the sailors – were matched by a high level of concern for them individually and collectively.

Order between the ranks – with all its inequalities, exploitations and oppressions – was maintained by a strict and often vicious discipline. Nelson was party to this; a captain's authority was to be respected absolutely, so long as the captain abided by the rules himself. Sailors knew that Nelson was only too aware of their conditions and hardships. He did what he could to improve food supplies, warmth and ventilation below decks. His proactive way of improving their pay was to win prize money through capturing enemy vessels.

Following the Battle of Cape St Vincent, Nelson and his flag captain Ralph Miller were celebrities, and he was one of the youngest admirals on the roster. Being in his fleet, especially being on board his ship, instantly presented prospects of potentially lucrative activity. Hence, on 15 June 1797, Nelson was able to write home that a note bearing the words quoted at the beginning of this chapter had been found, left where he took his nightly walks, confirming the crew's commitment to serving him.

On board the *Theseus* was not the only time Nelson had to win the hearts of a reluctant crew. In January 1797, the captain of the *Blanche* had been sent home for sexually abusing young sailors; the replacement was to be Captain Henry Hotham, a renowned authoritarian. An observer from the lower deck reported:

> *He came on board, had the officers armed on the quarter deck and all hands turned aft to hear his commission read at the capstan head. They all cried 'no, no, no'. He asked what they had to say against. One of the petty officers replied that his ships company informed us that he was a damn'd tartar and we would not have him and went forward and turned two of the forecastle guns aft with canister shot.*
>
> *Commodore Nelson's first lieutenant then came on board and ordered all hands aft. He called all the petty officers out and paraded*

*them in a line on the quarterdeck. 'Now, my lads, If you resist taking
Captain Hotham as your captain, every third man shall be hanged.' The
crew flew in a body forward to the guns with match in hand, likewise
crowbars, handspikes, and all kinds of weapons they could get hold of
and left him, Captain Hotham, and the officers standing looking at us.
They consulted for a moment and returned on board Commodore
Nelson's ship. In the space of half an hour the Commodore, Nelson,
came on board, call'd all hands aft, and enquired the reason of this disturbance. He was inform'd of Capt Hotham's character, which was the
reason that we refused him.*

*'Lads,' said he, 'you have the greatest character on board the
Blanche of any frigates crew in the navy. You have taken two frigates
superior to the frigate you are in, and now to rebel. If Captain Hotham
ill treats you, give me a letter and I will support you'. Immediately
there was three cheers given and Captain Hotham shed tears, and
Nelson went on board his ship.*

On many occasions Nelson also had to discipline junior officers, refusing
to let them get away with crimes for which seamen were regularly punished. Referring to a young officer's behaviour, he pointed out

*that it was upon the quarter-deck, in the face of the ship's company,
that he treated his captain with contempt; and I am duty bound to support the authority and consequence of every officer under my command... a poor ignorant Seaman is for ever punished for contempt to his
superior.*

There are differing views of the British seaman: the jolly Jack Tar of popular legend, and the less positive view of the hardened, uneducated man
pressed unwillingly into service. Whichever is the most authentic, these
were tough men in a physical world. A large ship was a kind of gang-
land of trained fighters. But for many it was by no means the worst of
their options. Recent research has suggested that conditions at sea were
not much worse – and were in many cases better – than those on land.

Basic rations at sea provided almost 5,000 calories per day per man: the victuals may not have been exciting, but there were plenty of them and they included a daily gallon of beer. In spite of the notoriety of the press gangs, it is likely that many volunteered for the service. Decommissioned crew members might relish some time on shore, but they faced dire unemployment – or grim jobs in the mills and mines of the early Industrial Revolution – and in wartime they could sometimes negotiate marginal improvements in terms because trained seamen were always preferred to pressed landsmen. Nonetheless, captains often struggled to find a full complement; and usually anchored well offshore to discourage desertion.

Perhaps the greatest challenge was managing junior officers and men living in the close confines of relatively small ships – a perennial feature of naval vessels, built as fighting machines and only incidentally for accommodation. Over 800 officers and men served on the *Victory*, a large ship for its day, but with a gun deck of only 186 feet (around 60 metres). Most men slept in hammocks slung on beams between the guns, with only around 10 inches to swing between them. This vast number was needed to work the guns in battle; far fewer worked the ship itself, hence the overcrowding and possibility of boredom. Junior officers fared little better, and only captains and admirals had their own cabins. It was in many ways a community of shared suffering, with a strong sense of identity captured, at its most romantic, in the reputation of the 'hearts of oak', Britain's premier fighting men.

A Spanish nobleman living in France gave an account of a British sailor, a midshipman captured at the Battle of the Nile and held as a prisoner of war. While the French navy was 'under a cloud and, at times, could scarcely be said to exist', the British navy was feared and powerful. 'Their Nelson was perpetually cruising off the coast, trying to entice our forces out of port... no boat was allowed out of harbour, for fear of capture by the English.' Napoleon was marooned in Egypt

> *and between us and him were those terrible ships of the English, with their victorious leader, Nelson, in command. It seemed we couldn't even manage our internal affairs without the consent of the barbarous Islanders.*

The English midshipman was described by the author (both were only 15 years of age) as 'a nice young lad, for all he was a barbarian, and an islander, and a John Bull, and a bit of a savage when he lost his temper. He often gave me a thrashing when I ventured to argue with him that he was not what could be called civilised by his nationality' and his captors soon gave up trying to 'turn him into a Frenchman'. He had been captured when the English 'had the temerity to believe that a mere boatload of them could capture any of our vessels that they set their fancy on', boarding a frigate with 350 seamen. As the English midshipman pointed out (and he was just a boy, alone, on enemy soil), 'it took a whole shipload of you to capture a little chap like me, and a dozen naked tars'. The French remained in awe of this aggressive and proud young chap, who soon stole a boat and escaped.

The system of casual marine labour was similar to that of the merchant navy, where each voyage was usually independently funded as a stand-alone venture. Like the new factories displacing people from their rural roots, these ships drew people off from the land into a place where they had few rights and no stake in the operation. In the face of this alienation, the navy eventually evolved into a coherent and professional corps, supporting the essential camaraderie of the service.

As we have seen, Nelson's first taste of command (of small boats and cutters) came at the age of 14, and he was promoted to post captain at only 21. He had sole authority over crews comprising hundreds of men from his early 20s.

Nelson, like all officers, depended on formal sources of power – legitimate, reward based and coercive. This was the way the navy operated. His influential uncle, Captain Suckling, pushed the point home when Nelson passed his examination as lieutenant. From the *Lowestoffe* in 1777 he wrote, 'my dear Horatio, pay every respect to your superior officers, as you wish to receive respect yourself'. Nelson himself was to give advice to young officers including 'obey orders implicitly, without forming any opinion of your own regarding their propriety'.

From this formal power accorded to all officers, Nelson developed informal influence through his knowledge of the navy, the workings of a ship and the needs of war, and through gaining the respect of his men. By the time of the peace in 1778, Nelson was building a new power base through the success of his relationships with his men. He was caring, thoughtful and sympathetic to their needs, and related easily to men of all ranks. This was perhaps one of his more unconventional traits: he remained one of the lads, even as an admiral and peer of the realm. As a midshipman on the *Agamemnon* wrote home, Nelson 'was acknowledged one of the first characters in the Service, and is universally beloved by his men and officers'. This was confirmed by his seamen as they faced the opening salvoes of the Battle of the Nile in 1798. He overheard 'two seamen quartered at a gun near me, talking, and one said to the other, "damn them, look at them! There they are, Jack, and if we don't beat them, they will beat us". I knew what stuff I had under me,' he reflected.

Nelson was driven by what we would now call 'intrinsic motivation' and he expected others to be the same. Being at sea, fighting the enemy, gaining recognition from his superior officers for a job well done and from the population at large for his heroic feats – this was what mattered to him. 'If my services have been of any value, let them be noticed in a way that the public may know me or them,' he commented in 1797 to Colonel Drinkwater, who went on to observe:

> *The attainment of public honour, and an ambition to be distinguished above his fellows, were his master passions. His conduct was constantly actuated by these predominant feelings.*

Nelson undoubtedly assumed honour and recognition to be as important for his crew as for him, and was generous in his praise of subordinates of all ranks. But he also recognised the importance of prize money in giving him the power to reward officers and men. However, Nelson was never particularly successful in securing financial reward for his own efforts:

> *Had I attended less than I have done to the service of my Country, I might have made some too: however, I trust my name will stand on record, when the money-makers will be forgot.*

His reward power was limited in terms of cash and material benefits, but he never rationed praise and recognition, nor affirmation of his belief in the superiority of the British seamen and the importance of their cause. After tough fighting in the Mediterranean on the *Agamemnon*, shared with his men and leading to close bonding, he spoke of their only reward being 'honour and salt beef'. There was no doubt as to which was the most appetising; but no one seriously pretended these were really sufficient. Many middle-ranking families sent their younger sons to sea in the hope that they might repair the family fortunes. William Hoste, a favourite protégé of Nelson's and also a parson's son, was one such.

The rewards to admirals generally combined honours with cash – Sir John Jervis won a pension of £3,000 per annum for three generations as well as his earldom for the victory at St Vincent. Nelson sued the Earl for his share of the prize money in a long-running court case that was resolved (in Nelson's favour) shortly before Trafalgar.

This all took place in a situation of evident and substantial lack of equity and fairness, and this was a strong demotivator against which Nelson had to constantly battle. A famous cartoon of the time shows a seaman on his knees on the deck on the eve of battle, his hands together in prayer. Asked by an officer for the reason for his entreaties to the Almighty, the seaman explains that he has been praying that the enemy's shot should be distributed in the same proportions as the prize money; that is, the greater part to the officers! Nelson himself often bemoaned the irony of having lost an eye and an arm in the service of his country, yet constantly being in debt. Many seamen who served with Nelson in his most famous battles ended their days in poverty, especially when disabilities and infirmities from their sea duties (such as amputated limbs and rheumatism) reduced their ability to work. That Nelson did as much as he could to help poor seamen by lobbying the Admiralty and other authorities, and often paying them out of his own pocket, was well known.

Winning hearts on the lower deck

Overall, Nelson appreciated the mettle of the men he was working with. There was none of the dismissive attitude of Wellington, who described his soldiers as 'the scrapings of the gallows'. The sailors' generally high levels of competence, commitment, experience and their alignment in fighting for the same goal – which also applied to the officers – meant that any admiral could delegate large tasks, such as fighting a ship, firing a broadside and boarding an enemy ship, to the captains. Only the most distant and loose monitoring was needed, as everyone knew what he had to do, and many crews led by his competent captains performed as heroically as Nelson's own.

They knew his track record. As Nelson had written to his brother during the 1794 Mediterranean campaign,

> *I am now pointed out as having been this war one hundred and twelve times engaged against the French, and always successful to some degree... Opportunities have been frequently offered me, and I have never lost one [chance] of distinguishing myself.*

By 1805 there had been many more opportunities. It was his constant search for action that so inspired others, because it gave meaning to lives so often sacrificed for temporary military gains or trading advantages that brought little benefit to the men who fought for them. Nelson knew how much he gained from his men's identification with him; for a very good reason he chose to have a sailor, wearing typical sailor's rig, as one of the supporters on his coat of arms when he entered the peerage.

When Nelson toured naval towns across Britain he was welcomed particularly enthusiastically by seamen, who regarded him as their special hero and showed their unique relationship with him by releasing the horses from his carriage and pulling him along the road by themselves. One of many such instances was at Haverfordwest (Nelson was visiting the brother of Captain Foley, one of his band of brothers), where his carriage was dragged by cheering seamen, and then again at nearby Swansea. In his native Norfolk the crowds were even larger and more devoted, cheering outside his hotel half the night.

Two stories from his tour of Wales and Monmouthshire in 1802 reveal his closeness to his seamen. Tom Cleaves, formerly a bo'sun on one of Nelson's ships, had become the licensee of the Plume and Feathers public house in Swansea. Jostling to get near to Nelson's carriage, Cleaves blew three distinct blasts on his bo'sun's pipe. At the sound, Nelson sprang up from his seat in the carriage and turned to the crowd, exclaiming 'Tom Cleaves' pipe, by Jove!' and calling the carriage to stop so he could shake him warmly by the hand.

At Chepstow, Nelson was at dinner when he received a message from a man who claimed to be one of his old sailors, who wanted to pay his respects. Nelson sent him a bowl of soup from the table, and the waiter was about to add a spoon. 'Nay,' said Nelson, 'by this token I shall know whether this be one of my tars.' The servant took the soup to the sailor, expecting him to drink it up, but to his surprise, and the enjoyment of the spectators, the sailor took from his pocket a box containing tobacco which he emptied and then used the box as a spoon. Immediately Nelson recognised the man as one of his sailors and gave him a guinea!

Inspiring courage

When Nelson was wounded at the Nile and taken down to the surgeon's cockpit, he refused to pull rank and jump the queue, insisting: 'I will take my turn with my brave fellows.' Of course, his brave fellows would have none of this and he was immediately attended to, but these were the gestures remembered on the messdecks, which became part of the Nelson legend.

Stories of his exploits were well known: dragging cannon over the Corsican hillsides in his attack on Bastia, attacking the *Ça Ira*, and especially leading boarding parties at the Battle of Cape St Vincent. People heard about the seamen saving his life at the raid on Tenerife. They heard about how his boat stopped to pick up survivors from the sinking cutter *Fox* as he returned to his ship for the amputation of his arm. Even when mortally wounded at Trafalgar, he sent the surgeon away to look after others.

Nelson did not leave this admiration of his courage to chance. Like many successful leaders, he saw his own career as an inspiration to others and wrote a book to facilitate the process. His *Short Biographical Sketch*, published by The Naval Chronicle in 1799, was written to emphasise his personal courage. After the Battle of Copenhagen in 1801 Nelson had the extraordinary self-assurance to write to Captain

Hans Sneedorff, the head of the Danish Naval Academy in Copenhagen, presenting the Academy with commemorative medals of his past actions and saying:

> *I send you also a Short account of my life, it cannot do harm to youth & may do good, as it will show that Perseverance and good conduct will raise a person to the very highest honours and rewards.*

Disciplining

Although he was willing to listen to grievances and complaints and to take them seriously, and he believed deeply in the bravery and professionalism of his men, there was always a bottom line in Nelson's attitude to discipline. Out-and-out mutineers were to be hanged.

Not all sailors were so enthused by the Nelson spirit that they would not desert when they had the chance. During the 1803 blockade of Toulon a number of sailors attempted to desert (and they must have had it comparatively easy – others were doing a similar job in the less clement seas off Brest). Nelson was willing to forgive the first band of deserters, sympathising with the monotony of the job, but he then cracked down heavily, sending a memo to the fleet in November 1803:

> *Lord Nelson is very sorry to find that, notwithstanding his forgiveness of the men who deserted in Spain, it has failed to have its proper effect, and there are still men who so far forget their duty to their King and Country, as to desert the Service at a time when every man in England is in arms to defend it against the French. Therefore Lord Nelson desires that it may be perfectly understood, that if any man be so infamous as to desert from the Service in future, he will not only be brought to a Court-Martial, but that if the sentence be Death, it will be most assuredly carried into execution.*

Nelson was always disappointed by poor performance and felt, probably correctly, that most officers and seamen who let themselves down would be amply punished by feelings of chagrin. Shame and pride are the twin guarantors of conduct in a community that values honour, and as

Nelson himself strove to do things he would be proud of, his greatest fear – perhaps his only fear – was that he might be thought to have acted shamefully. He was instinctively sympathetic to these dynamics in others. One example may be seen in a letter he wrote to a Lieutenant Waller, of whom little else is known, in 1804:

> *I am very sorry that by your misconduct you have been induced to change out of so fine a ship as the Superb where you have served so long into the Madras, but you must be sensible that under your circumstances allowing the exchange to take place has been a great act of lenity towards you. However I do not want to touch further upon this painful subject except to hope that you will take warning by the past, and that you will recover yourself in the Service by your future conduct. If you can get anyone to exchange with you from the Madras into any Ship going to England I shall have no objections. Your present feelings I am sure must be acute, and I sincerely hope that this very unpleasant circumstance in your life will conduce to your future benefit.*

Mentoring

Winning hearts meant starting when the hearts were young and impressionable, and Nelson was always glad to mentor young officers, starting with the boys serving in his ships. He would invite young officers to breakfasts and lunches, and after the loss of his arm these lads would help cut up his meat for him. These relationships would play a great part in the future, when the boys graduated to become members of a new 'band of brothers', a loyal generation after Trafalgar.

Many of these midshipmen were very young, mere boys. Asking a young officer at what age he entered the navy and being told that it was at 11 years, Nelson declared 'much too young' – having started at the age of 12, he knew only too well the loneliness and homesickness this caused.

To one young man about to be appointed midshipman, Nelson wrote:

> *as you from this day start in the world as a man, I trust that your future conduct in life will prove you both an Officer and a Gentleman.*

Recollect that you must be a Seaman to be an Officer, and that you can-
not be a good Officer without being a Gentleman.

He emphasised the need to earn his captain's respect and protection,
vital in the system of patronage then in place.

Nelson was active in giving youngsters the confidence they needed.
He had a habit of making a race to the masthead with nervous young
midshipmen, proving to them that it was nothing to worry about. When
chasing two French ships he noticed a young midshipman flinch as
enemy shot hit nearby; Nelson patted the quaking 14-year-old on the
head and told him the story of Charles XII of Sweden, who ran away
from the first shot he heard. But, Nelson added, they later called him
'the great' because he was so brave in action. 'Therefore, I hope much
from you in future!'

He was anxious to encourage young officers to use their talents for
the good of the service, including their 'inventions'. One was that suggested, in October 1805, by Lieutenant Francis Roskruge of the
Britannia, later killed in action at Trafalgar. Nelson wrote to him just
days before the battle:

Sir, I am most obliged by the perusal of your book of Night Signals,
which in many respects are very ingenious. But I fear the Multiplicity
of Guns & false fires & Rockets repeated by three Admirals and then
repetitions of false fires & Rockets as second parts of the Signals
together with the answering Signal Lights of the fleet would create
much confusion. The difficulty of making Night Signals perfectly dis-
tinct is perhaps impossible and several of yours I think might be
adopted with much advantage but it is not in the power of any admiral
to alter the Signals issued from the Admiralty.

Thus Nelson sandwiched his criticism of what sounds like an impossibly
complicated new approach to night signalling with praise, ending with
a guiding hint at the bureaucratic procedures through which any serious innovation must be piloted. Lieutenant Roskruge must have been
delighted to receive a personal reply from Nelson, taking his ideas seriously and going to the trouble of offering constructive comments.

Promoting

Promotion was a way to recognise honour and merit – and to give both more responsibility and rights to a bigger share of prize money. It was also a sign of a senior officer's power of patronage.

This related mostly to young officers, as promotions of seamen to officer rank were rare. There were exceptions, such as Nelson's support of Mr Atkinson, the sailing master of the *Victory*, in gaining his formal Master's certificate. Nelson was well known for his efforts in promoting officers, mostly deservedly. Those who arguably did not deserve their promotions – such as Josiah Nisbet, his stepson – were a source of heavy disappointment to him. Nelson encouraged fellow officers – his own protégés and those of his friends – to achieve their full potential and show that his confidence in them was not misplaced; by the same token, his confidence in them was an essential part of inspiring their best performance. It all added up to helping him achieve his victories.

He wrote letters to superiors and officials at the Admiralty praising outstanding officers. Nelson was a good talent-spotter, an astute judge of character and a generous observer of others. One of his favourite acolytes was William Hoste, a midshipman on the *Agamemnon*, who went on to a distinguished and very active naval career, helped along the way by Nelson with strategic promotions. Lieutenant William Charlton, who served with Nelson at Copenhagen, was recommended to the Admiralty as meriting 'my approbation and I can say with truth that Mr Charlton is well-deserving of your lordships influence to get him promoted'.

He provided opportunities for young officers to distinguish themselves. This sometimes ended badly: Lieutenant James Moutray died of illness during the siege of Calvi, for example. Later he sent a favourite to lead the attack on a well-defended force at Boulogne. As a result the young man lost a leg and died shortly thereafter of his wounds.

Nelson believed in public and profuse praise, openly acknowledging achievements. In a very Nelsonian phrase, typical of his willingness to give praise where it was due, he wrote of a young lad from the village around his home in Merton: 'William Hasleham went out with me in the *Victory* a Boy and came home with Me a Young Man.' He also saw fairness as very important. He was careful to ensure proper recognition of all who deserved it. Thus he omitted mentioning that the *Culloden* had gone aground in the dispatches after the Battle of the Nile, as he wanted to avoid its ship's company being excluded from the honours. All first lieutenants serving in this battle were promoted, and he was annoyed at the special case that needed to be made for the *Culloden's*.

Much of Nelson's time (an estimated 15 per cent of his correspondence) was taken up with recommendations for promotion, a major part of the elaborate system of patronage and thus integral to the social networks of favours and influence. Careful use of patronage could place important people in debt to Nelson, potentially useful in his political as well as military ambitions. He cultivated a relationship with William Windham, the Member of Parliament for Norwich and former Secretary of State for War, who sought a place for the son of a political supporter, Surgeon Coleman. In 1804 Captain Page of the *Caroline* had written to Nelson offering a vacancy, in his own way ingratiating himself with his superior. Nelson had emphasised to Windham the difficulties of making appointments, that most decisions were made by the Admiralty. This maximised the effect of his subsequent letter offering a place on Page's ship to the Coleman boy.

A system of favours owed and returned is central to most organisations, and this aspect of Nelson's work has a distinctly modern ring to it, although it may be practised in a more subtle manner today. Among hundreds of examples, Nelson found promotions for the sons and protégés of his peers, colleagues, friends, relatives and even one-time superiors, such as Admiral Lord Duncan, Sir Richard Bickerton, Charles Tyler, Lord Minto, Admiral Lord Radstock and Thomas Louis – the last named one of the band of brothers at the Nile. All this he managed himself – he had few staff and certainly no personnel manager – so it is little wonder that Nelson was often spending between eight to twelve hours per day writing letters.

Rewarding

Nelson appreciated that many of the complaints of seamen in mutinies and desertions were about lack of pay, and that wages had not been increased for literally centuries. He pursued prize money claims for them as much as for himself, following up after each battle and even speaking out at the House of Lords in 1803 against the ruses of prize agents to deprive sailors 'from the highest admiral in the service to the poorest cabin-boy' of their rewards, and a bill for a commission of inquiry was passed.

When the authorities failed in their duties, Nelson put them right. During his peacetime tour of several counties of Britain he met many sailors. They compared their wounds and amputated limbs, discussed battles in which they had served, and he gave them sovereigns as mementoes. On one occasion he met the mother of a sailor killed at the Nile, but who had not received the medal due to him. Without hesitation, Nelson gave her his own.

His eye for detail was impressive. For example, on the back of a recently discovered battle plan for Trafalgar is a 'to-do' list, which includes a reminder to provide a timepiece for Mr Bunce, the carpenter of the *Victory*. Bunce had been recommended to one of the band of brothers, Troubridge, as 'one of the very best men in that line I have ever met with'. He had asked for a watch, and Nelson wanted to give it to him.

Caring

In the same spirit, Nelson wanted to show he cared when seamen and young officers were wounded and sick, and when they worried about their families and their families worried about them. He visited the seamen wounded at the battle of Copenhagen in hospital in Yarmouth, giving a guinea to each of the nurses. It always irked him that the City of London would not recognise this battle.

> *For myself… if I was only personally concerned, I should bear the stigma, first placed upon my brow, with humility; but… I am the natural guardian of the characters of the officers of the navy, army and marines who fought and so profusely bled under my command on that day.*

He saw himself as personally responsible for the well-being of men engaged in his battles. Thus, when his young protégé and other officers were wounded at the ill-fated Boulogne expedition, he visited them in hospital in Deal and rented, at his own expense, a house and nurses to take care of them so they could be more private and comfortable than in a public ward.

As far as Nelson was concerned, any protégé of his had a right to be cared for, and this particularly applied to brave associates such as John Sykes, who saved Nelson at Cadiz. As we have seen, Sykes survived the loss of his hand, which he had interposed to save Nelson from a cutlass blow. Nelson assured his mother in 1797:

> *your son John Sykes is quite recovered of his wounds, & is now on board Lord St Vincent's ship the* Ville de Paris, *by whom he will be made a Gunner – & if he is not before he comes to England I will take care & provide for Him.*

There are many examples of Nelson requesting medical care for sick seamen ashore, using his connections with ministers across the Mediterranean, and obtaining pensions for the widows of admired colleagues. In requesting a pension for the widow of Dr Snipe, Physician of the Fleet in the Mediterranean, he insisted that 'a better man in Private life nor a more able Man in his profession I never met with'. He asked for another opportunity in the Mediterranean for a deserving lieutenant who had recently completed an intelligence mission for Nelson, saying that being sent back to England would be the 'death' of him.

The caring was no doubt a genuine expression of his unaffected sympathy with men of all ranks. It was also an integral part of the paternalistic culture of naval ships. Captains were like fathers to the midshipmen; beyond that, Nelson's opposition to republicanism and its claims to equality was balanced by an almost feudal sense of responsibility for those dependent on him. Care was more than a matter of sympathy: it was a moral and professional duty.

This applied also to his enemies; when they were belligerent, he was ruthless towards them; but when defeated and in his charge, he was generally magnanimous. Shortly after Spain re-entered the war at the end of 1804 Nelson captured a transport of Spanish soldiers. Rather than sending them to British-held Malta to await exchange, he allowed them to board a neutral vessel to be returned to Barcelona. He asked that Spanish officers held as prisoners of war on Malta be 'allowed to walk about the town'; with the Governor, Sir Alexander Ball, being one of the band of brothers, this could be easily arranged. He was angry and disappointed that he was accused of sending a Spanish regiment to die of hunger on a remote island when he had in fact repatriated them.

There is less evidence, however, that he was as forgiving and liberal to French prisoners, and he was brutally severe towards the Neapolitan republicans in 1799. Nevertheless, when he spoke of 'humanity after victory being the Predominant feature of the British fleet' in his prayer before Trafalgar, he undoubtedly meant it.

Entertaining

One of the worst aspects of life at sea was boredom. In the blockade of Toulon during 1803–4 Nelson alternated cruising grounds to give his seamen different coastlines to look at. He encouraged singing and dancing, bands playing on the poop before and after dinner, contests between ships in gunnery drill and seamanship, and Christian services every Sunday – anything to keep seamen busy and active during the inevitably long periods of monotony on blockade duties. One consequence was that while their French counterparts may have enjoyed some of the pleasures of the ports, the English were practising their seamanship. Admiral Villeneuve, commanding the French fleet, recognised the significance of this:

Our naval tactics are antiquated. We know nothing but how to place ourselves in line, and that is just what the enemy wants.

Celebrations with extra rum rations were held after all battles and engagements, after the necessary Christian services of thanks and burial. Nelson also encouraged the carving of ornaments, himself the delighted recipient of ship models and other mementoes as gifts and souvenirs from shipmates.

Dinners were often an opportunity for fun – what might these days be called teambuilding exercises. Nelson entertained well, taking great care to provide good wine for his guests though he drank little himself, seldom more than a few glasses. He would invite his young officers, both to give them exposure to more senior colleagues and because he enjoyed their pranks. When he went ashore on official and diplomatic missions – or simply to dine with friends at garrison ports – Nelson would often take these young officers. The better food, the wines, stories and songs not only entertained them, it also extended the range of his generosity: any man with Nelson's fleet would be sure to have opportunities for fun as well as honour.

The build-up to battle

1805 was a tough year for Nelson's seamen. After a year and a half of blockading, the French and Spanish fleets escaped into the Atlantic. By August 1805 the British were back blockading in the Mediterranean. Nelson went home on leave for a few short weeks in a situation of stalemate. There was no end to the war in sight: the Grand Armée in France was still building up, Britain was developing its alliance with Russia and Austria, and Cornwallis was actively blockading Brest.

Nelson's determination to rush to the West Indies was an attempt to bring them to battle even if he was greatly outnumbered: 'the enemy have 24 sail of the line. My force is very very inferior I take only nine with me and expect to be joined by six.' It sounds impulsive, but this was a carefully thought-out and proactive strategy, and the news of the extraordinary chase halfway across the world and back protecting the West Indies was enthusiastically greeted at home.

The French and Spanish did no serious harm to Britain's colonies or trade because of Nelson's hot pursuit. They returned across the Atlantic, encountering Admiral Calder's squadron off Finisterre in July. This inconclusive action nevertheless prevented them from sailing up the Channel.

In early September Nelson heard the news that battle was imminent. The seamen were raring to fight. They had waited a long time.

Touring the *Victory* before Trafalgar, walking the decks and talking with the gun crews, Nelson inspired great support and raised morale. He had a reassuring ability to remember individual seamen from previous ships and actions, and to recall enough about them to show he cared. In contrast, Napoleon had to be briefed by aides de camp about individual soldiers in order to achieve the same effect. Nelson's sincerity was more convincing.

His ability to attract men to want to follow him is clear from this story from lower-deck cynic Jack Nastyface, a rare voice to emerge from that world:

> *It had been a favourite mode with Lord Nelson to paint the sides of all the ships under his command in chequers, which made them to be distinguished with greater certainty in case of falling in with an enemy. This became a well-known and general term in a squadron or fleet. So much so that, when speaking of another ship, it was usual to say, 'oh! She's one of Nelson's chequer-players' signifying thereby that she had been one of the fighting ships. The seamen liked the distinction, and took great pride in being considered as a chequer-player, and could not wish to part with the name.*

The worst thing that Nastyface's tyrannical new captain did was to paint the ship in one stripe, thus destroying the chequer design. 'This single act caused so much disgust,' Nastyface reflected, that it 'robbed the seamen of their glory.'

The story refers to Nelson's instructions when he arrived to rejoin the fleet in the final few weeks before Trafalgar. The ships under his command would be painted 'Mediterranean style', like the *Victory*. The hull would be painted black with yellow bands around the ships along the lines of the portholes. The porthole covers were painted black so that, when they were closed, the entire hull gave a black and yellow chessboard effect. The painting kept the men busy for a day, and gave them a livery with which to identify, as Nastyface described. Thus Nelson created an élite and special identity, destined for glory, very much in the spirit of Shakespeare's portrayal of Henry V. If you were not there that day, if you were not fighting on board one of Nelson's chequer-players, you had missed out on something special.

Nelson strongly believed in the superiority of British seamen, British seamanship and British ships in their performance in battle, and was able to transmit this confidence to the men who served and sailed with him in a real and powerful way. Though many of the officers and most of the men had never served directly under Nelson, they nonetheless felt the impact of his presence and his confidence. After such a long wait, two years of blockade and a chase across the Atlantic, the officers and men could not wait to be at the enemy.

The 'Nelson touch' has been used to describe the battle plans for Trafalgar, and indeed that is how Nelson used the phrase. But many writers and observers have employed it to describe the almost mystical impact he had over his officers and men on the eve of battle. Nelson's unshakeable belief in himself and in his seamen, which he transmitted to the fleet, inspired daring and determination. But this was more than superstitious belief, for it was based on hard evidence.

The seamen at Trafalgar knew personally – or knew someone who knew personally, or heard stories and legends at the mess tables – how seriously Nelson was committed to the success of his campaigns. They saw him spend all night in a boat – without a boat cloak – sounding the depth of icy northern waters before he risked the dash through the shallows that was so instrumental in the outcome of the battle of Copenhagen. They knew the devastation of his attack on the French at the Nile. They knew that as a young man he had led dozens of land attacks and small boat actions, sword in hand, and that he was still leading from the front. They knew that the fresh meat, vegetables and fruit that relieved the tedium of salt beef and hard tack were obtained through his efforts, by his connections throughout the Mediterranean. Above all, they knew his track record for victory at the lowest possible human cost: casualties on the British side were always much less than the enemy. They were heavily outnumbered and outgunned as they approached the French and Spanish at Trafalgar, but if they were worried about this they did not show it.

At battle

As the two fleets closed range on 21 October 1805 the men realised that this would be the last day of boredom, but also that it might be the last day of their lives. This more sombre reflection did not stop them cheering and excitedly running up onto the deck to catch their first glimpse of the enemy. If they were frightened they kept it to themselves. 'We scrambled into battle as best we could,' wrote one officer, 'each man to take his bird.' There was a general eagerness to be at them, and matter-of-fact discussions about the disposal of one another's effects in the event of death. Bands played, some formal and in uniform with gleaming instruments, others volunteers from the crew, with drums made out of barrels, triangles bent out of ramrods, and a variety of instruments found in captured enemy ships. It all made a cheerful sound, and was in strong contrast with the grim view of the cannon of the enemy line. The British gun crews were in battle dress, stripped to the waist, bare-footed, wearing kerchiefs tied round their heads to deaden the blast of the guns to their ears. The marines were in their distinctive red coats, officers in blue dress coats and white breeches.

As they came within range of the enemy broadsides – long before they could return fire because the British were sailing straight at the enemy line – Nelson gave his famous signal. 'England expects that every man will do his duty' was the first use of a new signalling system that allowed more than a set of standard tactical instructions. Significantly, it has been suggested that his original plan of hoisting 'Nelson confides...' would have been more effective, that the men would have been more inspired by Nelson's confidence than England's expectation. By that stage in the build-up to battle – and in spite of some officers' exasperation at all these unnecessary flags – the men were ready to cheer anything; and they were certainly ready for Nelson's final trade-mark signal, 'Engage the enemy more closely'.

The gun decks represented the contrasts of the social strata, with the officers elegant in gleaming golden epaulettes, frock coats, frilly white shirts and white silk breeches and stockings, with polished shoes and golden buckles. But this contrast provided a measure of order and certainty as they approached the chaos of battle. The sailors were, according to reports, calm and confident, speaking of legends about Nelson and their expectations of victory. There was talk of glory, of going home and of retirement. There was particularly talk of prize money. Even a seaman's share of a few pounds was equal to months of wages.

How about the feelings of captains with their young sons on board as junior officers? Of course, they feared their possible death in battle, but they also worried that they should be brave and honourable and not let down the family. As Captain Duff of the *Mars* wrote home, with his only son, young Norwich, aged 13, with him, 'we are just going into action... I hope and trust in God we shall all behave as becomes us... Norwich is quite well and happy, I have however ordered him off the quarter deck.'

The captains had a lot to think about – they picked their opponents and altered course to attack them. Tension mounted, but not so much that the officers and men forgot it was dinnertime, so they ate their bread and cheese at the guns before going into action.

Reflecting on the battle – and relatively few accounts of seamen and junior officers survive, compared with those of the more senior officers – the men were getting on with the job, some even surprised that they were less afraid than they expected to be. 'When they had given us one duster,' a sailor wrote, 'and I found myself snug and tight, I bid fear kiss my bottom, and set to in good earnest.' One man sang 'Rule Britannia' all through the amputation of his smashed arm. Another described his similarly shattered limb, also an amputation case, as 'only a mere scratch, and I shall have to apologise for leaving the deck on so trifling an occasion'. Another, recovering from the amputation of his leg, cheered so loudly with his messmates on hearing an enemy ship strike her colours that he burst the ligatures and died of haemorrhaging.

On a happier note, one seaman – known for his elegant hornpipes – was thrown overboard, thought to be dead. He began to kick his legs and was hauled back just in time. As he said, without any complaints to his messmates, 'a good thing I showed you some dance steps, otherwise I would be snug in Davy Jones' locker'.

These were typical stories of British seamen – proud of their success, sad for their friends, glad to be alive, working out their share of the prize money – above all feeling confident, able and inspired. They were tired and emotional, and the news of Nelson's death when it came was a huge blow. Tough seamen were plunged into dismay, misery and tears – even Jack Nastyface:

It was... made known by one of our boat's crew, that Lord Nelson had received a fatal shot. Had this news been communicated through the fleet before the conflict was over, what effect it might have had on the hearts of our seamen I know not, for he was adored, and in fighting under him, every man thought himself sure of success. A momentary but naturally melancholy pause among the survivors of our brave crew ensued.

The ability of the British seaman and officer to survive fear, battle and the death of loved ones, and put a brave face on it, was all part of the legend of the navy. Nelson had built on this and reinforced it all his career, and was to leave behind him a navy that was stronger than ever. They revelled in the image that they 'minded shot no more than peas'.

The 13-year-old Norwich Duff had more to reflect on. His father, Captain George Duff, had been leaning over the taffrail looking at the enemy ships when a cannon ball had taken off his head. They left him lying on deck, covered with a Union Jack flag. Two of Nelson's band of brothers heard of young Norwich's fate: Admiral Collingwood found him and asked Captain Blackwood to look after him. In his elegant, childish but careful script he wrote a very difficult letter home:

My dear Mama, you cannot possibly imagine how unwilling I am to begin this melancholy letter. However as you must unavoidably hear of the fate of dear Papa, I write you these few lines to request you to bear it as patiently as you can. He died like a hero, having gallantly led his ship into action... Captain Blackwood has indeed been very polite and kind to me, and has said that on account of his acquaintance with my papa he will feel himself very happy in keeping me on board his ship... it has been the will of heaven and it is our duty to submit. Believe me, your obedient and affectionate son, Norwich Duff.

Nelson's ability to inspire his officers and men and maximise their performance, creating a culture of fearlessness and superiority, was a major factor in the success of his naval career and especially at Trafalgar. It was based on believing in his men and boasting of their prowess in seamanship and in warfare. It included supporting them against unfairness (although upholding discipline when required), trying to improve their food and conditions, arguing their case for prize money, and helping them gain promotions. He answered their letters and those from their families and helped them as much as he could. When ashore, every seaman he met was his friend.

Other officers practised humane acts and were encouraging to the seamen, but Nelson was special. With his reputation for leading from the front – supporting the '*allons*' rather than '*allez*' school of leadership – he presented himself as a role model. His ideals of the honour of the cause, pride in the vocation of the navy and belief in their invincibility matched their own feelings. They were not just firing a cannon or taking in a sail – they were saving their country. Even if they had never seen Nelson, the sailors knew what he looked like, with his empty sleeve and dim eye. These were the wounds that fighting men suffered. No wonder they identified with him and wanted to follow him.

Nelson also stood for an ideological position in times of tremendous uncertainty, arguably far more turbulent than the early twenty-first century. Britain had lost the war against the Americans, was a mere shout across the channel from the tumult of the French Revolution, was experiencing the collapse of the feudal order that had defined the rights and responsibilities of all, and faced open revolt in Ireland on religious and secular issues echoed on mainland England and Scotland. In the midst of all this Nelson stood clearly for monarchy, empire, British trading rights – and a simple enmity to the French, to which all his sailors could easily relate.

Nelson's Way
Inspiration

Inspiration is the action or power of stimulating the intellect or emotions in others through affection and communication. It is also being enthused, with an inspiring idea, agent or influence. Being inspired is to be outstanding and brilliant beyond the ordinary.

The inspirer is a muse or a genius, giving cheer and hope, who draws in, prompts, induces and fires people up to imaginative and lofty ideas. Inspiration is vivifying, vital and full of promise.

As a leader you may not be divinely influenced or be outstanding or brilliant, but you can show you care. You may be effective through Machiavellian and manipulative means, but you will only be respected as a great leader if you aspire to great ideals, and practise them personally and in the way you direct the organisation. You can't inspire others if you're not inspired yourself. Start with knowing what inspires you. What do you want to achieve? Whatever you say, this is what will communicate itself. Inspiration is infectious.

Colleagues and subordinates can be open to inspiration if it is well communicated. It may help everyone to develop skills in presentation, simplification and clarification to get their message across. In recruiting new staff members, look for those who have volunteered for projects beyond the call of duty and outside of their job descriptions – they are clearly inspired by something. Find out what, exactly. Look for animated people who are good communicators, with a heart to be stirred, good at thinking of and presenting new ideas.

Remember, you don't have to come up with something new all the time – just make sure that your words and deeds are the best your organisation can aspire to, and communicate them in a dynamic way.

Leadership comments
Greg Dyke

'Nelson was a great inspiration to his men, mostly because he earned their trust, they wanted to follow him, and they believed in him,' explains Greg Dyke, who was an inspirational BBC Director-General. When he left the BBC in 2004 in controversial circumstances, thousands of BBC staff took to the streets in protest. He inspired his colleagues in the same way that Nelson did his, by his actions and words.

'The people who work for you are going to see you, what you do and say. If you think that inspiring the people who work for you matters, you have to take this seriously,' he insists. 'If you believe you can only run an organisation if the people want to go in the same direction, then you have to be seen to be there. It's about the stories you tell and the stories they tell about you. You are inevitably high profile. If you treat people badly, everyone knows. Leaders may try to be quiet figures in the background, but the stories are told anyway. If you think people perform better when they respect and like you, you have to manage your visibility.'

Being inspiring, like being a legend and a hero, is based very much on stories, symbols and gestures. Thus Dyke described how Mo Mowlem, the popular Minister for Northern Ireland, would always talk to reception staff at places she visited and then ask after them on subsequent visits. These small gestures show that people matter and that you care. Dyke made a point of attending a meeting of BBC colleagues the morning after his house burned down. 'Stories were told about me doing that – and they would have been told about me if I hadn't gone,' he explains. 'And stories are told to customers as well as to colleagues – which can be very damaging if they're negative ones.'

'To inspire people, you need to make them think of you in a way that means that, when they are not sure about something, they will give you the benefit of the doubt,' Dyke considers. 'If you've done enough, been there with them, then people just have faith in you. It doesn't come automatically – you have to build it. Nelson had to, by getting to know people and appealing to their highest aspirations.'

Having knowledge and expertise gives confidence but, according to Dyke, 'You don't have to know everything, you haven't got time. When we introduced digital TV I didn't understand all the technology, but I knew what it did' and that is enough to inspire the necessary influential people with confidence. However, 'if you have only a couple of years experience in an industry you start with a disadvantage.' He feels that there is much in common between a business like broadcasting and an institution like the navy: 'You can't inspire people if they don't respect you, and you do need basic technical knowledge and understanding to gain respect.'

Nelson inspired his men as their leader and manager, and he knew enough about their jobs to convince them that he cared and depended on their contributions to achieve his objectives. In his stint at London Weekend Television, Dyke diagnosed the trouble as starting with 'something called "the management". They had "creatives" and "managers". All the smart people went into "creatives", so they outmanoeuvred and were more influential than the managers.' When Dyke arrived as CEO he forced the creatives to manage too, with no excuses for poor performance. 'Everyone has to work together to run the place as best they can,' he argues, and mentions the importance of dealing with discontent and promoting unity to the cause. Inspiration doesn't work on people who are divided.

He also makes the point that 'you can only inspire people by being sincere and honest, by demonstrating your sense of purpose with conviction. People don't care if you are eccentric as long as it's you. Some people try to "ape" the manager before them, then you see them changing, because they can't keep it up. There is no chance of aping Nelson, if it's not what you are. He was very successful at inspiring people, but you have to find your own way.'

Dyke believes that one of the most powerful ways to inspire people is to create effective teams. The Nelson approach of participative leadership and the creation of a band of brothers is right up his street. But he knows it's not easy. 'People who are close to you at the top are there partly because they are naturally competitive, ambitious and liable to shaft each other,' he insists. They will not normally work together as a team. 'You can get over that by getting people to become friends, to stop trying to kill each other. Instead of sending uncooperative and rude emails to each other, they can say "Can I help?"'

What has to come first, the creation of teams or the inspiration? It's a bit of both. Dyke considers that 'all those team-building things that people make fun of – outdoors with ropes and mountains – really work'. The practical experience that Nelson's officers and men went through bonded them into teams – and replicating it with experiential training can certainly help. Dyke sees the need to overcome conflict and the assumption that the best way to resolve it is to abuse each other. 'Good teams sort out the answers, or what should be done anyway,' he considers. 'And people will only buy in if they've been part of the team. You as a leader can't micromanage what they do – then you make them feel useless; people want to be part of something. And when they achieve something, they want to celebrate as a team, then that makes it even stronger. Actually most people are not Machiavellian; if they live in a system they'll play their part.'

For Dyke, another Nelson – Nelson Mandela – was also inspirational. 'He is an exception. I visited Robben Island and an ex-prisoner told how in the afternoons the place used to be silent, everyone was learning –

Mandela inspired them to use the time like a university.' Again, this was appealing to people's highest aspirations and sharing in their sense of pride in their achievements.

Leadership lessons
Inspiration

- ⚓ Ask yourself why you think others should follow you. The answers will be a mix of reasons, but if you hope to inspire them it must be something they recognise as special.
- ⚓ Remind everyone (regularly) what your work is for and demonstrate that you are fully dedicated to that great purpose – actions speak louder than words, but words inspire action.
- ⚓ Show that results can be achieved and that they are for an honourable and greater purpose, appealing to people's highest aspirations.
- ⚓ Know your people, know their jobs, know stories about them, and show you care with symbolic acts of kindness, responding to the needs of even the most junior employees.
- ⚓ Fight for the interests of your people, lobby for their cause; nothing can be achieved without them.
- ⚓ Be a hero to your people – and don't ask them to do anything you wouldn't do yourself. Leadership is based on trust earned through respect.
- ⚓ Represent the cause, the ideals and values of your people and be a role model, walking the talk and promoting unity through a common vision.
- ⚓ Offer stability and continuity in times of chaos, but also the possibility of reform and improvement.
- ⚓ Deal with discontent by appealing to your people's pride in their achievements. Offer to deal with genuine grievances fairly, and focus behaviour on urgent current tasks.
- ⚓ Use the sandwich technique of giving feedback – praise, criticise (gently) and praise again.
- ⚓ Even in the most extreme circumstances, always celebrate success – symbols and gestures matter.

8

GLORY

A hard act to follow, Trafalgar 1805

'Coup de Nelson: a surprise or unexpected blow, as in
"the Nelson Touch",'
Littré, *French Dictionary*

A romanticised interpretation, and strictly inaccurate as Nelson died below decks, around three hours after he had been struck. But the picture gives a flavour of the crowded scene and the burly sailors juxtaposed with the more gentlemanly officers.

'The Death of Nelson' by Benjamin West (artist), James Heath (engraver), Colnaghi & Puckle (publishers), 1841.

ON 29 SEPTEMBER 1805 IT WAS NELSON'S 47TH BIRTHDAY. He was thrilled to be back with the fleet, and they were overjoyed at his return. Able Seaman James Martin of the *Neptune* wrote:

> on the 28th September was joined by H.M. Ship Victory *Admirl Lord Nelson and the* Ajax *and the* Thunderer *it is Imposeble to Discribe the Heartfelt Satisfaction of the whole fleet upon this Occasion and the Confidance of Success with which we ware Inspired.*

Nelson had received a rapturous send-off from Portsmouth, the adoring throngs controlled by a military escort. In a typical winning-hearts gesture, he took a letter from a seaman's mother, asking her to kiss it so he could carry the kiss to her son too. As Southey, the poet laureate who wrote the first official biography of Nelson, described:

> *a crowd collected, pressing forward to obtain a sight of his face – many were in tears and many knelt down before him as he passed. All men knew that his heart was as humane as it was fearless... that with perfect and entire devotion he served his country with all his heart and with all his soul and with all his strength.*

His welcome from the seamen in the fleet and his popularity with officers set the scene for an unprecedented victory ahead, especially in contrast with low morale, confusion and conflict in the Combined Fleet of France and Spain. As one captain, Edward Codrington, remarked, 'Lord Nelson is arrived, and a sort of general joy is the consequence.'

On 29 September the master of the *Prince*, Richard Anderson, wrote, 'this is a Great Day all the Captns dine with Lord Nelson I Get a letter and some Clean Shirts from my dear Mary – Hurra.' Nelson liked to deliver letters to his captains personally, and they rowed over to the *Victory* in a state of excitement. Codrington wrote home to his wife:

> *he received me in an easy, polite manner, and on giving me your letter said that being entrusted with it by a lady, he made a point of deliver-ing it himself. I have no fear of obtaining his goodwill by the conduct of the* Orion *[Codrington's ship]; because I shall do my best to deserve it, and he is a man well able to appreciate my endeavours.*

Thomas Fremantle found him looking 'better than ever I saw him in my life, and is grown fatter'. Nelson – probably still quite thin but looking healthy and relieved now that action was at hand – knew that Betsey Fremantle had just delivered another baby, and asked his old comrade if he wanted a girl or a boy. 'I answered, the former, when he put the letter into my hand and told me to be satisfied.' It was a girl. Nelson then delighted him by

> *telling me that he should give me my old station, which is his second in the line of battle. This is very gratifying to me, as it puts me in a very prominent situation in the order of battle, and a very convenient and pleasant one in the order of sailing.*

So dinner on 29 September was very special. The junior admirals and senior captains gathered at the large mahogany table in the great cabin, with gleaming silverware and cut glass, good food and wines, and con-vivial company. The men were old friends from St Vincent and the Nile, as well as some Nelson had never met before, like Eliab Harvey of the *Temeraire* or Robert Moorsom of the *Revenge*. The old 'band of brothers' soon brought the newcomers into the fold.

Meanwhile, Nelson did his best to sort out personal problems and make everyone feel comfortable. Charles Tyler of the *Tonnant* was worrying about his son (for whom Nelson had arranged his lieutenant's examination and first commission), who had deserted his frigate and run off with an opera dancer in Malta. Nelson sympathised – and probably identified with the lad – but also alerted his contacts in Italy to find him, settle his debts and persuade him to return to sea. As he wrote to his old friend Ball, now Governor of Malta, 'I am not come forth to find difficulties, but to remove them.'

Dinner the next day was 'for all of us who did not dine on board *Victory* yesterday', as Codrington wrote home.

> *What our late chief [Collingwood] will think of this I don't know; but I well know what the fleet think of the difference; and even you, our good wives, who have some causes of disapprobation, will allow the superiority of Lord Nelson in all these social arrangements which bind his captains to their admiral.*

As Codrington indicated, the captains' pleasure at Nelson's return was partly because in only three weeks they had become fed up with Collingwood, his deputy. The latter's style serves to highlight why Nelson was so unusual and so popular. Collingwood, a trusted 'brother' for many years and a close friend, was nevertheless totally different from his chief. He was a dour Northumbrian, described by one of his officers as

> *a selfish old bear. That he was a brave, stubborn, persevering and determined officer everyone acknowledged; but he had few, if any, friends and no admirers. In body and mind he was iron, and very cold iron.*

Collingwood had been a friend of Nelson's during the Navigation Acts campaign in the 1780s, and they had sketched each other's portraits as young men in 1784. At Cape St Vincent Collingwood commanded the *Excellent* and strongly supported Nelson, who called him 'my dearest friend'. Having served at the Glorious First of June, he had been made a commodore after Tenerife and a rear-admiral after the Nile. Tall, bald and unsmiling, he was described as looking like a bishop. One of his few friends seems to have been his pet dog, Bounce, who unfortunately fell down a hatchway and died, leaving him more gloomy than ever.

Collingwood detested entertaining, discouraged the captains entertaining each other – they came to see a court-martial as a good enough excuse for a get-together – and forbade the innocuous and popular tradition of allowing neutral provision boats to enter the fleet so that officers and men could buy small treats and luxuries for themselves. No wonder that, after Collingwood's dull and kill-joy regime, the captains were writing to the Admiralty, 'for charity's sake, send us Lord Nelson, oh, ye men of power!'

Nelson, by contrast, took every chance to entertain his officers and captains, never eating a meal alone (in any case he needed help cutting up his meat) while inviting them in rotation, getting to know them one by one. Thus Captain Duff of the *Mars*, who had not met Nelson before, wrote: 'he is so good and pleasant a man that we all like to do what he likes without any kind of orders. He is the pleasantest admiral I ever served under.' When Nelson returned to the fleet, 'the signal is made that boats may be hoisted out to buy fresh fruit... or anything coming into the fleet'. After his arrival, Fremantle wrote to Betsey:

> *the whole system here is so completely changed that it wears quite a different aspect... [on 30th] the junior [captains] and I never passed a pleasanter day. I staid with him till eight at night – he would not let me leave him before. He has obligingly desired me to come to him without ceremony whenever I choose, and to dine with him as often as I found it convenient.*

Among the older band of brothers were Thomas Hardy, back from a brief convalescence for his rheumatism; Edward Berry, whom Nelson once described as his 'right arm'; and Ben Hallowell, he of the exotic souvenirs (Nelson still had the coffin that Hallowell had made for him, carved out of the mainmast of *L'Orient*). Another highly regarded officer, who certainly became a 'brother' in the upcoming action, was Blackwood, who played a vital communication role in his frigate *Euryalus*.

In April 1805 the French fleet evaded Nelson's blockade for the second time and set off for the West Indies. Under the command of Admiral Villeneuve, they planned to land 20,000 troops to disrupt British trade in the region, rendezvous with other French and Spanish squadrons and then sail back across the Atlantic and up the English Channel to support the invasion. Nelson gave chase, but he was a month behind them when he passed the Straits of Gibraltar and entered the Atlantic. Sailing hard, capitalising on the years of practice on blockade duty, Nelson's fleet arrived in the Caribbean just days behind the French, and so scared them that Villeneuve decided not to risk landing his troops and headed straight back towards the Channel.

The news of the escape of the enemy fleets caused predictable consternation back in England. First, people couldn't believe that the French and Spanish had escaped the blockade; didn't Nelson have the Mediterranean as tight as a drum? Secondly, they were stunned that Nelson had not been able to find the enemy, as if the Atlantic were a small place. Thirdly, the loss of colonies in the West Indies would be disastrous for trade and another sign of Napoleon's worldwide reach. Waiting anxiously for news, a small squadron led by Admiral Robert Calder was sent off to patrol the outer reaches of the Channel. On 22 July 1805 he sighted the larger Combined Fleet, which tried to evade him in their desire to reach the main French force blockaded in Ferrol. But Calder managed to attack and to take two Spanish ships, and the Spanish Admiral Gravina and his colleagues never forgave Villeneuve for abandoning them to Calder.

Villeneuve now seemed to have lost his nerve. In any case Napoleon had postponed the invasion of Britain in order to concentrate on countering a new alliance between Austria and Russia, so the Combined Fleet sailed south and sought refuge in Cadiz.

When Nelson came home to Spithead after the long blockade and epic chase, he was anxious about how he would be received. But the story of his rapid flight across the Atlantic, saving the Caribbean colonies from the enemy, assured him an enthusiastic welcome. At the peak of his heroic career, he was given command of the new force assembling off Cadiz.

Nelson was back in England for a little over three weeks. He spent the time in feverishly detailed planning and lobbying for the resources he needed for the campaign. Lord Minto, former diplomat and an old friend of Nelson's, remarked on seeing him mobbed wherever he went, 'it is really quite affecting to see the wonder and admiration and love and respect of the whole world'. Nelson realised, more and more, the weight of his responsibility.

After an emotional farewell from Emma and Horatia, he sailed on 14 September and joined the fleet two weeks later. His job now was to prepare for battle this force of 20–30 ships (the number varied as some went for supplies and others later joined the fleet off Cadiz). Two-thirds of the captains were new to Nelson, including his third-in-command. Alongside the routine administration of the fleet, Nelson worked on moulding this new team into a 'band of brothers'.

Preparing the battle plan

The whole force of the British campaign was directed towards a decisive battle. The tradition of fighting in two parallel lines was too slow, ponderous and indecisive. Nelson's idea was to form three lines of battle (later reduced to two) to pierce the enemy's line, concentrate his forces on the rear and centre, and especially to bring about a pell-mell battle in which the greater manoeuvrability of the British would present a chance to rake the enemy ships fore and aft. By firing a broadside down the length of the decks from the relatively undefended sterns, huge damage could be done to both men and guns far more effectively than by battering each other side to side. The tactic was not new; similar ideas had been developed by a French tactician and published in a late eighteenth-century manual. But never before had a fleet been so technically able to effect it, and Villeneuve fully expected Nelson to try.

Nelson was infectiously enthusiastic about the idea, and was delighted at the captains' response to the 'Nelson touch'. He thought the plan would 'surprise and confound the enemy. They won't know what I am about. It will bring forward a pell-mell battle, and that is what I want.' The surprise element was probably less significant, and Nelson's old adage from Locker was still the key deciding factor: 'Lay a Frenchman close and you will beat him.'

The final version of the plan of attack was shared with the captains in the first week of October. It was above all flexible, and aimed at saving time in order to be sure of annihilating as many enemy ships as possible before nightfall. The full memorandum, dated 9 October, concludes the detailed account of the plan on a practical note: 'nothing is sure in a sea fight... no captain can do very wrong if he places his ship alongside that of an enemy.'

By contrast with Nelson's fleet, the enemy was in a poor state of supply and riven by internal rivalries. Morale was low: Spanish civilians attacked French sailors in port, and outside the harbour the British were waiting. Nelson's squadron was reputed to be unbeatable at sea and feared for its deadly thunderous broadsides and cheering, bloodthirsty seamen. The French officers knew they had failed to deliver on their vital role in the invasion plans, and now Napoleon was sending a replacement admiral and new orders to head for the Mediterranean in support of his campaigns in Austria and Italy. By late September the fleets prepared to sail, and then heard that Nelson had returned and was about to blast them out of Cadiz by attacking them in port. What were they to do?

The British fleet, despite the years spent at sea, was more confident. However Nelson, as ever a diligent manager, was concerned that naval stores, food and water supplies were running low. The only thing to do was to send squadrons of ships to Gibraltar for repair and reprovisioning. But their captains, desperate not to miss the forthcoming battle, were most reluctant to go. The departure of six ships in mid-October actually served to help tempt the French and Spanish out of port, as they then reckoned that Nelson was now down to 23 sail. In fact he had been reinforced by individual ships sailing out from England (such as Berry's *Agamemnon*) and was now 27 strong. Gunnery drill was practised again and again, as were the complex manoeuvres that would make such a difference in the battle to come.

The Battle of Trafalgar

Villeneuve, tempted by his belief that Nelson was under strength and hearing that his own replacement was already at Madrid, decided to put to sea. He had no sooner made the signal than Blackwood reported it to Nelson. The Combined Fleets were trying to get a clear run to the Straits of Gibraltar, and Nelson stayed out of sight to stop them rushing back to port. Collingwood urged an immediate attack, but Nelson wanted a clear day to do the job properly. Having dinner that night with a group of awe-struck midshipmen, he announced:

> *tomorrow I will do that which will give you younger gentlemen some-thing to talk and think about for the rest of your lives. But I shall not live to know about it myself.*

This and similar stories of his premonitions of death are hard to verify, but they certainly lend a pathos to the narrative!

Cutting off Villeneuve's retreat to Cadiz in the early hours of the morning, Nelson signalled his 27 ships to form two columns to steer eastwards towards the enemy's 33 and form in line of battle, the same as the order of sailing. Villeneuve, going for the Straits, suddenly lost heart and headed back for Cadiz, but it was too late. Engagement was now inevitable. Everything was ready.

Nelson decided to send a signal 'to amuse the fleet'. He wanted to begin 'Nelson confides...' but was persuaded, in the interests of speed and brevity, to signal 'England expects that every man will do his duty'. Many cheered, but in their present mood they would have cheered any-thing. Keyed up for battle, after years of blockading and chasing, the men were excited. Bands were playing on poop decks throughout the fleet. Some seamen were dancing hornpipes, some polishing their guns as if for an inspection, others arranging the inheritance of one another's effects should they get hit by 'one of Johnny Crapeaud's shots'.

For Nelson, it was a time of reflection and recommitment to his God. His prayer, written out for posterity, was part of his legacy of a lifetime committed to service. And like many of his officers and men, he also rewrote his will that day. Witnessed by Blackwood and Hardy, he left Emma Hamilton and his 'adopted' daughter Horatia as a bequest to the country. Despite the gratitude of the nation to Nelson after the battle, and despite the efforts of these and other 'brothers', his last wishes were to be ignored.

As the two armadas slowly closed range, Nelson thrilled to the prospect of battle. He was calmer than usual, somehow sensing that the climax to everything he had worked for was arriving. Surrounded by the 'brothers', in his generosity he spared a thought for poor Calder, on his way to a court of inquiry for not living up to the standards that Nelson had created: 'Hardy, what would poor Sir Robert Calder give to be with us now?'

He said farewell to Blackwood, who replied, 'I trust, my Lord, that on my return to the *Victory* I shall find your Lordship well and in the possession of twenty prizes.'

'God bless you, Blackwood,' Nelson replied and, to the young man's horror, added, 'I shall never speak to you again.'

He was right. In taking charge at Trafalgar, Nelson as usual led from the front, and the *Victory* bore tremendous damage in the opening salvoes of the action. Until the British ships could manoeuvre to rake the stern of the enemy ships, they would be exposed to fire they could not return. His officers had tried to persuade him to shift his flag to the *Euryalus*, to wear a plain coat, to allow the ships immediately astern to overtake the *Victory*, but all to no avail.

Soon surrounded by three enemy ships, Nelson and his crew were exposed to immediate danger. The quarterdeck was constantly raked by fire, both from broadsides and soldiers in the tops. Nelson's secretary John Scott was one of the first casualties, smashed to pulp by a cannon ball and unceremoniously dumped over the side. Eight marines standing in a row were mown down by a single cannon ball. A huge splinter ripped the buckle off Hardy's shoe as he and Nelson were pacing the quarterdeck.

From only 50 feet away, with the ships fighting as close as he had always insisted they should, Nelson was hit by a musket ball from a sniper in the mizzen top of the *Redoubtable*. Covering his face and jacket with his handkerchief so that the men would not see he had been hit, he was carried down to the 'butcher's shambles' of the orlop deck. He never lost his attention to detail and concern for his ship, noticing that the tiller had been shot away and sending a midshipman to inform Hardy. Knowing that he had received a fatal wound, he told the distressed surgeon, Beatty, that he could do nothing for him. Overcome by emotion, Beatty concurred.

Nelson lived just long enough to know the enormity of his fleet's victory. Congratulating him in the arms of death, Hardy reported that at least 15 of the enemy had struck their colours. In the most poignant moment of both their lives, Nelson asked Hardy to kiss him. One of the least expressive but one of the most loyal and devoted of the band of brothers, Hardy kissed his dying chief again.

Even near death, Nelson was always the professional. In great pain and sinking fast, he nevertheless remembered that a rising swell indicated the coming of a storm. He would not give up command easily. Lying against a great timber on the orlop deck and covered with a bloodstained sheet, on Hardy's second and last visit, less than an hour from his final expiry, Nelson still tried to carry on directing the fleet. Instructing Hardy to anchor in order to secure the prizes during the storm, he tried to raise himself from his bed with his last ounce of strength. He wished he had never the left the deck because he would soon be gone – and he wanted to continue to command the fleet while he had breath in his body. At half past four, just over three hours after he had been hit, Nelson died.

The aftermath

Collingwood unfortunately never received the order to anchor, and by the time he thought of it, it was too late. In the next four days most of the prizes were lost in the storm. Collingwood seemed to go to pieces, issuing orders and cancelling them minutes later. As Fremantle reflected, 'the poor man does not own his own mind five minutes together.' They were all stunned by the loss of their commander, which robbed them of the joy of victory. It seemed to have affected Collingwood particularly badly. He wrote:

> it was about the middle of the action, when an officer came from the Victory to tell me he was wounded. He sent his love to me and desired me to conduct the fleet. I asked the officer if the wound was dangerous and he, by his look told what he could not speak, nor I reflect upon now without suffering again the anguish of that moment.

They all suffered in their own way. Blackwood wrote that he had never been so shocked or upset in his life. Hallowell, the giant prizefighter of a captain, could not stand upright. The Rev. Dr Scott, Nelson's chaplain, translator and foreign secretary, was 'stupid with grief for what I have lost'. Hardy, the last to see him alive, also outlived Nelson the longest, dying in 1839. He asked that a favourite miniature of Nelson be placed alongside him in his coffin. All the captains remaining in the Mediterranean fleet felt 'it was formerly a pleasure to serve; it has now become a toil'.

For the junior officers and men, the blow was just as hard. 'He was as great a hero as ever existed,' a young lieutenant wrote, 'a seaman's friend, and the father of the fleet.' Across the fleet they wrote letters, not just of respect or admiration, but about 'a friend I loved', 'our beloved Admiral', 'our dear Admiral Nelson'. As a sailor in the *Royal Sovereign* wrote,

we have paid pretty sharply for licking 'em. I never set eyes on him, for which I am both sorry and glad; for, to be sure, I should like to have seen him. But then, all the men in our ships who have seen him are such soft toads, they have done nothing but blast their eyes, and cry, ever since he was killed.

The reception of the news in England mirrored the feelings in the fleet, emphasised by Lieutenant Lapenotiere's dramatic announcement to the First Secretary of the Admiralty in the early hours of the morning of 6 November, 16 days after the battle: 'Sir, we have gained a great victory, but we have lost Lord Nelson!' There was little public joy. The king was rendered speechless and people in the streets wept openly as if they had lost a close relative or intimate friend. In Naples, Coleridge was stopped by passers-by who noticed the tears running down his cheek and comforted him.

The high point of Nelson's magnificent state funeral in January 1806, one of the most elaborate before or since, was when seamen from the *Victory* were supposed to lower the shot-rent colours onto the coffin. Instead, they ripped the flag to pieces, each saving his precious souvenir inside his shirt. This was a leader they loved.

The war against Napoleon would continue for another decade, but it was a war predominantly fought on land. For many years invasion had been a real threat, with Napoleon's Marshal Massena claiming that Britain would be conquered and ruined and left in such a state that no one would doubt the French possession. A number of factors had already drawn Napoleon's ambitions away from the immediate invasion of Britain, and in reality it had been prevented by Cornwallis's Channel Fleet. The enemy fleets were rebuilt: nine years after Trafalgar the French navy was back to strength. But after 1805 no nation was prepared to take on the might of the British navy for over 100 years.

Nelson was great while he was alive, but when he died he became cosmic. He had always seen his career leading to his most dramatic victory, and his hero's death at the ultimate moment of success brilliantly expressed his brand of leadership. Nevertheless, this total dedication, almost martyrdom, is not for everyone, certainly not anyone who values a quiet life and comfortable retirement!

Nelson wanted to go out in a blaze of glory and dying a hero's death in battle was his trump card. After Trafalgar, the salient image was of a leader who profoundly respected each individual with whom he came in contact. All his men, from admirals to seamen, had hopes and wishes of their own, and were not there simply to receive orders. He took them into his confidence and trust freely and willingly, and they bought into his ideas with a strong sense of personal responsibility. Even the French admiral Villeneuve admitted that at Trafalgar, 'every captain was a Nelson'. The Spanish admiral Gravina called Nelson 'the greatest hero that the world perhaps has produced'.

Nelson's Way
Glory

People can possess or deserve glory and can confer glory on others. A glorious achievement can be marked by great beauty or splendour, be delightful, wonderful and renowned. A commendable asset is known as a crowning glory. The act of glorifying is to make eminent, heavenly, sanctified, or merely glamorised and intoxicated. Glorious means grandiose, illustrious, superb, gorgeous, radiating grandeur, notability and brightness.

A glorious leader is an exaggeration, but that's what glory is all about. A leader aspiring to glory places honour and great deeds above getting money, position or power. To be glorious is to become an archetype of humanity, to be a model of greatness, transcending particular circumstances of time and place. Every society has its marks of glory, bestowed on those it deems great and exemplary, such as knighthoods and other honours.

Heroes of the Ancient World aspired to glory because it meant that their names would live on in the songs and legends of their people. Anyone who hopes to be remembered by future generations thereby aspires to glory. Many people do good works anonymously; but many want to be recognised for the legacy they leave. Endowments to foundations, universities and charities often glorify the donors' names; streets, pubs and parks are public glorifications of people who have contributed much to society.

Glory is also about reputation, which can only be built and maintained if everyone believes in it. A reputation can take years to build and minutes to destroy. So take care what you will be remembered for.

Leadership comments
Sir John Harvey-Jones

'Nelson's legacy was mirrored in the feelings of others about him: loyalty, love, trust, brotherhood. That's what being a participative leader is all about. His captains were committed because he shared the objectives with them,' Sir John Harvey-Jones points out. 'He gave glory to others because they felt such a strong sense of achievement because of his sharing approach.' His honour and glory became their honour and glory too.

In terms of his own legacy, Harvey-Jones sees himself as continuing to learn and not looking back, as Nelson did. 'People want leaders they can respect, on whom they can model themselves. Heroes are examples from whom you can go on learning. For all of us, life is a continually developing pattern – until the last trump. I think I am slightly like

Nelson in this respect: I never look back; I can't do anything about what's gone, but keep developing towards the future,' Harvey-Jones reflects.

Nelson's loyalty to his officers and men – sharing glory with them – was a significant part of his legacy, Harvey-Jones feels. 'Most leaders have the wish to leave behind them something worthwhile – it's a much more powerful driver than money or publicity, or anything else. People get to the top by ambition, and when they get to the top their ambition stretches beyond that – but the longevity of your legacy depends on what you believe and what you leave in terms of the beliefs for those you lead.'

Having served in the navy, Harvey-Jones has experienced the impact of the Nelson legend first-hand. For a young naval officer, identifying with Nelson's legacy is essential, he feels, agreeing with Sir Jonathon Band. 'The image of Nelson presents a powerful role model. There is a deep sense of reverence, on the part of every naval officer and seaman, on a visit to the *Victory* in Portsmouth, especially when he (or she) reaches that small brass plaque on the deck that simply states "here Nelson fell". The emotion intensifies in the 'tween decks of the orlop, where even the shortest person has to stoop, to see another simple memorial: "here Nelson died".'

But Harvey-Jones warns against seeking glory as potentially producing a leader's downfall. Few people, before or since, have been as clear as Nelson about their legacy, and his was closely aligned to what his country needed. But for many this is dangerous ground. Many don't think about their legacies at all, and some become obsessed by seeking glory, doing everything now based on what succeeding generations may think of them. They may be missing the point: what is needed now and for whose benefit?

Leadership lessons
Glory

⚓ Will you leave your part of the world in a better state than you found it?

⚓ Do you want to achieve glory and be remembered, or do you want to do your job quietly and just as quietly slip away? Leaving behind a glorious legacy is not for everyone.

⚓ To leave something really glorious, you will probably have to make sacrifices, to give up current pleasure for future benefits. So it's worth choosing something worthwhile to aim for.

⚓ The cause you serve is important – it should be bigger than any individual, bigger than the self-interests of a minority or a corporation; it should be worthy of your best efforts, tangible and real.

⚓ Results matter and so do examples. Setting an example can have a bigger long-term impact. Live your life according to ideals that will be admired by others for generations to come.

⚓ Build your legacy into the culture and woodwork of your organisation, so that everyone joining it and becoming aware of the culture becomes aware of your legacy – the rituals, stories, values, norms, rites of passage, language and reputation.

⚓ Present a clear, common vision that everyone can buy into and make their own commitment to, and celebrate its achievement.

⚓ Create memorable stories about your exploits, mixing great achievements with little touches that reveal your human qualities – being glorious must be larger than life.

9

LEADERSHIP LESSONS FROM THE GREAT COMMANDER

'When I came to explain to them the "Nelson Touch", it was like an electric shock. Some shed tears, all approved – it was new – it was singular – it was simple! And from Admirals downwards, it was repeated – "it must succeed, if ever they will allow us to get at them! You are, my Lord, surrounded by friends, whom you inspire with confidence".'

Nelson

NELSON'S STORY REMAINS RELEVANT TODAY BECAUSE THE leadership challenges he faced are still immediately recognisable, in terms of the virtues he espoused and the leadership questions he had to answer.

Nelson needed to promote himself and publicise his achievements in order to be recognised as a hero. He had to learn his trade and pass professional examinations to show his commitment to his vocation. He needed influence – which can be seen as patronage and networking skills – to succeed. He needed sheer guts and courage to get on. He faced the timeless choice between his passion for the pleasures of the flesh and the call of duty. He could have been autocratic and dictatorial, but he chose to be a team player, to be a participative leader, to be loyal to his captains. He loved hanging out with the lads, he was a man's man but he could be a lady's man. He needed his favourite lads around him and he managed to strike a rare balance between being 'one of the boys' and 'the boss'. He was an outstandingly diligent manager as well as a leader. He was powerfully inspirational to all who knew him and to a vast population beyond that. So his legacy is wide-ranging, modern and complex.

Nelson was ambitious, aggressive, confident and impulsive. He was determined, risk taking and courageous. But he was also emotional and expressed his feelings openly in his caring, loving, passionate and trusting relationships. He was (in the context of his society) classless, concerned with fairness, encouraging, inspirational, optimistic and humane. He made huge personal sacrifices and was spiritual, committed and energetically self-actualising. He found it difficult to get on with his superiors, was self-promoting, unconventional and, like any survivor, depended on luck. When the enemy made more mistakes than he did, it worked. He was xenophobic in a way that would be unacceptable in modern liberal societies, though it remains a potent force in the more war-mongering nations of west and east. He was rarely cautious or circumspect. He was immodest, impatient, intolerant and often imprudent, in both his public and private life.

In this book, in a mix of chronological and thematic approaches, we have looked at Nelson's development as a leader, from his early life to the build-up to and climax of Trafalgar. We have seen the positives and negatives of his leadership style in each aspect as the story unfolds. Clearly, Nelson's way of leadership is not the only way, nor an ideal for all circumstances. But Nelson stands as an example of a certain and very distinctive style.

Leadership questions

Why be a leader?

Above all Nelson wanted to be a hero. He realised that heroes have to be created, so he made a conscious effort at developing his own hype. In the process he may have exaggerated his own heroism, as not all of the anecdotes are true. He loved the hero worship and this may have led him into some unwise decisions, but it was an essential part of who he was.

Enthusiasm for heroism has ebbed and flowed over time. Immediately after Nelson's death it was at its height, with the fleet and the country plunged into mourning. The gloom among officers and men, the weeping and sense of personal loss were all about the death of a hero. The massive public attendance at his huge state funeral, the monuments, the plays in the West End and the souvenir hunting celebrated the hero. Now heroism has become confused with celebrity, but even Nelson was conscious of needing to be a celebrity to be a hero.

It is obviously impossible to be a hero quietly. We may guide our actions with a private internal reference to heroic ideals, but being a hero requires the social construction of a person identified with the ideals advanced by others – preferably masses of others. Heroes are genuinely outstanding and have a lasting impact, not to be confused with the air time and column inches given over to mere celebrities. Nevertheless, Nelson's experience shows the value of media coverage and developing a popular following.

If being a hero in the Nelson mould is your choice, you can't hide your light under a bushel, but don't get carried away by hype and celebrity building. There's an important difference between a real, lasting hero and a passing fad. And don't set your heart on gaining and enjoying hero worship, it may not last. Decide what true heroism is for you.

On the other hand, you may prefer a low profile, considering that heroism suggests a macho, arrogant and egotistical approach. Getting things done in an organisation often requires a facilitative and modest way of operating. You don't have to be a hero to be a leader, and remember that leadership may be the domain of a group rather than an individual.

Does a leader need to be an expert?

Nelson learned his business thoroughly and was committed to it, always seeing part of his credibility as stemming from his technical ability as a good seaman, navigator and fighting naval officer. He was not the best, but was good enough to hold his head high with his captains. Once he wrote to St Vincent 'I was very seasick today – don't laugh', but he was still a seaman through and through.

The idea of vocation is less popular these days with the increase in corporate job hopping and non-expert leaders, but the desire for work that is more of a calling than 'just a job' remains strong, expressed in concepts such as self-actualisation.

Nelson's achievements can also be seen as contributing to the expert or generalist debate. These are two distinctly different routes to the top of a company, unit, team or whatever. One is starting at the bottom and working up to the top (this was and is the traditional way in the armed services), which involves knowing the business inside out through years of service. The alternative is flitting between different sectors, rising to the top by being a strong professional manager and leader regardless of the field, and moving around as a mid-career executive, to whatever walk of life offers itself.

Nelson rose through the ranks rapidly partly because of his expert knowledge of his chosen profession. A commanding officer had to know how to interpret sketchy information that was often weeks or even months out of date; entrust missions to people who may have to act on their own initiative because further communication was impossible once they were out of sight; and any officer from captain upwards needed a deeply ingrained knowledge of ships and the sea to make sound judgements about specific manoeuvres, tactical risks and medium-term campaign strategies. Having said that, highly effective naval commanders such as Earl St Vincent made appalling mistakes as admiralty administrators, crippling the supply chain via a set of so-called reforms that showed no evidence of his practical experience. A confident commander can become a monomaniac manager!

So specialist expertise that may be essential at one level in an organisation is no guarantee of success at more senior levels. Conversely, a successful manager of one business can often move to another, and the higher up you are the easier it gets. Leadership may in this respect be different, because it depends so much on the respect of others. Here real expertise in the work of the organisation is often essential.

The authority to lead always comes partly from experience of some kind – technical or managerial. Your interest and competence in each may change over time and as you rise up the managerial ladder the emphasis of your workload will inevitably change too. Organisations differ in what they expect of their leaders. Some require a long apprenticeship, others welcome newcomers with different ideas. So there is no simple formula for balancing technical and managerial expertise in all circumstances, but being clear about your vocation is the main thing. What are you called to do?

Does a leader have to lead from the front?

Nelson always wanted to be in the thick of the action, in the front line, prominent and visible. But he exposed himself to great danger, suffered injuries and wounds, and clashed with senior officers in his zeal for action. Luckily most of his choices worked; but when they did not, he suffered as much as anyone. For example, when he sent a protégé to command at Boulogne in 1803, leading to conspicuous failure and a fatal wound to the young man, he blamed himself and wept openly at the man's funeral. He could cope with his own wounds, but not those of others.

The courage exemplified by leading from the front embraces moral integrity as well as battlefield bravery, having the courage of your convictions and making ethical stands. Nelson frequently crossed pens with Admiralty officials, and not knowing what life was like in the front line was only one of his criticisms. 'I hate your pen and ink men,' he wrote just before the Battle of Copenhagen. 'A fleet of ships of war are the best negotiators in Europe.' It was not just that he wanted to be a showman; he felt it necessary to be a role model, even when he reached more senior ranks.

It is no longer essential for a commander to be at the front line. In many industries, the real progress is made behind the scenes by powerful people who are noticed little. For example, the current consolidation in the global insurance and financial services industries is led by people who may well instil confidence in their immediate teams and among shareholders, but they are not visible leaders in the Nelsonian mould. On the other hand, visible leadership remains tremendously valuable in helping these organisations through their transitions and restructuring. So sometimes a quiet leader may have to come into the limelight in order to provide what's needed; or find someone else, another member of the team, to do so. In the absence of a visible leader groups tend to lose focus – a person is more memorable than an event, and an event is more memorable than a principle.

If you are always in the thick of the action, prominent and visible, your successes and failures are equally exposed. Working quietly behind the scenes can be just as effective, and not everyone has to be a super-star. It depends on how important it is for you to gain the credit, and how much others need a visible leader.

How can you balance work and private life?

Nelson's private life became an open book, he wore his heart on his sleeve and he found it hard to be discreet over his private affairs. His rep-utation became tarnished in high places, especially when his passion began to influence his judgement and led to him selectively responding to orders from superiors. It was as if he had dedicated his whole life to duty to the exclusion of all else – then suddenly he fell in love and it was like a volcano erupting. It took years for the passion to subside and for him to reconcile it with his duty.

Especially when a senior executive becomes well known and a media property, how should he or she handle the private aspects of an increas-ingly public life? Passion for work and for a cause is lauded, but not the kind of passion that can lead to narrow-mindedness.

Passion declares what you really care about and balance may be impossible: great achievements are usually the result of obsessive effort. Few leaders are promoted on the strength of their work/life balance. On the other hand, who on their deathbed wishes they had spent more time at the office? Nelson followed his passions – all of them!

As a successful and high-profile leader, there will be more attention given to all aspects of your life, including your private life. If this poses a problem for your continuing leadership status, you will need to be par-ticularly discreet, otherwise you might have to give up the leadership status. Seeing things in context and keeping them in proportion are not easy when it's happening to you.

Should a leader be a team player?

Nelson valued his friendships with his brother officers, sought their inputs in decision making about plans and tactics, and trusted them completely to think and act as he did. He was a strong team player, but depended on his band of brothers heavily for social interaction and support. Fortunately they were able and willing, and they were always there for him. Even at home in England, there were seldom fewer than 15–20 at dinner every night. At sea, especially in the build-up to Trafalgar, he had to get to know a new set of 'brothers', and sharing dinners, plans and ideas was all part of the relationship building. Then trust and confidence followed.

The nature of command in the navy at that time, with the difficulties of signalling during battles, made participative leadership obvious and necessary (although not all of Nelson's contemporaries followed this dictum, and Collingwood's taciturn personality was certainly at odds with it). The levels of competence and commitment of subordinates were also high, and delegating large tasks to them without close monitoring made a lot of sense. Loyalty is still the bedrock of delegation in any organisation, as it is in subcultures in the workplace, in sports and among friends.

A more autocratic style of leadership, referred to as 'command and control', also has a role to play, in the military context and beyond. It can depend on the culture, the context, the nature of the work, the situation and the followers. A participatory leadership style, emphasising teamwork, requires strong relationships and a high degree of trust. Followers must be ready, willing and able, and the leader must be comfortable that they are. Which works best depends on the situation and the leader's personality – and the jury is still out.

Should a leader also be a manager?

Nelson learned early on the importance of victualling and supplies in maintaining morale and battle readiness. Noble listeners in the House of Lords were shocked and disappointed when Nelson, evaluating the worth of different colonial possessions, talked about the price of cabbages. The availability of cabbages at a good price was just as important as bravery and courage.

Nelson did not see leadership as being different to management, or these functions as being carried out by different people. On the other hand, many authorities see a clear distinction between the two. Admiral Sir Jonathon Band, for example, suggests that management is about maintaining the status quo, while leadership is about instigating change. But Sir David Ormand points out that sustained operational performance requires leadership at all levels, particularly in administration.

Diligence is hardly fashionable – it never was a glamorous virtue – but attention to detail, follow-up and persistence are essential to success in most areas of endeavour. Being a good manager is much less fashionable than being a good leader, but its value is unquestioned.

Why should others follow you?

Nelson was an inspiration to his men, just as much as to his captains and other officers. He reminded them of their deepest values and he lived by them himself. They also knew he was one of them. He had worked his way up from the lower deck and remembered what it was like. He demonstrated his care for them in practical ways, procuring fresh fruit and vegetables and fresh meat. He tried to improve conditions below deck. He fought for their share of prize money. He remembered the faces, names and stories of dozens of them. In a tough world, they loved him.

An inspirational leader needs to build relationships, share values, present a common vision, and be convincing and confident. Of course, you can offer rewards or threaten punishment. The carrot-and-stick approach is very simple and can be effective. It depends on what works for your particular type of follower and their expectations.

Inspiration is always at a premium. Those who can get more out of their people by inspiring them are seen as adding considerable value, and most creative work is inspired by the example, words or ideas of other people.

What about the so-called followers? What turns them on? Do they really depend on you for inspiration and direction? What can you do to help them succeed? Maybe you'll be inspired by them!

What will be your legacy as a leader?
Nelson decided early on that he wanted a hero's death in battle at the moment of victory, and his whole life bore the death or glory theme. With his almost stage-managed death at the high point of his career, his legacy was firmly in place.

Nelson had dreams, but no real idea about retiring. He was not adept at laying foundations for his future wealth. If he made any money Emma spent it, or he gave it away in the generosity that was so much a part of his passionate nature. Because he died when he did there was also little risk of dilution of the glory by subsequent events, such as Napoleon's sad demise on St Helena or Wellington's necessarily compromised career in politics.

In business a glorious reputation is often based on the most recent feat, not the best one, and few are prescient enough to die at the moment of their greatest achievement! Legends are now less durable and more immediate. Everyone can have five minutes of fame, but what will you leave behind as your contribution? Of course, the problem is that we can't control how our legacy will be interpreted and used. However, being a memorable role model can be of real value to those seeking direction in the immediate or more distant future.

The Nelson legend

The Nelson legend has been subject to varying interpretations through the ages – some judgemental, some seeking understanding. Some of the concepts with which Nelson has been associated have gone out of fashion, such as antagonism towards the French and Spanish (now seen as fellow Europeans); defending the empire (now that it has more or less disappeared, and with it the concept of imperialism); defending trade (now largely the domain of politicians rather than military men); maintaining a large navy (now that peacetime is more the norm); making sure that 'Britannia rules the waves' (now that Pax Americana has long since replaced Pax Britannica).

In many ways Nelson's iconic status was a huge boost to the navy; yet it also became something of a burden. As Joseph Conrad summed it up, 'he brought heroism to the line of duty... but verily he was a terrible ancestor'. His legend inspired others to serve in the spirit of the great leader, but the danger of the legend was that in naval battles after Trafalgar, all admirals would be compared with Nelson and found wanting.

For every naval officer Nelson left a legacy of professionalism, heroism, pride and dedication to the service, celebrated in anniversaries of his battles, especially of Trafalgar, every year. British naval ships have been named after Nelson and his captains. Second World War Captain-class corvettes included *Berry*, *Blackwood*, *Foley* and *Hallowell*; *Saumarez*, *Hardy* and *Troubridge* were fleet destroyers.

The Nelson legend has ebbed and flowed in popularity, reaching a high immediately after his death, sinking a little in the 1830s and 1840s with the reform acts and a change of emphasis away from war. That was also the time of the publication of his letters to Emma Hamilton. The Victorians were shocked to discover that their great hero had a torrid affair with a married woman who was formerly a prostitute!

Once the excitement of the hundredth anniversary of Trafalgar had died down, and especially after the First World War and the change in attitude to warfare that it brought, there was a more sober re-evaluation of Nelson. Simplistic sentimentality over the past was seen as escapism in the face of the country's declining influence. The old-style Nelson legend – of Nelson as swashbuckling hero engaged in glorious war – was shattered by the bloodshed of the First World War.

Then a new-style legend emerged, One of the most remarkable efforts of the propaganda campaign to persuade America to enter the war was the celebrated 1941 movie *Lady Hamilton* (known in the USA as *That Hamilton Woman*) starring Laurence Olivier and Vivien Leigh. With powerful battle scenes and strong acting, Winston Churchill – involved in the making of the film – is quoted as saying that the effect of the film on morale was equal to the presence of four army divisions.

In the 1950s there was a boom in the use of Nelson's name in post-war housing developments and the 1980s and 1990s saw the creation of the Nelson Society and the 1805 Club. The build-up to the 200th anniversary in 2005 occasioned another boom, already evidenced as we go to press by the International Fleet Review on 28 June 2005, attended by 167 ships from 57 nations. Her Majesty the Queen, the daughter, wife and mother of naval officers and holding the rank of Lord High Admiral, paid tribute:

> *The presence of such a large international fleet is a mark... of the high esteem in which Nelson, one of the world's most inspirational maritime leaders, continues to be held... [and] of the special bond that exists between all mariners... Admiral Lord Nelson's supreme qualities of seamanship, leadership with humanity and courage in the face of danger are shared among our maritime community today. He could wish for no greater legacy.*

The collecting of Nelson relics has continued with a sort of religious fervour, not so much the grisly exhibiting of bones and bodily artifacts (safely buried in St Paul's) but of items that once belonged to Nelson, which still turn up in auction rooms around the world. Mostly owned by museums, many are also in private hands, and Nelson's letters – in their thousands – are scattered all over the world and are probably the most accessible and collectable item available. Whole books have been written on the collecting of Nelsoniana, an activity popular since Nelson's day and started by himself, with his own 'Nelson Room' at Merton.

Books written about Nelson and his era – his captains, ships, men, women, mistresses, relatives – have flooded bookshelves in their thousands over the last 200 years and are read by everyone from schoolchildren to academics to business people. They have been representative of their eras, but show the impressive resilience of the subject matter.

Music hall traditions from the early nineteenth century until recent times also kept the Nelson legend going for a type of audience looking for fun and enjoyment rather than intellectual stimulus. Nelson himself enjoyed such boisterous and noisy entertainment and audience participation was always part of the evening. This is in considerable contrast with more serious Nelson plays in the 1930s, 1950s and 1960s, culminating in Terence Rattigan's *A Bequest to the Nation* of 1970, later made into a film of the same name, starring Peter Finch and Glenda Jackson. Based on the Nelson–Emma relationship through the eyes of Nelson's young nephew George Matcham, the play is a post-romantic interpretation of the lovers' tempestuous relationship.

The newest genre of Nelson-related films are realist portrayals of the hardships of life at sea, showing horrific wounds and grim conditions as if trying to take comfortable viewers back to a tougher world. Examples include the popular BBC series of C. S. Forester's *Hornblower* and the film version of Patrick O'Brien's *Master and Commander*, complete with amputations, disease, crowded living conditions and weevily ship's biscuits, but also taking a hard look at the timeless challenge of leadership – not omitting the sex appeal of the hero!

Nelson and the shadow side of leadership

It is important to consider the shadow side of leadership and the possible negative impacts of its misuse. This is not just in the case of leaders who have been selfish or deluded, but where personal greed and ambition can be negative for organisations. In Nelson's case his desire for leadership and the needs of the situation coincided most of the time – his desire for combat was exactly what the navy wanted. But in peacetime there wasn't really a place for him.

Leadership can be seen as an alienating social myth, so that rather than empowering subordinates it can deskill them and cause excessive dependency on the leader. Organisational members become mere followers, depending on their leaders to offer a sense of meaning, direction and purpose. Then followers become seekers, waiting for a miracle or a messiah to alleviate their problems. This can be a challenge to charismatic and inspirational leaders (and their organisations). Subordinates may be left alienated, helpless and passive, and far from reaching their maximum potential.

The blind desire of followers to be led can be as dangerous as the blind ambition of the leader to do the leading, but this is too simplistic an account of Nelson's case. The individual members of the band of brothers were also ambitious for themselves. They wanted a leader, but each of them was also able to lead. Commanding a ship of up to 1,000 men was already a high level of achievement. What was true, however, was that a trusted sidekick was needed to challenge the leader's assumptions and encourage the consideration of alternatives. Nelson had, and wanted, men like this, such as Collingwood, Blackwood, Hardy and

Fremantle, to name just a few. When Nelson did not have these men around him, such as when he was alienated from the band of brothers in Naples, things started to go wrong.

Leaders can also lose touch with reality. First, through their strength of vision and personal commitment to achieving their goals, they can stubbornly refuse to consider other approaches. In their obsession with themselves, in their narcissism, they seek the power to make the vision come true. There are elements of Nelson here – certainly his judgement was affected by his overwhelming need for hero worship. But he had so many years of learning his trade, making many mistakes and also many smart moves in the process, that he was not wedded to any one way of achieving his goal. If his goals were to climb to the top of his profession, be a hero and defeat the enemy, he was less concerned with how he would achieve these than with the overall outcome. He was a pragmatist and an opportunist. Life was so uncertain, information so unreliable and the enemy so elusive that he had to take opportunities as they came.

A second way leaders can lose touch with reality is through communication and impression management, selectively presenting information to promote a particular message, which can delude themselves too. In a sense here Nelson believed he was a hero to a greater extent than he really was, or before he had truly achieved heroic status. But in heroism, perception is reality. It became a self-fulfilling prophecy.

Thirdly, leaders can become fixated on processes and procedures, obscuring overall objectives – which change, often quite rapidly. This is usually connected to position and privilege: a leader at the top of a hierarchy can easily be convinced that the organisation's survival depends on keeping him or her there; and the best way to do that is to keep everyone focused on self-perpetuating procedures. While Nelson loved naval traditions and rituals, he was ruthlessly inventive when new circumstances required it.

Larger-than-life leaders can be driven by a need for recognition and power and by their own self-promotion, and this can be the key to their success and sometimes their downfall. These leaders are good at expressing a vision, are charismatic and are strong communicators. But by the same token they can be overly sensitive to criticism and intensely competitive. In some ways this applied to Nelson, who became very upset at real and perceived slights by his superiors. By the time he was in charge, however, this was less of an issue and the situation was too dire to worry about such things. He may have been vain, but he was a good listener, with a capacity for empathy and a committed mentor – not common qualities of the arrogant narcissist.

Nelson's contribution to leadership

Is the concept of Nelson as leader rooted in one leadership theory, or are the principles or lessons relevant to ongoing studies of leadership? The answer lies between the two. We can learn much from studying him as a person; and more by coming to appreciate how his particular genius worked in his time and circumstances.

Trait theory

Nelson as a leader can be applied as an example of trait theory in action: he possessed the traits or tendencies to feel, think and act in certain ways that showed he had the characteristics of a leader. Leadership studies of the 1930s focused on identifying the traits that related most strongly to effective leaders. Eight in particular emerged as especially important, and Nelson certainly exhibited these:

- ⚓ *Intelligence* in solving complex problems such as deploying limited resources of ships, guns and men to maximum effectiveness.
- ⚓ *Task-related knowledge* in knowing what has to be done and how, through his extensive hands-on experience in seamanship and navigation.
- ⚓ *Dominance* in his need to exert influence and control over others, as in his ambition to command first a ship of the line and then an entire fleet.
- ⚓ *Self-confidence* in influencing others in the face of difficulties, especially in his belief that the British fleet could succeed against overwhelming odds because of its superiority in gunnery and discipline.
- ⚓ *Energy/activity levels* of a higher magnitude than others in dealing with the demands of the job and taking on the necessary tasks on a daily basis, such as writing hundreds of letters.

- ⚓ *Tolerance for stress* in dealing with the uncertainty of the job, which Nelson found especially challenging because of his impatience with delay and inaction.
- ⚓ *Integrity and honesty* in being worthy of the trust and confidence of others, such as his support for seamen in the face of poor-quality victuals supplied by corrupt vendors to the Admiralty.
- ⚓ *Emotional maturity* in not being too self-centred, in controlling his feelings and accepting criticism. Nelson may have shown a lack of maturity – or just an open playfulness – in some aspects of his personal life, but his confidence was revealed in his sharing of battle tactics and vision with his band of brothers and seeking feedback.

Are these traits that we notice in any leader and ascribe to Nelson *post hoc*, or did he possess the traits first and then use them in his leadership role? Again, there may be a mixture of both answers here. Many of these personality characteristics were already evident in Nelson's character, such as confidence, ambition to lead, natural intelligence, integrity and work ethic. But it was through taking command at increasingly senior levels that all these traits, together with task-relevant knowledge, came into play in the particular way that we recognise as leadership.

Contingency theory

Trait theory (and other behavioural approaches) are of limited use in exploring leadership overall. It is always worth looking at the conditions in which leadership takes place for a more rounded view. Why in some situations were Nelson's characteristics of confidence, ambition and high energy levels dangerously misplaced, such as in the disastrous attack on Tenerife in which he lost his right arm? Why did they work so well in other situations, such as leaving the line of battle at Cape St Vincent to prevent the enemy regrouping? It depended on other factors, such as the element of surprise, the power of opposing forces, the ability to use technical superiority, and so forth.

In trying to identify what makes a leader effective the debate is often between being *relationship* oriented and *task* oriented. Nelson exhibited both characteristics, but in some cases he was too task oriented. He was so impatient and determined that a task should and could be completed that he would rush to action and would not take advice. However, he matured over time and in doing so became more skilled at handling complex political relationships as well as the more familiar world of naval colleagues. But he was always more comfortable doing so in the context of a clear-cut goal. Nelson was best deployed in situations where there was an overwhelming need to complete a task and that task could be defined in simple terms that were appealing and immediate to others – such as saving the country from invasion by defeating the French and Spanish fleets.

One of the ways of defining whether a leader is task or relationship oriented is to examine their attitudes to someone they find it difficult to work with. A relationship-oriented leader will see some good in them and see at least an element of potential for positive outcomes, even on a human scale and outside of the working context. Nelson could be fair and reasonable to other officers, such as letting the disgraced Sir Robert Calder go home in his own flagship rather than having to transfer to a lowly frigate or a worn-out ship returning for repairs. Collingwood was cold and unfriendly as a leader and the band of brothers couldn't wait for Nelson's return to the fleet, but Nelson always maintained a good relationship with him, trying to overlook his defects and concentrating on his better qualities. He also tried to do his best for his disappointing stepson, Josiah Nisbet, attempting to see positive attributes in him.

Overall, in his relationships with his patrons and mentors, with his peers and with his seamen – especially with the men of the *Agamemnon*, one of his favourite ships – Nelson was strongly relationship oriented. But leadership relies on much more than having good relations with subordinates. By and large, people will follow those who both know what to do and how to do it. This implies that who leads depends on what needs to be done and the circumstances in which it all happens, the *situation*. It makes sense to be led by a qualified captain if there is a battle to be fought. Nelson had shown he was able to fight and to command ships; he was strong on both 'what' and 'how'.

Situational theory

A situation comprises much more than a leader and followers. Some tasks are inherently more complex than others, and often the competing interests of all those involved mean that the focus of authority is constantly shifting. If we look at it dispassionately it can be hard to see where leadership is coming from. For example, the outcome of Trafalgar was strongly influenced by Napoleon's impatience with Villeneuve and the latter's decision to leave port, playing into the hands of the British fleet, which had the wind in its favour.

Situational theory urges us to seek the manner of leadership most appropriate for a specific context rather than assuming that leadership is located in the official leader. For example, where both the tasks and the relationships have a high degree of complexity and uncertainty, we would expect leadership to involve a good deal of selling of the overall mission and the encouragement of commitment. Over time, people need less support, and can accept delegated authority so that leadership is then distributed. The traditions and disciplines of the navy provided a degree of structure, and the war provided clear goals, so that leadership could be delegated to a surprisingly large cadre of senior officers around the world. Nelson relied on this in delegating authority to others and his inspirational brilliance was rendered more effective by this distributed leadership.

John Adair distils this into a simple and accessible model that he calls 'action-centred leadership'. Leadership, he says, requires competence in three interlocking circles of activity: identifying tasks, building teams and developing individuals.

Motivation: 'honour and salt beef'

Nelson believed in intrinsic motivation – hence 'honour' rather than 'salt beef'. Honour was why you joined the navy – the work was challenging, but you could make a contribution recognised and valued by family and friends. You were saving your country from invasion and protecting its trade and prosperity. You learned a skill, you could take more and more responsibility and enjoy limited scope for creativity. This is certainly what motivated Nelson, and he encouraged others to share it too. The extrinsic motivators were not always there – pay, security and benefits were often lacking and the 'salt beef' was not always appetising.

So Nelson, supported by centuries of naval tradition, emphasised the sense of identity and status in being a sailor, a 'heart of oak', invincible, 'minding shot no more than peas'. For many who had only transient relations back on shore, the social contacts aboard ship, being part of a mess or a gun crew, were also significant benefits.

Transformational and transactional leadership

In recent years, much has been made of a distinction between transformational and transactional leadership. The former describes a leader who heightens subordinates' awareness of the importance of their tasks, and encourages them to find new and better ways of doing things in pursuit of even more ambitious goals. Thus Nelson, in insisting on gunnery drill and pitting gun crews competitively against each other to fire the most rapid and accurate broadsides, encouraged seamen to excel themselves in the vital job of defending their country. The work of 'manning a gun' was transformed into 'defending the country'.

Transformational leaders also typically help subordinates to gain promotion and a sense of achievement in their work, which Nelson certainly did for younger and more junior officers under his care, trying to arrange opportunities for promotion, command and prize money in the same way as his mentors did for him.

A third characteristic of this style of leadership is the encouragement of subordinates to work for the organisation as a whole rather than just personal gain. Of course, success is more likely if personal incentives are aligned with corporate goals, and winning battles potentially brought prize money and wealth. But Nelson strongly represented the transcendent priority of the survival of the country and the success of the navy. He showed a vision of the future: winning a great victory, bringing an end to the long, tedious blockade and freeing Britain from the onerous fear of invasion and terror of Napoleon. He emphasised the role of his officers and men in sharing that responsibility. As far as he could, within the confines of the navy's bureaucracy, he gave subordinates the chance to improve themselves, by recognising their individual talents and giving them opportunities for command.

Nelson stood out from other naval leaders in all these respects, but he was no slouch at the more transactional aspects of leadership. In his ships, like others, performance was rewarded by an increased rum ration and disobedience was met with punishment, including flogging and withheld rations. But because these disciplines were placed clearly in the context of a wider purpose, they could be justified, at least in the value sets that sustained the power relations of the navy.

Mintzberg's managerial roles

By studying what managers actually spend their time doing, one of our interviewees, Henry Mintzberg, has delineated ten managerial roles. How do these illuminate Nelson's practice?

- As a *figurehead* he personified the navy and carried great credibility with his track record of success in battle, awards, medals and war wounds.
- He was a *leader* in commanding his ships and men in battle and in managing the resources of the fleet.
- He carried out *liaison* work by coordinating his captains and provision suppliers all over the Mediterranean.
- He acted as a *monitor* of performance by singling out officers for promotion, and setting targets for speed in gunnery and dexterity in ship handling.
- He was a *disseminator* of information through his huge output of letters to insiders and outsiders, superiors, peers and subordinates.
- He was a *spokesperson* in speaking up for his captains and other protégés to the authorities to gain the advancement he felt they deserved.
- As an *entrepreneur* – although he was more of an intrapreneur – he encouraged change by introducing a new signal system, improving conditions below decks and reducing costs through more economical purchasing.
- He was at his best as a *disturbance handler*, such as dealing with the disgruntled crew of the frigate *Blanche*, who rejected their new commander, Captain Hotham, and had to be recalled to their duty.
- He was an excellent *resource allocator*, making sure all his ships were supplied and repaired, even when resources were hard to come by.
- He learned to become a strong *negotiator*, showing his skills at Copenhagen at a high level and solving disputes between his officers and men at a much lower one.

A recent and related study, by Gosling and Mintzberg, suggests that a successful manager should weave different mindsets into a comprehensible whole. Reflectiveness is the first, using experience, successes and failures to develop self-awareness and the ability to manage oneself as appropriate. Nelson, who was hugely self-critical of failure (as at Tenerife), closely analytical of success (as at the Nile) and also appreciative of near-run things (as at Copenhagen), put all his reflections of the past into his Trafalgar memo of 9 October 1805.

Managing organisations through an analytical mindset, understanding the essential meanings of structures and systems, was also important for Nelson. He had a tremendous eye for detail, such as knowing the cheapest place to buy lemon juice for the crew. and could capture complexity simply as, after detailed fleet depositions, he could declare that 'in case signals can neither be seen or perfectly understood no Captain can do very wrong if he places his Ship alongside that of the Enemy'. He was concerned with specific measures, such as the health of seamen on individual ships – how many were on the sick list? And what was the state of the ships – stock of spares and speed of sailing? How long did it take to fire a broadside? How fast was the enemy? Could we be even faster?

Developing a worldly mindset to manage the context was another challenge that Nelson embraced, and he was exceptionally international for a man of his era. By 18 years of age he had voyaged to the West Indies, to the Arctic, to India and the Arabian Gulf. He came to know the Americas and Europe, lived in Italy and, with his power of reflection, developed an understanding of the differences in local social and economic contexts, giving him a unique understanding of international politics, though much circumscribed by his overarching patriotism.

Nelson developed a collaborative mindset in managing relationships, one of his greatest strengths. Although he wanted to be a hero, he did not necessarily engage in self-oriented 'heroic management' but pursued 'engaging management', based on collaboration. He fundamentally assumed that naval actions could be effective only through deep-rooted understanding and mutual appreciation among a ship's crew and the captains of a squadron. The band of brothers is the archetype of a collaborative mindset at work. For Nelson, leadership was 'a sacred trust earned through the respect of others' rather than being 'thrust upon those who thrust their will upon others'.

Finally, Nelson embodied an action mindset, setting and maintaining direction and coaxing everyone along. He pushed for changes in naval tactics, provisioning and manning, while preserving the best of naval tradition.

Nelson's Way of leadership illuminates and illustrates existing theories of leadership, providing us with concrete examples and bringing them to life. His approach to leadership raises important questions that are relevant to anyone facing the challenge of leading and managing any group of people, anywhere.

In this book we have attempted to distil some of the more useful insights for today's executives in the leadership lessons at the end of each chapter and the interviews with corporate leaders, commentators and educators. But Nelson's way of leadership comes with a health warning – it is not for the faint-hearted!

The virtues by which he lived his life – heroism, vocation, courage, passion, loyalty, diligence, inspiration and glory – are the building blocks of his style. They are ideals to which any leader may aspire, though few will pursue them with such passion.

CONTRIBUTORS

John Adair, author of 30 books on leadership and internationally recognised as a writer, teacher and adviser on leadership

More than a million managers throughout the world have been through the Action-Centred Leadership (ACL) course that John Adair pioneered in the 1970s. After Cambridge University he joined the Scots Guards and then became the only national serviceman to serve in the Arab Legion, where he was adjutant of a Bedouin regiment. He became Senior Lecturer in Military History and Adviser in Leadership Training at the Royal Military Academy, Sandhurst. With degrees from Cambridge, Oxford and London, Adair was appointed as the world's first Professor of Leadership Studies at the University of Surrey. Other firsts include introducing the world's first university degree course in Leadership Studies at the University of Exeter, and subsequently playing a part in establishing Europe's first university-based Centre for Leadership Studies at the same university.

Adair's clients include ICI, Exxon Chemicals, Mitsubishi, Lehman Brothers, BAE Systems, British Airways, the Church of England and the Department of Education. His 30 books, such as *Effective Leadership* and *Not Bosses But Leaders*, have been translated into 18 different languages. *How To Find Your Vocation* and *Effective Strategic Leadership* are among the more recent.

Admiral Sir Jonathon Band KCB, Commander-in-Chief Fleet, Commander Allied Maritime Component Command Northwood

Sir Jonathon Band joined the Royal Navy in 1967 and, having trained at Dartmouth, underwent fleet training in ships in the Far East. This was followed by three years at Exeter University as an undergraduate. Then he served in junior officer appointments in Lewiston and Rothesay and on exchange with the United States Navy in Belknap. Following junior officer staff and warfare training in *Eskimo* in the West Indies and South Atlantic, he then commanded the minesweeper *Soberton* in the Fishery Protection Squadron around the UK coast, then served as Flag Lieutenant to Commander-in-Chief Fleet, a period that included the Falklands Campaign.

Promoted Commander in 1983, he assumed command of *Phoebe*, operating in the NATO area, and was subsequently appointed to the Defence Staff in the Ministry of Defence in the Directorate of Defence Policy. Promoted Captain and helping in the formation of Flag Officer Naval Aviation, he commanded *Norfolk* and established the first Type 23 Frigate Squadron. He then became the Assistant Director Navy Plans and Programmes in the MOD, and was a member of the Defence Costs Study. His last Sea Command was *Illustrious*, an aircraft carrier, including two operational deployments to the Adriatic in support of the United Nations, and then NATO, operations in Bosnia, and the start of a major Royal Navy deployment to the Middle and Far East.

As Rear Admiral, he returned to the MOD as Assistant Chief of Naval Staff and became Team Leader of the Defence Education and Training Study. As Vice-Admiral, he became the Deputy C-in-C Fleet and was appointed a Knight Commander of the Most Honourable Order of the Bath. As Admiral, he took up the appointment of Commander-in-Chief Fleet, Commander Allied Maritime Component Command Northwood.

Greg Dyke, former Director General of the British Broadcasting Corporation and head of many other television stations

Greg Dyke went to York University and, after an early career as a journalist, started his broadcasting career in 1977 at London Weekend Television. He became Editor-in-Chief of TV-am in 1983 and the following year Director of Programmes for TVS (Television South), rising to Group Chief Executive of LWT (Holdings) by 1990. After the Granada takeover of LWT, Dyke joined Pearson Television as Chief Executive and built it into the largest non-US independent production company in the world. He also guided the consortium that created Channel 5 and became its first Chairman.

While at Pearson, Dyke undertook a review of the Patients' Charter of the NHS at the request of the Secretary of State for Health. He became Director-General of the BBC in January 2000. At the BBC he reorganised its structure to put him closer to programme makers and to spend less on running the organisation. He also made major commitments to using digital technology. Leaving the BBC in January 2004 in controversial circumstances, he was recently made the new Chancellor of the University of York. He has been Chairman of the Independent Television Association; Chairman of GMTV; and at various times a director of Pearson plc, Channel Four Television, ITN, BskyB and a non-Executive Director of Manchester United Football Club.

Sir John Harvey-Jones, former chairman of ICI, star of television series *Troubleshooter*, business consultant and bestselling author

One of Europe's most respected and internationally recognised business leaders, Sir John Harvey-Jones has the rare ability to make complex business and management issues understandable to a wide range of multicultural audiences from different socioeconomic groups. He is one of the very few business leaders to have had a television programme – the *Troubleshooter* series (1990, 1992, 1995–6) – built around his ability to identify quickly the problems affecting today's business, in the fast-changing corporate world of global competition.

Harvey-Jones began his career in the Royal Navy, before moving to ICI, where he eventually became Chairman at a time when the giant British industrial group was in difficulties. In just over two years, the company had doubled in share value and turned a loss into an annual profit of more than £1 billion.

Knighted in 1985, he has also been voted (by his peers) Industrialist of the Year in 1986, 1987 and 1988. He was voted Motivator of the Year in 1992 and received a coveted BAFTA Award (the British Oscar) for his television work. He has published a number of bestselling books, including *Making It Happen: Reflections on Leadership* (1994), *Getting It Together* (1992), *Managing to Survive* (1993–4) and *All Together Now* (1994). His areas of interest include managing in the twenty-first century, the leadership imperative, maximising growth and business potential, global industrial trends, developing people, and structuring the workforce in the new organisation.

Dr Henry Mintzberg, Cleghorn Professor of Management Studies at McGill University in Montreal and author of 12 books on management

Henry Mintzberg's research has dealt with issues of general management and organisations, focusing on the nature of managerial work, forms of organising, and the strategy formation process. Recent publications include *Developing Managers, Not MBAs* and an electronic pamphlet entitled 'Getting Past Smith and Marx... Towards a Balanced Society'. Educated at the M.I.T. Sloan School of Management and McGill University, he holds honorary degrees from 13 universities and is an elected Fellow of the Royal Society of Canada, the Academy of Management and the International Academy of Management. He was named Distinguished Scholar for the year 2000 by the Academy of Management.

Mintzberg is the author of 12 books, including *The Nature of Managerial Work* (1973), *The Structuring of Organizations* (1979), *Mintzberg on Management* (1989) and *The Rise and Fall of Strategic Planning* (1994). His management articles number over 100, including two *Harvard Business Review* prize winners: 'The Manager's Job: Folklore and Fact' (first place in 1975) and 'Crafting Strategy' (second place in 1987). His books are 'written for those of us who spend our public lives dealing with organisations and our private lives escaping from them'.

Sir David Omand, former Security and Intelligence Coordinator and Permanent Secretary, Cabinet Office, Her Majesty's Government

Sir David Omand joined the Government Communications Headquarters (GCHQ) in 1969, before transferring to the Ministry of Defence (MOD), where he served in policy and private office posts, including that of Principal Private Secretary to the Secretary of State during the Falklands War. His MOD experience spanned two Defence Reviews, two changes of Government and six Secretaries of State.

In 1985, Omand took up the post of Defence Counsellor to the UK Delegation to NATO in Brussels. He returned to the MOD in 1988 and introduced a new management strategy for defence and on appointment to Assistant Under Secretary (Programmes) ran the MOD's long-term planning and resource allocation system. In 1992 as Deputy Under Secretary of State for Policy, he was especially concerned with the British military contribution to alleviating the crisis in former Yugoslavia.

On promotion to Permanent Secretary he took up the post of Director of GCHQ in 1996. He was Permanent Secretary at the Home Office until 2000, and was then appointed Chairman of the Centre for Management and Policy Studies before moving to the Cabinet Office. In 2002 he became Security and Intelligence Coordinator and Permanent Secretary, Cabinet Office, retiring from this post in spring 2005.

Professor Dr Danica Purg, founder and director of the IEDC-Bled School of Management, Slovenia, the first business school in Eastern Europe

The founding and current director of the IEDC-Bled School of Management, Slovenia, and the first President of the Central and East European Management Development Association (CEEMAN), Danica Purg is also chairperson and director of the European Leadership Centre (ELC). She is the author of several books and numerous articles on technological and organisational change, comparative HRM practices, team building, economic reforms and management development. She co-authored and edited the book *Leaders and Teams; The Winning Partnership* with Pierre Casse, Lynn Isabella, Paul Claudel and Arnold Walravens. Her special field of interest is looking for inspiration for managers from art and other professions.

After graduating from the Faculty of Political Science in Ljubljana, she completed her PhD at the Faculty of Political Sciences, University of Belgrade, and extensively studied in the USA (Harvard Business School), UK, France, the Netherlands and Switzerland. She has been awarded the Honorary Order of Freedom by the President of the Republic of Slovenia for her contribution to management development in Slovenia and Europe.

BIBLIOGRAPHY

Nelson

Adams, Max (2005) *Admiral Collingwood: Nelson's Own Hero*, London: Weidenfeld & Nicolson.

Adkin, Mark (2005) *The Trafalgar Companion: The Complete Guide to History's Most Famous Sea Battle and the Life of Admiral Lord Nelson*, London: Aurum Press.

Adkins, Roy (2004) *Trafalgar: The Biography of a Battle*, Boston, MA: Little Brown.

Beresford, Charles & Wilson, H. W. (1897–8) *Nelson and his Times*, London: Eyre and Spottiswoode.

Brown, Stephen (2003) *The Age of Scurvy*, Chichester: Summersdale.

Callo, Joseph F. (1999) *Legacy of Leadership: Lessons from Admiral Lord Nelson*, New York: Hellgate Press.

Cannadine, David (2005) *Admiral Lord Nelson: Context and Legacy*, London: Palgrave Macmillan.

Charnock, John (1806) *Biographical Memoirs of Lord Viscount Nelson*, London: Symonds.

Clayton, Tim & Craig, Phil (2004) *Trafalgar: The Men, the Battle, the Storm*, London: Hodder & Stoughton.

Coleman, Terry (2002) *Nelson: The Man and the Legend*, London: Bloomsbury.

Coleman, Terry (2004) *The Nelson Touch: The Life and Legend of Horatio Nelson*, Oxford: Oxford University Press.

Cordingly, David (2003) *Billy Ruffian – The Bellerophon and the Downfall of Napoleon: The Biography of a Ship of the Line, 1782–1836*, London: Bloomsbury.

Downer, Martyn (2004) *Nelson's Purse*, London: Bantam Press.

Drinkwater Bethune, Colonel (1840) *A Narrative of the Battle of St Vincent*, London: Saunders & Otley.

Fraser, Edward (1906, reissued 2004) *The Enemy at Trafalgar: Eyewitness Narratives, Dispatches and Letters from the French and Spanish Fleets*, London: Chatham Publishing.

Gardiner, Robert & Morriss, Roger (1998) *The Campaign of Trafalgar 1803–1805*, London: Chatham Publishing.

Hattersley, Roy (1974) *Nelson* (The Great Commanders series), London: Weidenfeld & Nicolson.

Hayward, Joel (2003) *For God and Glory: Lord Nelson and His Way of War*, Annapolis, MD: Naval Institute Press.

Hibbert, Christopher (1995) *Nelson: A Personal History*, Harmondsworth: Penguin Books.

Howarth, David (1969) *Trafalgar: The Nelson Touch*, London: Collins.

Jeaffreson, John (1888) *Lady Hamilton and Lord Nelson*, London: Hurst & Blackett.

Kennedy, Ludovic (1951) *Nelson's Band of Brothers*, Glasgow: Collins.

Knight, Roger (2005) *The Pursuit of Victory*, London: Allen Lane.

Lambert, Andrew (2004) *Nelson: Britannia's God of War*, London: Faber & Faber.

Laughton, John Knox (1895) *Nelson*, London: Macmillan.

Lavery, Brian (1989) *Nelson's Navy: The Ships, Men and Organisation, 1793–1815*, London: Conway Maritime Press.

Lavery, Brian (2003) *Nelson and the Nile: The Naval War against Bonaparte 1798*, London: Caxton Editions.

Lavery, Brian (2005) *Nelson's Fleet at Trafalgar*, Greenwich: National Maritime Museum.

Lewis, Michael (1960, reissued 2004) *The Social History of the Navy 1793–1815*, London: Chatham Publishing.

Macdonald, Janet (2004) *Feeding Nelson's Navy: The True Story of Food at Sea in the Georgian Era*, London: Chatham Publishing.

Mahan, A. T. (1897) *The Life of Nelson, the Embodiment of the Sea Power of Great Britain*, Boston, MA: Little Brown.

Moore, Lucy (2002) 'Horatio Nelson' in Cooper, John (ed.), *Great Britons: The Great Debate*, London: National Portrait Gallery.

Nicolson, Adam (2005) *Men of Honour: Trafalgar and the Making of the English Hero*, London/New York: HarperCollins.

Oman, Carola (1947) *Nelson*, London: Hodder & Stoughton.

Pack, James (1982) *Nelson's Blood: The Story of Naval Rum*, Annapolis, MD: Naval Institute Press.

Parsons, G. S. (1843) *Nelsonian Reminiscences*, London: Saunders & Otley.

Pocock, Tom (1968) *Nelson and His World*, London: Thames & Hudson.

Pocock, Tom (1980) *The Young Nelson in the Americas*, London: Collins.

Pocock, Tom (1987) *Horatio Nelson*, London: Bodley Head.

Pocock, Tom (2002a) *The Terror before Trafalgar: Nelson, Napoleon and the Secret War*, London: John Murray.

Pocock, Tom (2002b) *Nelson's Women*, London: Andre Deutsch.

Pope, Dudley (1972) *The Great Gamble: Nelson at Copenhagen*, London: Weidenfeld & Nicolson.

Pope, Dudley (1999) *Decision at Trafalgar* (Heart of Oak Sea Classics Series), New York: Owl Books.

Pugh, P. D. Gordon (1968) *Nelson and his Surgeons*, Edinburgh/London: E & S Livingstone.

Rattigan, Terence (1970) *A Bequest to the Nation*, London: Hamish Hamilton.

Rodger, N. A. M. (1986) *The Wooden World: An Anatomy of the Georgian Navy*, London: Fontana.

Rodger, N. A. M. (2004) *The Command of the Ocean: A Naval History of Britain, 1649–1815*, London: Allen Lane.

Royal Navy (2005) 'Trafalgar 200: The International Fleet Review, 28 June 2005', *Trafalgar 200 Summer Programme*, official commemorative brochure.

Russell, Jack (1969) *Nelson and the Hamiltons*, Harmondsworth: Penguin Books.

Schom, Alan (1992) *Trafalgar: Countdown to Battle, 1803–1805*, Harmondsworth: Penguin.

Southey, Robert (1813) *The Life of Nelson*, London: John Murray.

Vincent, Edgar (2003) *Nelson: Love and Fame*, Newhaven, CT/London: Yale University Press.

Warner, Oliver (1955) *Lord Nelson: A Guide to Reading with a Note on Contemporary Portraits*, London: Caravel.

Warner, Oliver (1958) *A Portrait of Lord Nelson*, London: Chatto & Windus.

Warner, Oliver (1959) *Trafalgar* (British Battles Series), London: Batsford.

Warner, Oliver (ed.) (1971) *Nelson's Last Diary*, Kent, WA: KSU Press.

White, Colin (ed.) (1995) *The Nelson Companion*, London: Bramley Books.

White, Colin (2001) *1797: Nelson's Year of Destiny*, London: Sutton Publishing.

White, Colin (ed.) (2005) *Nelson: The New Letters*, Woodbridge/Rochester, NY: Boydell Press.

Wilkinson, Clennell (1931) *Nelson*, London: Harrap.

Websites

www.admiralnelson.org
www.bbc.co.uk/history
www.hms-victory.com
www.nelson1805.com
www.nelson-society.org.uk
www.nmm.ac.uk
www.royal-navy.mod.uk
www.seabritain2005.com
www.trafalgar200.com
www.wtj.com/archives/nelson

Leadership

Adair, John (1989) *Great Leaders*, Guildford: Talbot Adair Press.

Adair, John (2002) *Effective Strategic Leadership*, London: Macmillan

Barnard, Chester (1938, reissued 1966) *The Functions of the Executive*, Cambridge, MA: Harvard University Press.

Bass, Bernard M. (1990) *Bass and Stogdill's Handbook of Leadership*, New York: Free Press.

Bennis, Warren & Thomas, R. (2002) *Geeks and Geezers*, Cambridge, MA: Harvard University Press.

Binney, G., Wilke, G. & Williams, C. (2005) *Living Leadership*, London: FT/Prentice Hall.

Blanchard, Kenneth (1994) *Leadership and the One Minute Manager*, London: HarperCollins.

Blanchard, Kenneth (2002a) *The One Minute Manager*, London: HarperCollins.

Blanchard, Kenneth (2002b) *Whale Done!*, London: Nicholas Brealey Publishing.

Boulden, Richard (2004) 'What is Leadership?', Research Report, Exeter: Centre for Leadership Studies.

Boulden, Richard (2005) 'What is Leadership Development?', Research Report, Exeter: Centre for Leadership Studies.

Burns, J. McGregor (1978) *Leadership*, New York: Harper & Row.

Ciulla, Joanna (1998) *Ethics: The Heart of Leadership*, Westport, CT: Praeger.

Daft, Richard (2002) *The Leadership Experience*, New York: Harcourt.

Freemantle, David (1995) *Eighty Things You Must Do To Be a Great Boss*, London: McGraw-Hill.

George, Jennifer M. & Jones, Gareth R. (2002) *Organizational Behavior*, Englewood Cliffs, NJ: Prentice Hall.

Goffee, Robert & Jones, Gareth R. (2000) 'Why Should Anyone Be Led By You?', *Harvard Business Review*, September–October: 62–70.

Gosling, Jonathan (1996) 'Plato on the Education of Managers', in French, Robert & Grey, Christopher (eds), *Rethinking Management Education*, London: Sage.

Gosling, Jonathan & Mintzberg, Henry (2003) 'The Five Minds of a Manager', *Harvard Business Review*, November: 54–63.

Gosling, Jonathan & Mintzberg, Henry (2004) 'Education of Practising Managers', *MIT Sloan Management Review*, Summer: 19–22.

Grint, Keith (2000) *Arts of Leadership*, Oxford: Oxford University Press.

Harvey-Jones, John (1988) *Making It Happen: Reflections on Leadership*, London: Collins.

Hersey, P. & Blanchard, K. (1988) *Management of Organizational Behavior*, Englewood Cliffs, NJ: Prentice Hall.

Jones, Stephanie (1992) *Psychometric Testing for Managers*, London: Piatkus.

Jones, Stephanie (2003) 'On Top of the World: Leadership and Management Lessons from Everest', *Human Assets Middle East*, Autumn: 16–19.

Jones, Stephanie & Awamleh, Raed (2004) 'A Comparison between the Leadership Styles, Subordinate Styles and Team Roles of New Recruits and Experienced Managers: A United Arab Emirates Case Study', *Leadership Refrains: Encounters, Conversations and Enchantments, Studying Leadership*, 3rd International Workshop, Exeter: Centre for Leadership Studies, University of Exeter.

Keegan, John (1987) *The Mask of Command*, London: Jonathan Cape.

Lipman-Blumen, Jean (1996) *Connective Management*, Oxford: Oxford University Press.

Machiavelli, Niccolo (1981) *The Prince*, Harmondsworth: Penguin.

Mant, A. (1983) *Leaders We Deserve*, London: Martin Robertson.

Mintzberg, Henry (1973) *The Nature of Managerial Work*, New York: Harper & Row.

Morrell, Margot & Capparell, Stephanie (2001) *Shackleton's Way: Leadership Lessons from the Great Antarctic Explorer*, London: Nicholas Brealey Publishing.

Peace, William (2001) 'The Hard Work of Being a Soft Manager', *Harvard Business Review*, December: 99–104.

Sun Tzu (1981) Clavell, J. (ed.), *The Art of War*, London: Hodder & Stoughton.

Useem, Michael (2001) 'The Leadership Lessons of Mount Everest', *Harvard Business Review*, October: 51–8.

Yukl, Gary (2002) *Leadership in Organisations*, Englewood Cliffe, NJ: Prentice Hall.

Website

www.leadership-studies.com

INDEX

ACKNOWLEDGEMENTS

W E ARE BOTH EXTREMELY OBLIGED TO PROFESSOR Nicholas Rodger, also at Exeter in the Centre for Maritime Historical Studies and a distinguished and prolific naval historian, for his encouragement and interest, and for submitting such a thoughtful foreword. Also to Professor Roger Knight, formerly Chief Curator and Deputy Director of the National Maritime Museum and now Visiting Professor of Naval History at the Greenwich Maritime Institute at the University of Greenwich, the author of a groundbreaking new biography of Nelson, who read and commented on our manuscript.

In our research and interpretation, we have benefited from the hundreds of publications on Nelson produced over the last 200 years, from those that started us off on the trail as teenagers to those we have consulted for the present study. If we are to name any one in particular, we must join the applause of all Nelson scholars for Colin White's *Nelson: The New Letters*. Described as reading like a leadership manual, it is the closest we are likely to get to a book by Nelson himself and represents massive research on primary sources, providing intriguing new insights to a man we thought we knew.

We have also relied heavily on research and writing on leadership by colleagues across the world, part of a dynamic community of which the Centre for Leadership Studies at Exeter is an active member.

We also thank most sincerely our seven interviewees. They brought a wealth of experience, thoughtfulness and originality to the questions we posed. Most were Nelson fans already, and all provided critical observations on leadership past and present and helped to bring Nelson's way of leadership to life.

Lastly we would both like to thank our families who have suffered several *coups de Nelson* over the last year, with missed family events and neglected household duties. Even when on temporary shore leave we have been unable to keep our eyes from scanning the metaphorical horizon for Nelson and his fleet!

ILLUSTRATION CREDITS

All illustrations are reproduced with permission from the National Maritime Museum, London. See www.nmm.ac.uk. All rights reserved.

Cover: 'Nelson Boarding the American Prize', Artist Richard Westall, 1806, National Maritime Museum, Greenwich Hospital Collection.

p8: 'Nelson's Signal', Artist Thomas Davidson, undated,

p22: 'Captain Horatio Nelson', Artist John Francis Rigaud, 1781,

p48: 'Nelson Boarding the San Josef at the Battle of Cape St Vincent, 14th February, 1797', Artist George Jones, undated, National Maritime Museum, Greenwich Hospital Collection.

p74: 'Lady Emma Hamilton', Artist Johann Schmidt, 1800,

p98: 'Victors of the Nile', William Bromley & John Landseer (engravers) after Sir Robert Smirke (artist), 1803,

p128: 'England expects every man to do his duty. Lord Nelson explaining to the Officers the Plan of Attack previous to the Battle of Trafalgar, and Position of the Combined Forces of France & Spain', William Marshall Craig (artist), James Godby (engraver), 9 January 1806,

p152: 'Admiral Nelson Recreating with his Brave Tars after the Glorious Battle of the Nile', Artist Thomas Rowlandson, undated,

p182: 'The Death of Nelson', Benjamin West (artist), James Heath (engraver), Colnaghi & Puckle (publishers), 1841,